THAILAND'S CRISIS

THAILAND'S CRISIS

PASUK PHONGPAICHIT AND CHRIS BAKER

SILKWORM BOOKS

ISBN 974-7551-38-9

First published by Silkworm Books in 2000

Silkworm Books
Suriwong Book Centre Building
54/1 Sridonchai Road, Chiang Mai, Thailand
E-mail address: silkworm@pobox.com
Website: http://www.silkwormbooks.com

All photographs courtesy of *The Nation*
Typeset by Silk Type in Garamond 10 pt.
Design by T. Jittidecharak
Printed in Thailand by O.S. Printing House, Bangkok

CONTENTS

PREFACE

This book is not so much about getting into a crisis as getting through one.

A lot has been written on the origins of the Asian crisis. The first two chapters below are on this theme. But the bulk of this book is about what happened during the Thai crisis—how it was managed, who got hurt, what changed, and what are the implications for the future. It is not intended as a detached, olympian account. All of the essays included here have evolved out of debates, lectures, press articles, and other writings developed through the period of the crisis. Some crystallized into essays when we were asked to contribute to an international conference or publication.[1] Some have been pulled together here for the first time. We feel that this has been such an extraordinary event that it is worth putting down these views before they pale with age and soften with reflection. Also we think there are some important lessons.

The book has four main themes. The first is about the management of the crisis, both economic and social. We are not surprised that the economic measures imposed by the IMF had many disastrous results. This was a new sort of crisis and the IMF is a very old-fashioned institution. Besides, the IMF was more intent on forcing Thailand to accept neoliberal reforms than on achieving the fastest and least painful recovery. Neither are we so surprised that the social programmes designed by the World Bank and Asian Development Bank (ADB) were relatively ineffectual. These programmes were part of a new and highly experimental project in international social policy for which Thailand happened to become a guinea-pig. We are not recording these failures in a spirit of blame, but of learning. We can understand the IMF's defensiveness in view of the severe threats to the institution. But we think it's important for Thailand, and other countries subject to financially generated crises, to lay out these failures so something can be learned.

The second theme is about the economic changes which this crisis has left behind. We believe that in the light of history, these few years will appear as a major turning point in the Thai political economy. The changes that have happened may appear inevitable for a relatively open economy in the post–cold war world. But somehow in the early 1990s Thailand was partially shielded from outside pressures so that the changes during the crisis seemed very sudden. The major shift, we think, is a withdrawal from the strategy, begun since the 1950s, to build a strong local capitalism. As a result, Thailand emerges from the crisis as an economy more than ever oriented to export-led growth in sectors dependent upon foreign capital and technologies. This shift has social and political implications which will emerge over the years to come. Unless policy orientations change, we expect to see a deepening of the existing trend to social division, and a growing conflict between economic and social goals.

The third theme is that the crisis has been both economic and political—political in its origins and in its impact. Thailand emerges from the crisis with an extraordinary (and increasingly controversial) new constitution which may never have been passed if its fate had not become entwined with the economic crisis. This charter has the potential to assist many processes of social and economic change. Besides this, the crisis has realigned Thailand's party political system more in line with global forces, and has helped to stir up civil society. These changes—and their reaction with the economic shifts—will reverberate through Thailand's relatively open political system over the years to come.

The fourth theme focuses on internal debates about the crisis and future social directions. The crisis stimulated discussion, both at an articulate academic level, and in many less articulate public forms. Much of this debate was about turning inwards and re-examining social foundations and social goals as a strategy both to survive the crisis in the short term, and to survive in a globalized world over a longer horizon. Much of this debate is hidden from outsiders either by language or just by its ephemeral nature.

Much is easily misunderstood through the use of terms like "nationalism" and slippery concepts like "sufficiency" and "self-reliance." Here we bring some of this debate out into the open, and try to assess its importance.

In the last two chapters we bring these four themes together and peer into the future. The first of these chapters summarizes the impact of the crisis, and lays out the (rather elusive) debate about Thailand's options for the near future, their potential, and their danger. The final chapter is a summary of lessons, sprinkled with a few hopes.

We would like to thank Anis Chowdhury, Ha-joon Chang, Peter Warr, Karel van Wolferen, and Takashi Shiraishi who originally pressured us to write various of these pieces. We are grateful to Kevin Hewison, Ted Bardacke, and Thongchai Winichakul who read and criticized parts of the manuscript. We would like to thank the Japan Foundation who invited us to Japan at a critical point in the international history of the crisis, and the Center for Southeast Asian Studies, Kyoto which gave us some breathing space to write and the setting for a stimulating seminar. Thanks to Sauwalak Kittiprapas, Yukio Ikemoto, Kanishka Jayasuriya, and Sungsidh Piriyarangsan who helped with source material. Thanks to Pana Janviroj and *The Nation* for permission to reuse material, and for help in obtaining photographs. Finally, thanks to all at Silkworm Books for speed and professionalism.

NOTES

1. Some of the essays in this book originated as articles in academic journals and collections, but none are reproduced here in their earlier form. We have updated them substantially, and also removed material which would be duplicated across chapters. An earlier version of chapter 2 appeared in *Journal of Asia Pacific Economy* 4 (1) 1999, and we are grateful to the publishers, Routledge, and to the editor, Anis Chowdhury, for permission to reproduce. Earlier versions of chapters 5 and 6 (combined as one article) and 7 appear in the collection, *Thailand Beyond Crisis*, and we are grateful to the editor, Peter Warr, the National Thai Studies Centre of the Australian National University, and its director, Cavan Hogue, for permission.

MANY CRISES

First, what happened?

Over 1990–93, Thailand opened up its capital account, removing most restrictions on the inflow and outflow of money. The funds immediately poured in. Thai firms gulped up these funds because the interest rates were a fraction of what they were used to. Western and Japanese financial firms stuffed funds into the market because low returns in their home markets had generated a faddish enthusiasm for "emerging markets" and "Asian miracles." Some of the funds were lent directly to Thai firms, and some placed on the Thai stock market. Most however were short-term bank loans which Thai financial firms lent on to customers, often for long-term projects.

Economic theory says that a country cannot have both an open capital account and a fixed exchange rate without losing control over monetary policy. But the Thai monetary authorities had come to believe that a fixed exchange rate (roughly tied to the US dollar) made Thailand attractively "stable" for foreign investors and trading partners. So they resisted the advice to relax control of the exchange rate. Then they struggled to manage the impact of this unprecedented flood of money.

The economy quickly became distorted. The capital inflows stoked inflation. Because the exchange rate remained fixed, the baht became overvalued, Thai products became less competitive in international markets, and exports declined. At the same time, the flood of money boosted consumption, including consumption of imports, so the balance of trade slumped into deficit.

1

The flood of capital had nowhere much to go. The underlying economy was already into a cyclical downturn after several years of boom. The Japanese economy, which had underlain the dynamism of the Asian region over the previous decade, had collapsed into a severe structural recession. The falling prospects for export industries deterred further investments in this sector. Most of the inflowing capital went into projects for the domestic market—heavy upstream industries (steel, petrochemicals), infrastructure (highways, telecommunications), services (finance, insurance, real estate), consumer finance, and stock speculation. Over-investment in these sectors generated over-capacity and falling returns (Phatra Research Institute 1997). But with the inflow of money seemingly infinite, nobody was looking too closely at returns. Everyone from *The Economist* to the local analysts of firms like Merrill Lynch were drawing straight-line projections towards a profitable future.

The cracks first showed in the property market. The sector was easy to enter, and investors in the late 1980s had made huge profits which encouraged others to follow. By 1994, this boom was clearly over. But money still flooded into this sector, with increasing amounts coming from abroad (especially from Hong Kong, also through the BIBF offshore banks). By 1995, with supply far outrunning demand, property firms began to go bad. The problem backed up into the finance industry. On one side, property firms stopped paying their debts to finance houses, while on the other, perceptive foreign creditors refused to roll over their loans. Finance firms' balance sheets and cash flow deteriorated. In early 1997, the largest finance company (Finance One) collapsed. One of the largest real estate firms (Somprasong) reneged on its debts and its owner fled.

International financial speculators now saw an opportunity to profit by undercutting the baht. They had tried earlier, in the aftermath of the 1994 Mexican crisis, but without full commitment. By late 1996, Thailand's high balance-of-payments deficit, large volume of short-term foreign debt, export decline, and evident financial problems made the country's currency a sitting duck. The attacks started in November 1996, and were repeated with greater intensity in February and May 1997.

Since the 1990–93 liberalization, Thai economists (and the IMF) had occasionally called on the government to relax control over the baht so that exchange rate changes would counter the distortions in the economy. But capital inflows and economic distortions create their own coalitions of supporters. The companies and finance houses which had contracted foreign debt (and by now this was virtually any company of any significance) resisted the idea of allowing the baht's value to fall because it would raise the baht-equivalent value of their foreign debt. Driven by its own ingrained beliefs, and backed up by this background of political support, the central bank tried to hold the line. It allowed the collapsing finance firms to stagger along by borrowing from the Financial Institutions Development Fund (FIDF)[1] to cover the gap in their accounts caused by falling repayments on one side and increasing withdrawals of foreign loans on the other. It confronted the hedge funds and other currency speculators by playing poker in the foreign currency market with the international reserves. By the end of June 1997, the reserves were almost fully committed to this game, and the baht was defenceless.

The baht was floated on 2 July 1997. In early August, the US forced the Thai government to reveal the true state of the foreign reserves and the true extent of lending through the FIDF as preconditions for assistance from the IMF. Once this information was out, the currency speculators knew they could hammer the baht with impunity, and foreign creditors rushed to withdraw their loans as rapidly as possible. The currency began to drop like a stone. Over the next twelve months, the private capital outflows, net of foreign direct investment, were equivalent to almost a fifth of GDP. The currency bottomed just under half of its pre-float value.

Finance firms and companies whose foreign loans were withdrawn saw their liquidity evaporate. Those with foreign loans still on their books saw their liabilities soar in value and their balance sheets go bad (Bhanupong 1998). Many firms stopped operating. The impact of the outflows soon backed up into consumption levels. Layoffs increased. Sales dropped. More companies went out of business. Loans were not serviced or repaid. Banks restricted further credit. The economy tipped into a headlong downward spiral that continued unabated for eighteen months.

DISEASES, DIAGNOSES, AND CURES

The above sequence of events is generally accepted. But *why* this should have come about, and with what implications, are matters on which there are countless interpretations. Particularly during the early stages, there were many voices offering different explanations of the crisis. Most of these explanations were determined by what their protagonists hoped would be the outcome of the crisis.

American triumphalists argued the crisis proved the superiority of American-style capitalism, and expected the dismantling and replacement of Asian-style variants.[2] International Marxists argued there was an underconsumption crisis and expected a resurgence of labour politics (Beams 1998). Neoliberals blamed the crisis on governmental interference with the laws of the market, and expected reforms to advance liberalization (see below). Anti-modernists placed the blame on Thai development policy's emphasis on industrial growth and called for a return to agriculture and a community focus. Japanese economists pointed to Thailand's failure to cultivate its export industries with skills and R&D, and urged change towards a more Japanese approach towards industrial policy (Suehiro 1999). Opponents of export-oriented growth attributed the crisis to the resulting unbalanced shape of the economy, and expected new political forces to demand a shift towards growth powered by domestic demand (Bello et al. 1998; Bernard 1999). Institutional economists attributed the crisis to Thailand's poor stock of the fashionably new concept of "social capital," and argued that the solution lay in institutional reforms (Unger 1998). And so on.

Here we want to describe three of these teleological explanations in a little more detail. The reader must understand that this is not an academic review of analyses of the crisis. We have chosen these three because they were important to what subsequently happened.

The Washington version

Alan Greenspan, chairman of the US Federal Reserve, spoke about the Asia crisis in New York at the end of 1997. He started with the faith that market liberalization "offers enormous benefits to all nations over the long run." He went on to argue that in Asia "mistakes arose from government-directed or influenced investments." This was a problem because, "Policy loans, in too many instances foster misuse of resources, unprofitable expansions, losses and eventually loan defaults." Thus it was perfectly proper for capital to flee from Asia in such circumstances (though not at all clear why it should have entered in the first place). He concluded (Greenspan 1997) that:

4

The current crisis is likely to accelerate the dismantling in many Asian countries of the remnants of a system with large elements of government-directed investment, in which finance played a key role in carrying out the state's objectives.

Larry Summers, the deputy secretary[3] of the US Treasury, laid out the argument in more detail in a series of speeches and papers about the Asia crisis. He dismissed the idea that the crisis was caused by financial speculators, ignored any broader arguments about the nature of the international financial system, and paid little attention to macroeconomic policies in the crisis countries.[4] He emphasized that the origins of the crisis were "microeconomic" and "disproportionately involved the judgements of [the affected] countries' own citizens," by which he meant that Asian firms were the guilty parties. They had engaged in a "reckless pursuit of low cost capital" (Summers 1998a). Like Greenspan, he attributed this to political linkages: "In Asia, the problems related to 'crony capitalism' were at the heart of the crisis and that was why structural reforms had to be a major part of the IMF's solution" (Summers, 1999a). Close links between businessmen and politicians, Summers argued, could deliver fast growth for a time. But profits were made more by "rent seeking" than by productivity and efficiency, and there was a high risk of over-investment in unprofitable ventures.[5]

This combination of bad business and bad politics meant that the people of these countries were condemned to slower growth and lower welfare than would occur under free market conditions. Hence the US had a duty to the people of these countries to take the opportunity of the Asia crisis to force change. Summers liked to cite the fact that one of the two written characters in the Chinese word for "crisis" meant "opportunity," and he titled one of his key speeches of this period "Opportunities Out of Crises: Lessons From Asia" (Summers 1998b). Other speeches by Summers (*TN*, 16 Aug 1997) had a missionary tone about the American role in building a new Asia, in part by exporting the ideas and institutions which were the foundations of US economic power:

> The American financial sector is the largest—and most successful—financial sector in the world. It goes without saying that we believe countries will only

enjoy the benefits of a truly global capital market if our firms are given greater access to their markets.

Summers emphasized that the Clinton government had already embarked on this mission by pressuring the IMF to broaden its crisis programmes beyond macroeconomic tinkering to include measures "to reduce trade barriers and unproductive expenditures, promote core labor standards and mitigate the social costs of economic adjustments." Later he noted that under US guidance, the IMF had "for the first time explicitly endorsed the principle that conditions on the use of IMF resources should include requirements to liberalize trade and eliminate directed lending and other unfair or market-distorting subsidies" (Summers 1999b).

Summers emphasized that in pressuring for these changes in the IMF's scope, "the United States has made real progress in furthering some key American values," and had "been able to make a difference in areas of particular importance to the United States" (Summers 1999b). The advantages to the US were noticed by others in the policy establishment. A former undersecretary for commerce in the Clinton administration (Jeff Garten, *New York Times*, 14 Jan 1998) wrote:

> Most of these countries are going to go through a deep and dark tunnel. . . . But on the other end there is going to be significantly different Asia in which American firms have achieved much deeper market penetration, much greater access.

Charlene Barshevsky, the US trade representative, noted in February 1988 that the IMF programmes included "commitments to restructure public enterprises and accelerate privatization of certain key sectors—including energy, transportation, utilities and communications" which would "create new business opportunities for US firms" (*TN*, 3 Apr 1998).

Summers put the importance of gaining market access for US firms in historical perspective. He argued that, "The major industrial nations are crossing the threshold into an era of rising rates of retirement and much lower rates of labor force growth. . . . All of the world's population growth over the next 25 years—and the lion's share of its growth in productivity—will take place in the developing countries" (Summers

1999c). Hence for the future benefit of Americans, US economic diplomacy had to break down any barriers and gain access to these markets.

But unlike simple boosters of US self-interest, Summers recognized that there was a delicate issue at stake over sovereignty. Gaining market access meant not only breaking down formal economic barriers, but also changing legal, accounting, financial, and even political systems to create an institutional environment which US firms would find safe and familiar. But Summers noted that countries often resisted attempts by the US to integrate their economies more closely into the international economy, particularly when this involved efforts to force institutional changes. He attributed this resistance to "the widespread sense that international integration interferes with governments' ability to deliver the benefits the citizenry want" (Summers 1999a). To get round this problem, the US would need "to finesse sovereignty problems by highlighting the national benefits of internationally congenial behavior," in other words, persuade these countries that it was in their own best interests to approximate their financial, legal, and other systems to those in the US. Summers (1999a) noted what an important part US-trained economists played in this task:

> Just think of the Berkeley Mafia in Indonesia, the Chicago boys in Chile, and the MIT and Harvard graduates who have played such a large role over the last decade in Mexico and Argentina, or the historic changes wrought by Mahomon Singh as India's finance minister.

In sum, the dominant explanation in the US policy establishment at the outset of the crisis attributed the event to obstructions of the free market, contrived by coalitions of businessmen and politicians, which delivered returns more through "rent seeking" than through market-generated profits—a model often shorthanded as "crony capitalism." This explanation was important because it implicitly legitimated crisis-management policies which entailed widespread bankruptcies (the market's "creative destruction") and which obliged governments to accept programmes of institutional restructuring. This was nothing less than a mission to rescue the crisis countries from bad capitalism and bad government. In his retirement addresses, the IMF managing director, Michel Camdessus (*BP*, 15 Feb 2000; *TN*, 14 Feb 2000) portrayed his role in the crisis as an economic knight errant jousting with forces of evil:[6]

When we fight corruption, nepotism, cronyism, the *chaebols* in Korea, all the cronies are against us, all the institutions are against us. . . .
You have vested interests in the world trying to destroy us because, of course, they know that we destroy them. You cannot go and confront the family monopoly in Indonesia or the *chaebol* in Korea, and so on, without, well, provoking some adverse negative campaigns.

The resulting market opening would benefit the US because of the power of the US's highly developed capitalism. This was important because the developing countries, and those in Asia in particular, were expected to play a major part in world economic growth in the future. For the US policy establishment, the crisis was a danger to the international financial system, but an opportunity for American business.

Ammar's version

Ammar Siamwalla is one of Thailand's most senior professional economists and almost unique in being independent of both government and the financial sector.[7] He wrote one of the earliest explanations of the crisis available in the national press (Ammar 1997), and later expanded it in publications of the Thailand Development Research Institute (TDRI), where he was the retired president and presiding eminence. He was a key figure in the writing of the influential Nukul Report on the central bank's role in creating the crisis (see pp. 115–6). In his commentary on the crisis, he became the nation's most publicly prominent academic economist. It can be argued that his views were influential on—or roughly congruent with—the main policy makers in the Democrat-led government.

Ammar traced the crisis to two main causes: bad firms and bad technocrats. The bubble blew up, he argued, because Thai firms borrowed too much debt. The bust was so disastrous because bank debt could be withdrawn easily. Thai firms relied so heavily on bank debt because most were family businesses and because of "the reluctance of family businesses to cede control to outsiders" (Ammar 1997). These firms had also plunged enthusiastically into the newly vibrant stock market, but this had not changed their overall stance: "During the stock market boom, equity was raised merely to leverage more debt."

This debt dependence was not inherently wrong. Indeed Ammar recognized that bank lending was fundamental to "a system which worked for 40 years" and delivered Thailand high growth (*TN*, 4 Mar 1999). But the circumstances had changed with financial liberalization, and "the crisis has shown that the almost exclusive reliance on bank capital is fraught with greater risks for the country than most Thais had thought" (Ammar and Orapin 1998, 30). He noted that politics could interfere with bank lending (particularly in the case of the Bangkok Bank of Commerce). But he knew that Thailand had nothing like the government directed system of "policy loans" which the Washington version imagined was prevalent across Asia. He attributed the misallocation of capital during the boom to excess inflows, poor entrepreneurship, and the fixed exchange rate, not to any imagined "crony capitalism" or "Asian model."

In late 1997, Ammar predicted the "mother of all fire sales" (*TN*, 8 Sep 1997) with widespread bankruptcies and foreign takeovers. He presented this simply as a realistic projection, but his condemnation of "family businesses" also implicitly legitimated this result. Banks would be a major part of this fire sale. Long before the crisis, Ammar had criticized the protection given to the Thai domestic banks, arguing in particular that this protection allowed excessive profit margins. In the crisis, he advocated development of the capital market to reduce the dependence on banks. Some time later, when the financial crunch seemed to block prospects of recovery, he had doubts whether the attempt to move so rapidly away from a bank-based system would work: "I'm not sure the bankers or borrowers are ready for this new culture. . . . It's easy in retrospect to say that many things are weak in the system but do we need to dismantle it?" (*TN*, 4 Mar 1999). When prospects brightened, he justified the destruction of Thai financial institutions on grounds that they had not upgraded their technology and practice in line with the economy's needs.

Besides the problem of family businesses and protected banks, Ammar's second explanation of the crisis focused on the failure of Thailand's technocrats and in particular those in the Bank of Thailand. He argued that financial liberalization had led so quickly to a bubble economy because the Bank of Thailand had resisted unpegging the exchange rate, and had gone on using monetary rather than fiscal measures to control demand even though liberalization made monetary tools ineffective. He pointed out that the crash was deep and disastrous because of the central bank's failed defence of the baht, and its use of the FIDF to cover up the implosion in the finance industry.

Ammar believed these policy failures were the result of a decline of the technocracy, which he attributed to two main causes. First, the machinery of policy-making had ossified, especially the Bank of Thailand. From the 1960s to the 1980s, the central bank had been famed as the most capable, uncorrupt, dedicated, and effective public institution in Thailand. But since then it had suffered a rapid and catastrophic decline. It had initially been organized as an absolute monarchy—with all the power in the hands of the governor—at a time when the talent pool was limited. But it had not changed this structure after the ranks of skilled middle-rank personnel expanded. This had caused frustration, factionalization, waste of talent, and power games. As a result, the institution had totally failed to adjust to the new policy environment created by liberalization and other changes in the Thai economy and the international context. (Nukul 1998, paras 426–442).

Ammar's second reason for the decline of the technocracy lay in politics. Technocrats had become vulnerable to political pressures. Talented people had either been pulled away to the private sector or discouraged from entering public service. The Bank of Thailand had lost its independence after two governors were removed by the finance minister, and other pressures were applied during the time Banharn Silpa-archa was prime minister. Ammar (1997) concluded, "It is doubtful whether an autonomous technocracy exists any more."

For Thailand's politicians, chosen mostly by an unsophisticated electorate, "the public treasury was a milk-cow. The MPs' central chore was to milk that cow and bring the cream back home to their constituents" (Ammar 1997). The politicians not only pressured the technocrats for corrupt pork-barrel reasons. But they had no interest in "*national* economic policies" because these had no meaning for the people who elected them. The politicians not only undercut the technocrats, but also failed to take responsibility for economic management.

Over recent years, Ammar's thinking had become increasingly influenced by institutional economics. This was reflected in his diagnosis of the crisis which he attributed to failures in banking institutions and policy making institutions. In his analysis, the capital account liberalization was a given. The crisis stemmed from failures to adapt institutions to the changes which liberalization entailed. The solution would have to be institutional change. Thailand's old banking practices, whatever their pre-liberalization record, had become irrelevant and unsustainable. Better banking regulation was now necessary, and foreign bank takeovers were predictable. Thailand's old machinery for economic policy making had been sapped by political pressures and internal ossification. It had failed to adapt to a new era. This diagnosis led Ammar to place some (but not much) hope on political reform under the new constitution, but also to advocate major change in the machinery and objectives of economic policy making, especially in the central bank.

Mo Prawase's version

By the early 1990s, Dr Prawase Wasi had built a formidable reputation. He was a medic by training, had served as doctor to the king, was widely believed to maintain close royal connections, had won the Magsaysay award[8] for work with health NGOs, and was a recognized leader of the NGO movement. He spoke often in public about Buddhism, environmental issues, and Thai culture. He was also closely involved in politics (in a broad, non-party sense) and had played roles in the promotion of constitutional reform, the framing of the Eighth Plan, and change in the educational system.[9] His interpretation of the crisis was important because he was very public in his views, his angle was strikingly different from the mainstream, and because he commanded great respect on account of his connections and achievements.

Prawase argued that the crisis resulted from bad development policies which undermined the foundations of society. The idea of development which originated from the West promoted capitalism, industry, and greed. In doing so, it destroyed the "foundations of society" which were local communities, the natural environment, morality, and social harmony: "In search of big money, we do not hesitate to oppress, exploit, or destroy just about anyone and anything that we cannot turn into money" (*BP*, 14 Jan 1998). This development created an economy which was "heavy at the top but shaky at the bottom" and eventually collapsed like the Korat Royal Plaza Hotel which caved in because structural pillars had been removed during modifications.

Prawase argued that it was senseless to revive the old development path as this would only lead to further social destruction and repetitive crises. Instead Thailand should turn away from Western-style capitalism, develop on the basis of its own resources, both cultural and natural, and build a balanced economy which truly suited the needs of humanity. This task

11

would require nothing less than a "war of national salvation" (*TN*, 21 Jul 1998).

Although the urban or "upper" economy had collapsed, the local economy was still functioning "because the upper economy is fake but the lower economy is real" (*BP*, 28 Dec 1997). The foundations for the new economy would be local communities. They should concentrate on activities which drew on local resources and hence were self-reliant, such as integrated agriculture, handicraft production, cottage industries, herbal medicine, Thai food, and tourism. But this self-reliance was not the same as isolation. Once communities had developed their own strong foundations, they should network together to form more complex institutions such as savings banks, cooperative welfare schemes, and other businesses. The objective would not be growth in GDP but in GDH—gross domestic happiness—which Prawase proposed as "an economic indicator, Thai-style" (*BP*, 14 Jan 1998) whose components were "learning families, strong communities, sustainable environment" (Prawase 1998, 37).

MANY CRISES

These were three of many interpretations of the 1997 crisis in Thailand and in Asia. These three were chosen here because they were important in shaping the events which followed. The Washington version, so explicitly laid out by Larry Summers, provided the framework for the IMF package with its emphasis on market access and financial restructuring. It also had a bearing on the international organizations' interest in social policy (see chapter 4). Ammar's version is roughly congruent with the priorities of the main Thai policymakers from late 1997 onwards. It lacked the religious commitment to market liberalization in the Washington version, but promoted the practical need for financial and bureaucratic reform. Prawase's version reflects the inward-looking emphasis which characterized much of the popular reaction to the crisis. It also influenced the emphasis which came to be placed on the *social* management of the crisis, and the "retreat to the locality" which characterized that approach.

The contrast between these three approaches cautions against single, monolithic explanations of events as complex as a modern, finance-based crisis of this scope. The short descriptions above indicate the subtle gap between the Washington and Ammar versions, and the huge gulf between the Washington and the Prawase versions. One is focused on the financial crisis, while the other criticizes the development strategy of the previous half-century. One argues for the unfettered working of market economics, while the other rejects economics wholesale (Prawase lumped economists along with politicians and bureaucrats as those guilty of causing the crisis). One urges Thailand to look outward, the other is focused inward. This book will argue that all three of these views have influenced the way the crisis was managed, and how the future beyond the crisis will be shaped.

NOTES

1. A fund financed by a small tax on finance firms' operations, and managed by the central bank, with the objective of assisting finance firms which hit short-term difficulties.

2. "Just as the fate of the Berlin Wall in 1989 marked the triumph of the American political system over communism, so the latest crisis marks the triumph of the American economic system of open markets over state-run economies." James Flanagan in *Los Angeles Times* (*TN*, 5 Nov 1997).

3. He became secretary when Robert Rubin resigned in May 1999.

4. We stress that this summary represents Summers' early analysis of the crisis. Later he became more sensitive to the roles of macro policy and financial markets.

5. "Governments targeted particular industries, promoted selected exports, and protected domestic industry. There was a reliance on debt rather than equity, relationship-driven finance not capital markets, and informal rather than formal enforcement mechanisms." (Summers 1998b)

6. A few weeks earlier, Camdessus had claimed that the famous photo of him standing over President Suharto with his arms folded had been misinterpreted. It was not a display of arrogance, he said, he just didn't know where to put his hands. These more ebullient remarks on the occasion of his retirement may be less diplomatic, more heart-felt, more true.

7. He started his career at Thammasat University, and spent the latter part with the Thailand Development Research Institute. He officially retired in 1999.

8. An Asian prize for social contributions.

9. At the 7th International Conference in Thai Studies in Amsterdam in July 1999, Prawase described with great pride his manipulation of Banharn and other political figures to secure constitutional reform. Prawase would of course deny that he was in any sense a politician.

THE POLITICAL ECONOMY
OF THE THAI CRISIS

The economic crisis which began in Thailand in mid 1997 spread by
contagion through the regional and international economy. In parallel,
analysis of the crisis was just as contagious. It began in currency theory and
international economics, then infected development economics,
comparative economic systems, theory of the state, international relations,
and much more. In the course of this epidemic, diagnosis of the original
local roots of the crisis in Thailand became rather obscured.[1] In this chapter,
we examine the political economy background of the crisis—more
specifically, the key pressures on policy making from the financial
liberalization of the early 1990s through to the baht float and IMF entry in
July–August 1997.

The causes and sequencing of the Thai economic crisis have been
extensively discussed (Ammar and Orapin 1998; Chandrasekhar and Ghosh
1998; Hewison 2000; Lauridsen 1998; Phatra Research Institute 1997;
Warr 1998a). Most accounts of events leading up to the unpegging of the
baht in July 1997 cover the following four main points.

1. Rapid growth of export-oriented industrialization from the mid
   1980s, aided by a large inflow of foreign direct investment,[2] created
   large structural problems which undermined export competitiveness. First, the supply of some factors of production was
   exhausted—particularly skilled labour and infrastructure—leading
   to supply constraints and rising costs. Second, the capital inflows
   led to a version of "Dutch disease"—a rise in the price of non-

traded goods (especially property) relative to traded goods, causing a misallocation of resources and real appreciation of the currency to the detriment of the export economy.[3]

2. These difficulties created a slowdown by the early 1990s, but were then masked by financial liberalization. Deregulation and capital account convertibility in 1991–93—carried out in the context of excessive enthusiasm about Asia in the international financial markets—led to massive money inflows. Gross domestic investment rose above 40 percent of GDP, more than the economy could absorb. In the absence of any policing of these inflows, a large proportion of the debt was denominated short term (portfolio holdings and bank loans), and vulnerable to market sentiment.

3. Given the structural fall in export competitiveness and the structural distortion of tradable/non-tradable prices, the financial inflows generated a sharp rise in domestic consumption, a similarly sharp decline in the current account balance, an asset price bubble, and excessive investment in property and many domestically oriented industries (steel, automobiles, petrochemicals, services).

4. Economic policymakers failed to control these forces either by unpegging the baht from the dollar, properly sterilizing the inflows, or using fiscal and other measures to manipulate resource allocation. In fact they compounded the crisis by attempts to maintain the existing policy regime. They sacrificed financial reserves in a futile defence of the currency value, and created a stopgap fund (FIDF)[4] which allowed the financial industry to accumulate massive bad debts.

Among different schools of thought, there are variations in the weight given to each of these factors and the implications derived from them. But the general outline of the crisis is not in serious dispute.

However, there still remains a difficulty of explaining *why* all this happened. Why did Thailand's policymakers opt for such rapid liberalization of the financial sector? Why was little or nothing done between 1994 and 1997 to counter the obvious problems accumulating in the economy? Why did the government defend the policy regime in 1996–97 so ardently and so disastrously?

There have been three main approaches to answering this question. First, for those who fundamentally oppose the policy regime, including some Marxists and advocates of sustainable growth, the failure is integral to the strategy and does not require any extra explanation (Hewison 2000; Srisuwan 1998; Suthy 1997; Bello 1999). Second, for neoclassicals, the failures are simply "mistakes" by the policymakers (Ammar and Orapin 1998; Phatra Research Institute 1997; Warr 1998b). Third, for neoliberals, the failure is attributed to some combination of corruption and excessive government intervention, summarized by the term "cronyism," more subtly phrased as "bad banking" under political protection (Krugman 1998) or "noncommercial relationships amongst the banks, governments, and industrial companies" (Rubin 1998), and sometimes magnified as an intrinsic failure of a specifically Asian brand of capitalism.

Here we want to put some political economy behind the answer to the question of why the Thai crisis took this form. Any explanation of the crisis must look not just at economic mechanisms but at the politics of economic policy making. Our argument focuses on the new economic and political forces which emerged from the second oil crisis recession of 1984–86.[5] However, first it is necessary to look back before this turning point.

Chart 2.1: Real GDP growth 1959–96

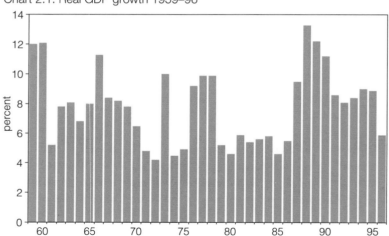

THE THAI ECONOMY BEFORE THE MID 1980s

From 1959 to 1996, Thailand's annual GDP increase averaged 7.8 percent and never fell below 4 percent (chart 2.1). This long period of sustained and relatively stable growth was based on a specific political economy and policy-making regime.

This regime was different from the Japan-derived "Asian model" often used to characterize the successful Asian economies of this era. The key features of that model included: a powerful, authoritarian state which sought economic growth through market-defying industrial policy and an assertive role in the allocation of credit; close cooperative or dependent relationships between an economic technocracy and the leaders of business; high levels of domestic savings and their conversion into industrial investment; the creation of a docile urban working class through repression and paternalism; high investments in education, skill, and technology development; and relatively high insulation of the economy from external forces through exchange controls, trade barriers, and other filters.[6]

Very few of these features hold good for Thailand for the single reason that the government played a much more limited role in industrialization. There was no industrial policy; virtually no guided credit; low levels of investment in skill and technology; relatively distant relationships between businessmen and policymakers; and a trend away from dictatorship to parliamentary rule. Yet, many of the achievements of the Asian model do hold good for Thailand: high rates of savings, a growth-oriented allocation of credit, and plentiful supplies of cheap labour. However, in the Thai case, the mechanisms and the resulting industrial structure were rather different from East Asian examples.

Capital market

Until the early 1990s, there were two main sources of capital formation: the Thai commercial banks and foreign direct investment.

Government set out incentives to attract foreign investment into sectors prioritized by government, but this incentive regime was only minimally restrictive, and more investment took place outside the incentive framework than within it. Foreign investment was conditioned more by international business's perception of Thailand than by specific Thai government policies.

After 1975 the US, previously the largest foreign investor, saw Thailand as unsafe and unpromising. Apart from oil companies and a few consumer goods vendors, very little Western investment flowed into Thailand until the mid 1990s. By contrast, Japan identified Thailand as a site for offshore manufacture and cultivated its knowledge of and relations with Thailand over the long term. From 1973 onwards Japan was Thailand's largest source of FDI.

The Thai government took only a minimal role in the allocation of domestic credit, but provided protection for a cartel of Thai commercial banks.

These banks emerged between the 1940s and 1960s when Western banks had little interest in Thailand. From the 1950s they secured government protection against foreign competition. They amassed capital from the high-saving propensities of the largely rural population. They prospered by spotting the high potential sectors in the economy and allocating capital to these sectors either through investment in subsidiary companies, or by supporting groups of associates (Suehiro 1989, 154–72). Four or five major banks became such a large factor in the whole economy that their decisions on allocating credit were fundamental not only to their own profits but to the overall direction and health of the economy. These banks became the centres of sprawling business conglomerates.

With the big banks often acting as their planners and consultants, these conglomerates dominated each area of business opportunity which opened up through this era—first agriprocessing, then import-substituting consumer industries, then basic process industries, and then urban services. In the period from the 1950s to the 1970s, these conglomerates were assisted by links with the military politicians who controlled the state. In the late 1970s when dictatorship gave way to a transitional form of "semi-democracy" (the coexistence of an elected parliament and a military strong-man as prime minister), business leaders maintained their political links by becoming players and sponsors of the new party politics (Anek 1992; Hewison 1989; Pasuk and Baker 1995). But there was no stable "cronyism." Rather, the competition between business groups was reflected in competition between fragmented political parties and factions.

Government had no overt policy to favour these corporate groups, but government machinery was susceptible to their great influence. Government agencies sometimes policed business competition by creating monopolies, but this was rare. It preferred instead to ringmaster competing oligopolies which were more efficient and more competitive in sharing their profits with the regulators (Khan 1998). The result was a high degree of concentration under thirty or so major business conglomerates. Because government encouraged foreign investors to enter into joint ventures with domestic partners, FDI also became part of this process (Suehiro 1989; Pasuk and Baker 1995).

A key factor in this crudely developed capital market was knowledge. The Thai banks and the Japanese investors built their own data banks and information networks about the Thai economy, its prospects, and its participants. The major banks developed economic research departments which gathered statistical data that was often more extensive than the official data. The heads of the banks cultivated extensive networks of trust with allied entrepreneurs. The Japanese government funded information gathering and personal networking through institutions such as JICA and JETRO, while major Japanese firms developed relationships with counterpart Thai business groups in order to acquire market knowledge and other advantages.

Labour market

Thailand has a large rural sector whose population increased from 20 million in 1960 to around 45 million in the mid 1980s.[7] From around 1980, investment in agriculture declined, and this sector's pace of growth fell behind that of the economy as a whole. From this point on, the countryside was managed as a source of labour and other inputs for urban growth (land, water, electricity generation). The countryside released plentiful supplies of labour into the urban economy at a price which was subsidized by the village's role as a social welfare system providing unemployment relief, retirement support, and many other social functions. This labour force remained cheap and largely docile, requiring only selective exercises of repression and careful control over labour laws.

Technology and skills

The openness to FDI provided access to technology, relieving the government of any imperative to divert funds towards technology development, or to force firms to do likewise (Westphal 1989). Similarly, government's role in education and skill development was limited. School education concentrated on creating mass basic literacy, while higher education was oriented to staffing the bureaucracy. Secondary schooling and technical education were neglected. The demand for high-level educated manpower in industry and commerce was met by self-financed overseas education. Labour skills were acquired on the job.

Policy making

A technocrat cadre was developed from the 1960s onwards, but was engaged mostly in the technical management of the economy—infrastructure planning, and tight macro management under a fixed exchange rate regime. The main direction of policy was laid down by the military rulers under the influence of the World Bank, and adjusted in practice by business lobbies. Technocrats *administered* policy, but in this era had only a limited role in *making* policy. From the mid 1970s, as the political system eased, some technocrats formed a lobby for greater liberalization and for a switch towards the East Asian pattern of export-oriented industrialization. While this advocacy was written into the five-year plans and other policy documents, it was ineffectual in face of the vested interests of the conglomerates and their political allies who wished to retain the old regime of agricultural exports and import-substituting industry (Snoh 1987; Pasuk 1992).

In sum, Thailand from the 1950s to 1980s did not approximate any Asian model of state-driven growth, but delivered some of the same results, namely, high savings, reasonably well-directed allocation of scarce capital, manufacturing relying on plentiful supplies of docile and cheap labour, access to technology, and the absence of major political threats to urban-based economic growth. These were achieved not through directed credit, industrial policy, and labour repression, but rather through the control of capital allocation by a handful of major banks and one major FDI source (Japan); the exploitation of a large and dependent rural sector; and the gradual development of both business and political competition.

THE TURNING POINT IN THE MID 1980s

The period came to an end in the mid 1980s. The second oil crisis led to a balance-of-payments crisis, devaluation, and banking shake-out in 1984–86. Four changes emerged from this crisis and its aftermath: first, a significant expansion in the role of technocrats; second, financial liberalization; third, a reorientation of the conglomerates; and fourth, the emergence of new business groups. Moreover, these economic changes ran in parallel with the expansion of democratic politics.

Democratization

The dissolution of the cold war and the decline of US tutelage in the 1970s paved the way for a gradual transition from military dictatorship to parliamentary systems. The transition was not smooth. Generals and their coalitions of supporters were reluctant to cede power, and there was a continuous series of clashes and standoffs. But the trend was clear. In 1988, the general who presided over the "semi-democracy" stepped down and was replaced by an elected prime minister whose government moved quickly to shift power from bureaucrats to politicians. The army reacted with a coup in February 1991, which was reversed by the popular protests of May 1992, and a restoration of elected governments from September 1992 onwards (Pasuk and Baker 1995, ch. 9). Parliamentary politics became an arena of competition between business interests, and between competing claims on the government budget. The resulting public life—characterized by fluid parliamentary coalitions, immature parties, fierce electoral competition, and raucous public debate—provoked concern about "stability" and "corruption." But in the absence of severe rural disorder or strident labour demands, attempts to revive dictatorship or one-party statism to defend urban growth from internal threats found only limited support. From the mid 1980s, party politics, press, and civil society organizations developed very rapidly (Hewison 1997).

The rise of the technocrats

The crisis of 1984–86 saw a significant transfer of power over economic policy making into the hands of technocrats.

This transfer was graphically symbolized. In November 1984 technocrats in the Finance Ministry and central bank persuaded the cabinet to devalue the baht by 14.7 percent. The army chief appeared on TV to demand they reverse the devaluation. He subsequently had to accept defeat and soon after lost his job.

The influence of the technocrats had begun to increase from the early 1980s when Thailand accepted World Bank structural adjustment financing to counter the impact of the second oil crisis and worldwide recession. The World Bank worked with Thai technocrats to plan the transition to an export-oriented strategy. Until 1984, however, these plans were blocked. But resistance was destroyed in 1984 by the recession, devaluation, and financial crisis which saw the collapse of two banks and the closure of many finance companies. After the devaluation, the main parts of the export-oriented industrialization plan were implemented. Key conglomerate leaders recognized that the era of import substitution industrialization was over and backed the transition to export orientation (Naris 1995: Snoh 1987; World Bank 1983, 1985).

Through the mid 1980s, technocrats acquired additional influence because of their technical skills for managing the transition of the economy to export-oriented industrialization. Several technocrats became key public figures and had a lead role in formulating the new strategy. They formed a loose network across major institutions, including: in the planning board, Snoh Unakul and a group of subordinates and associates such as Phisit Pakkasem, Kosit Panpiemras, and Sippanonda Ketudhat; in the Finance Ministry, Suthy Singsaneh and Panas Simasthien who had managed the devaluation; in the central bank, Chavalit Tanachanan, Nukul Prachuab-moh, and a group of younger subordinates ("Dr Puey's children"[8]) including Vichit Suphinit, Chaiyawat Wibulswasdi, and Ekkamon Khiriwat; and some academics such as Virabhongse Ramangkura who acted as adviser to the prime minister, and Narongchai Akrasanee who worked as consultant to the planning agency.

The senior figures in this group were mostly educated in Europe. The more junior members had been educated in the US during the time of US patronage of Thailand in the 1960s and early 1970s. Many were undoubtedly affected by World Bank thinking, particularly the advocacy of export-oriented industrialization associated with Bela Belassa. Moreover, many of them shared a belief that the dominance of the conglomerates in the Thai economy hampered growth and contributed to the poor distribution of the gains from growth. They argued that the persistence of oligopolistic market restrictions sacrificed the interests of consumers, and subsidized backward and inefficient business structures and practices. The protection of the banking cartel led to a high price for capital as well as unfair restrictions on access. These technocrats were attracted to the notion that liberalizing markets would abolish rents, expose inefficient business practices, and maximize welfare (Snoh 1987; Narongchai and Paitoon 1990; Chittima and Mathee 1996). They also believed that liberalization offered Thailand the opportunity to make a rapid economic transition. Snoh Unakul, who headed the planning board from 1980 to 1989 and was in many ways the key figure in this technocrat network, wrote in 1987:

> Thailand will rank among the forefront countries capable of adjusting and performing strongly. The current trend is useful for Thailand as it will open up opportunities for investment and trade. More countries will pay attention to the region and us. . . . What needs to be done is to continue our restructuring. . . . The government must change from controlling to promoting and supporting. . . . What is unnecessary in terms of investment must be left to the private sector. . . . We must adjust the country to export orientation. . . . Bangkok will become a centre for business and air transport. (Snoh 1987, 57, 65, 67, 92, 207)

The growing influence of the technocrats was disrupted in 1988, when an elected government came to power and set about shifting power from government official to politician. The role of the planning board—which had become a coordinating centre for technocrat policy making—was diminished. At the central bank a key technocrat was sacked and replaced by a more ineffectual figure. The Finance Ministry was controlled by a succession of business politicians.

But this disruption was temporary. After the military coup of 1991, the technocrats returned in force, without the complications of an elected parliament. The coup generals chose as prime minister Anand Panyarachun, an ex-diplomat who had become chairman of one of the conglomerates. He had played a role in the business diplomacy between corporate leaders and technocrats in the mid 1980s. He filled his cabinets with many of the technocrats who had been prominent in the years 1984–88. Snoh Unakul returned as the deputy prime minister in overall charge of economic matters. Kosit and Suthy also became ministers.

Anand's cabinets took most of the major decisions on financial liberalization, in the belief that these moves would not only spur the economy but also make Thailand a financial centre for the region (Finance and Banking 1992). When elected governments were restored in late 1992, the Democrat Party cajoled Tarrin Nimmanhaeminda, a US-educated professional who had had a meteoric career at the establishment Siam Commercial Bank, to become finance minister and to continue the policy of liberalization.

Financial liberalization

Under this technocrat regime, the financial system was liberalized over 1990–93. Restrictions on convertibility were removed in 1990. The domestic banking cartel was left in place, but in 1993 an offshore banking facility (BIBF) was established to enable foreign banks to lend into the Thai market. In addition, rules and supervision arrangements in the stock market were reformed to increase its attractiveness for foreign investors.

The liberalization of the capital account not only opened up an unprepared financial market to eccentric movements of short-term money, but also supplanted the existing mechanism for allocating capital within the economy. The dominant role of the major Thai banks was diminished by the multiplication of domestic credit institutions, and by domestic

Chart 2.2: Capital account, 1985–96

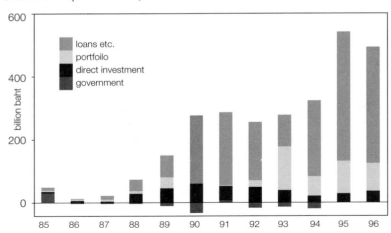

borrowers' direct access to overseas financial markets. At the same time, the ranks of foreign direct investors expanded, with increasing inflows from non-Japan sites in East Asia and from the West. In addition, the dominant form of capital inflows changed from FDI to bank loans and portfolio investments (chart 2.2). Capital was no longer scarce; between 1988 and 1990, net private inflows quadrupled, and then maintained that new level until a final bubbly surge in 1995–96.

Foreign debt accumulated rapidly. Between 1988 and 1996, the private sector's foreign debt increased almost ten times from 7.8 to 73.7 billion US dollars (chart 2.3). Much of the inflow came from new sources, through institutions which were new to the market and which made little investment in local knowledge. The opportunities for profitable investment did not expand at this rate. As a result, much investment was poorly planned and redundant, resulting in falling rates of return, rising over-capacity in certain sectors, and then a self-feeding bubble in finance and real estate (Phatra Research Institute 1997). Much of the evidence cited to condemn Thai firms for malpractice comes from this terminal, money-mad period. By 1996, Thailand's total foreign debt stood at 90.5 billion US dollars (equivalent to half of GDP), of which 81 percent was held by the private sector.

Chart 2.3: Foreign debt, 1988–99

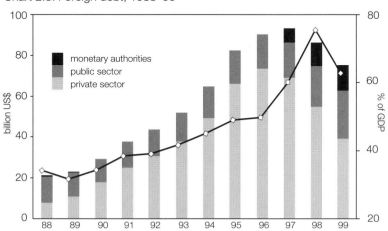

The reorientation of the conglomerates

From the 1984–86 crisis and the upturn of 1987–88, the role of the conglomerates in the Thai economy changed. They became separated from the main motor of growth in the economy, and also more detached from politics and policy making.

Between 1984 and 1986, currency realignments and policy reforms transformed Thailand's competitive advantage as an industrial exporter. The initial benefits from this transformation accrued to existing firms which could transfer spare capacity to export production or in other ways expand quickly. The firms which benefited included many small firms which were flexible, but also some of the conglomerates (including joint ventures) which had spare capacity (Narongchai, Jansen, and Jeerasak 1993).

However, after FDI began to flood in from 1986 onwards, multinationals took a much larger role than Thai firms in export industrialization. There are no figures to demonstrate this point. However, towards the end of the 1980s, the export mix changed from classic cheap labour industries (textiles, shoes) and resource based industries (processed food) to technology based industries including computer parts, auto parts, and electrical goods (TDRI 1994). Multinational firms controlled the technology required. Japanese companies in particular had advantage of access to export markets for these products through their extensive network of trading companies across the world. Often the units in Thailand were part of dispersed production networks spread across several countries under the control of a multinational.

From this period, the expansion strategies of the Thai conglomerates focused less on the export economy and more on the growth in the domestic market caused by the export-led boom. Their new investments went into property development, service industries (retail, finance, hotels, media), infrastructure development (roads, telecommunications, power generation), and secondary import substitution (petrochemicals, cement, steel). In these sectors they often had advantages over the multinationals in terms of market knowledge and marketing networks—the reverse of the situation in export industries where an increasing proportion of exports were intrafirm trade. In addition, in these sectors they were often able to leverage direct assistance from the government to maintain oligopolistic or at least privileged market positions. The property market was still partially protected by restrictions on foreign ownership of land. The financial market remained incompletely liberalized. The spectacular growth of telecommunications was cartelized by a system of government concessions. Investors in steel and petro-chemicals were able to persuade government to extend the life of protective tariff regimes (Pasuk and Baker 1998, ch. 3). Finally too, the conglomerates' focus on these domestic sectors was encouraged by the "Dutch disease" inflation of domestic prices, induced by the large inflow of foreign capital and the appreciation of the Thai baht.

However, the over investment in these sectors was not only the result of "crowding in" of domestic investment. The local firms were more agile in moving into these areas, but multinational capital was only four to five years behind. From 1993 onwards, most FDI and other capital inflows were directed towards these same sectors—especially property and finance—and contributed a large part of the asset bubble in the latter years of the boom. Foreign firms also began to invest in many service industries (retail), infrastructure (power generation), and secondary import substitution (petrochemicals, automobiles).

New business groups

The double-digit growth rates of the export-led boom in the late 1980s created the setting for the rapid rise of new groups of domestic firms. Two main new groups can be identified.

The first consisted of new Bangkok-based firms. Most emerged from existing small-scale businesses. They focused on the same growth sectors of the domestic economy as the conglomerates, namely property, services (finance, media, telecommunications), infrastructure, and secondary import-substitution industries. Crucial to their growth was the liberalization and expansion of the capital market. The most successful of these new firms expanded rapidly through their ability to raise money from the growing stock market, from the BIBF offshore banks, and from direct access to overseas capital markets. Often business growth and the acquisition of assets was more important than cash flow and short-term profitability in securing access to successive new sources of capital (Phatra Research Institute 1997; Handley 1997).

The second group consisted of provincial businessmen whose expansion was mainly based on infrastructure and services for local markets. The roots of their growth were often found before this period, but again the acceleration was rapid, and the access to new sources of capital was often critical in overcoming earlier constraints.

Although these two groups differed in many respects, they acted similarly in three ways which were crucial for the political economy of the mid 1990s. First, they followed the earlier pattern of the conglomerates in investing time and money in acquiring political influence as a strategy to extend or defend their business position. Many of the leading provincial businessmen became players in the expanded democratic politics.[9] Some key figures from the Bangkok-based groups also took a direct role as MPs, but more participated as financiers and "advisers" of leading political figures (Pasuk and Baker 1995, 331–54; Pasuk and Sungsidh 1996, ch. 3). Second, their rapid commercial success was tied to the expansion of the financial market, and they were aware of this. When it came to the crunch in 1996–97, they would put their political weight behind attempts to prop up the crumbling finance industry (Handley 1997). Third, like "new men" in many economies, they opposed any regulatory control imposed either formally by bureaucrats or informally by more established business groups.

The result was a very rapid decline in the technocratic management of the economy from 1995 onwards. All of the key institutions (and especially the central bank) were weakened by the defection of senior and mid-level personnel, lured away by high salaries in the private sector. The remaining personal links between old colleagues, now facing one another across the regulatory divide, served to blunt the impact of government regulation of the economy (Nukul 1998). From mid 1995 cabinets dominated by these new business groups interfered with senior technocrats to such an extent that they caused a "technocrat flight." Prominent and able figures refused to accept key jobs because they could expect political interference and a short career span.[10]

FROM DOWNTURN TO CRISIS

The technocrats spearheaded the financial liberalization in 1991–93, but then lost control over economic management. By mid 1995, it was clear to many that the economy was in trouble. This trouble was diagnosed and debated under three main headings.

First, export slowdown and current account strain. Although export growth collapsed only in 1996, the signs of a dramatic slowdown of labour-intensive exports was visible from 1992, and more so from 1994. This was attributed to infrastructure bottlenecks, rising costs (especially labour), and increased competition from countries such as China, Indonesia, and Vietnam.

Second, loss of macroeconomic control. By attempting to maintain a pegged currency while liberalizing the capital account, the government had lost control over macroeconomic management. Previously, government had reacted against overheating by raising interest rates and restricting liquidity. After financial liberalization, they continued much the same policy (Aroonsri 1995). However, the high rates only served to attract capital inflows, particularly of short-term funds, or encouraged Thai firms to borrow at better rates offshore. This problem was widely discussed by 1994.

Third, the asset bubble. While the property market was already seen as over-extended and over-priced by 1994, new capital (especially from overseas) was still entering the sector and further inflating asset values.

Despite awareness of these problems, for around three years down to the currency float of 2 July 1997, very little was done by government to address these problems. From 1994, the Bank of Thailand imposed some penalties on short-term loan inflows which brought the ratio of short-term loans down from half to a third of the total. The central bank also restricted bank lending to the property market, but failed to extend any similar restriction to finance companies. Leading central bankers ruled out any more drastic policy change (Chaiyawat 1996).

In the pre-1984 period, the Thai banks and conglomerates had played the key role in allocating capital to growth areas and lobbying government for appropriate policies. But the conglomerates had become detached from the export-led industrialization which was now the motor of the economy, and detached from the political milieu. In the debates over responses to the emerging economic crisis, the conglomerates did not have a significant voice or a clear strategy. Only Banthun Lamsam of Thai Farmers Bank predicted the severity of the coming crisis. Besides, the critical debate focused on exchange rate policy—whether to float or devalue the baht to promote exports, or maintain the peg to protect the finance industry and its loan clients. Most of the conglomerates had become heavily involved in the domestic market, heavily implicated in the growing finance and property bubble as well as being deeply involved in dollar-denominated offshore loans themselves. Therefore in the end they also opposed devaluation as this would hurt them very badly.

The major force in export industrialization—Asian multinationals, especially the Japanese—did raise concerns over the trend of slowdown in exports. In February and again in April 1997, the president of the Japanese Chamber of Commerce in Thailand took the unusual step of publicly criticizing government economic policy, and commenting on the political constraints (*TN*, 17 Feb 1997, 15 Apr 1997). But this lobby did not have any political weight.

The new business groups, which had a dominant political role from 1995 to 1997, were tied to the financial market and involved in the asset bubble. Their interests would be affected by any devaluation of the currency, or any stricter control of the financial market. The successive prime ministers of this era, Banharn Silpa-archa (1995–96) and Chavalit Yongchaiyudh (1996–97), were surrounded by ministers and advisers from the financial world and from heavily foreign-leveraged sectors such as telecommunications. Under pressure to act over the economy, these prime ministers assembled committees composed of similar people. Through the two-year slide from 1995 to 1997, the main direction of policy was to smother the gathering bad news by extending ineffective bailouts, first to the stock market, then to the finance companies (FIDF), and then to the property sector (PLMO).[11] The central bank's policy to defend the baht was politically supported by financial institutions and other firms which feared the impact of currency depreciation on their leveraged balance sheets.

CONCLUSION

Because of the extraordinary extent of the Asian crisis, analysis of the event has been taken over by all the great political economy debates of the era: states versus markets; the merits of competing capitalisms; finance versus the real economy; the changing role of the state under globalization. Amid the clash of great ideas, the reality of local cases can get lost.

We argue that the oft noted and much vaunted stable growth of the Thai economy until the mid 1980s depended on three factors: the enforced discipline imposed by a controlled capital market; the role of a small group of Thai banks and associated conglomerates in directing the economy by managing the allocation of capital; and a government which largely complied with, protected, and supported the policy directions of the conglomerates. This was not the East Asian "developmental state," but it shared some of its features and delivered some of the same results.

Between roughly 1986 and 1993 this configuration was replaced by a very different trinity: capital convertibility which, in the environment of international finance's enthusiasm for Asia, removed all discipline from the capital market; the displacement of the conglomerates from their central role in the political economy, and the advent of competition between capital groups (old and new, domestic and foreign) and between policy agendas; the expansion in parallel of democratic politics giving scope for interplay between new political players, new capital groups, and new policy agendas.

From this perspective, the origins of the Thai crisis lie not in a random set of policy "mistakes," nor in the inherent failures of an economic model, but in the systematic disordering of economic policy making as a result of economic growth, neoliberal-inspired financial liberalization, and democratization. This change did not come about by chance but as the result of the formation of a specific political coalition encompassing the World Bank and IMF, the network of newly empowered Thai technocrats, and ambitious new Thai business groups.

The participants in this pro-liberalization coalition were motivated by differing agendas. For the World Bank, liberalization would theoretically bring welfare benefits through more rational capital allocation, and would also increase market access for the bank's Western patrons. For the Thai technocrats who were suddenly empowered to handle rapid change in the economy, liberalization would sweep away old oligopolies which hampered growth and welfare. For the new business groups, liberalization was a windfall which opened up access to capital on an unimagined scale. Ultimately this was a disastrous coalition as the World Bank and technocrats could not control the political consequences of liberalization, and the new business groups did not understand the macroeconomic consequences. The new coalition did not have either the ideological or political coherence to establish a workable policy regime.

Similarly the failure to react to the downturn in 1995–97 was not simply a "mistake" or the result of bad policy choices. New business groups, whose wealth and political influence had been boosted by the foreign inflows,

31

dominated parliament and cabinet. They also dominated debate on policy, often taking the lead from foreign financial firms which advocated further liberalization and fewer controls. Through the swelling of the bubble, Merrill Lynch in particular consistently promoted an optimistic view of the Thai economy, and urged further liberalization (for instance *TN*, 5 Nov 1996). SocGen Crosby published its last boosterish analysis of the Thai economy just two weeks before the crisis hit (*TN*, 13 Jun 1997).

In retrospect, it was naive to expect—as the World Bank, Thai technocrats, and Western financiers appeared to believe—that liberalization would substantially alter a system in which political power and capital were so tightly entwined. But describing this political-capital nexus as "cronyism" and blaming this cronyism for the crisis is misleading. Cronyism implies the existence of a powerful business-political alliance able to extract rents, as in the models of the Philippines under Marcos and Indonesia under the Suharto clan. But Thailand fell into crisis after it had abandoned the relative stability of a similar system, and had entered a period of greater competition in the markets both for political success and for business success. Cronyism is much less to blame than the expectation that liberalized markets would quickly acquire an internally generated logic, fairness, and discipline in circumstances when such markets were populated by ambitious new business groups, ambitious new political players, and the speculative fringes of international finance.

We are not arguing that "Thailand is different." Rather we are suggesting that the genesis of the crisis appears different if you look closely at the local origins, instead of beginning from some grand theory of millennial change. There are strong parallels between our argument and bottom-up analyses of the origins of the crisis in Korea and Malaysia (Chang 1998; Jomo 1998). In all three countries, the cyclical upswing after the second oil crisis brought into play new capital groups and new pro-democratization forces which combined with the neoliberal agenda of the World Bank to bring about liberalization; and in all three cases, liberalization led to competitive over-investment in similar domestic-oriented sectors, neglect of export-led growth, and subsequently financial panic when these trends threw up the danger signals of rising short-term debt levels and deteriorating current account positions.

These three cases suggest that the *local* origins of the Asian crisis lie in the difficulties of transition from an old, stable "Asian" model of policy management, aggravated by the politically naïve interventions of coalitions of technocrats, international organizations, and international finance in favour of rapid liberalization.

NOTES

1. On Nouriel Roubini's Asia Crisis homepage (www.stern.nyu.edu/~nroubini/asia/asiahomepage.html), there was no article specifically on the Thai crisis until around August 1998, a year after the IMF bailout, and thereafter there was still only one (transcript of a speech by Surasak Nananukul). By contrast, the Indonesian section had over fifty entries.

2. After the Plaza Accord of 1985 and the rise in the currencies of Japan and other East Asian countries, East Asian capital migrated to Southeast Asia on a large scale. The registered capital of Japanese firms in Thailand rose from 2,836 million baht in 1986 to 38,755 million baht in 1991 (Pasuk and Baker 1995, 155).

3. Peter Warr (1998a) estimates that the real exchange rate appreciated by 30 percent between 1988 and 1997.

4. The Financial Institutions Development Fund (FIDF) was set up as a result of the financial crises in 1979 and in 1983 to rehabilitate ailing financial institutions. In the crisis of 1996–97, the role of the FIDF was expanded. By the time of the float, the FIDF had paid out 700 billion baht to assist ailing financial institutions (Nukul 1998).

5. Like other countries in the region Thailand was hit by the second oil price hike and the slump in commodity prices in the world market. The GDP growth rate which averaged 7.2 percent per annum in real terms between 1974 and 1983 fell to 4.9 percent between 1984 and 1986. On the recession and subsequent economic reforms see Pasuk (1992).

6. The two major pre-crisis versions of an Asian model are World Bank (1993) and UNCTAD (1996).

7. Definitions of the urban and rural population are not straightforward. Officially only around 13 million live in the municipal area and 48 million outside. But this classification understates the extent of urbanization. Around half of the total of 61 million belong to households whose main employment is in agriculture.

8. Dr Puey Ungphakorn was governor of the Bank of Thailand in the 1960s and early 1970s. He started a scholarship programme to send bright young economists to acquire overseas Ph.D.s and then return to work in the central bank.

9. Most obviously, the "Group of 16," a set of younger provincial politicians who came together in the early 1990s under a shared belief in the importance of political influence for business success. Members of the set figured in some of the great scandals of the period, including the Bangkok Bank of Commerce crash.

10. During the governments of Banharn and Chavalit, several technocrats publicly

refused offers to run the Finance Ministry or central bank. Before the 1996 election, Chavalit announced a "dream team" of economic managers but all but one refused to comply. During this period, some key figures left the country and others turned off their mobile phones. Difficulties also arose over finding candidates to head the Stock Exchange and the Stock Exchange Commission. When Virabhongse Ramangkura, the prime minister's adviser from the technocrat period of the mid 1980s, agreed to act as Chavalit's liaison with the IMF, he felt impelled to announce publicly that he had been "forced by the Royal Thai Army" to assume this post.

11. The Property Loan Management Office (PLMO) was established to take over viable property projects from virtually bankrupt developers, but the organization never got off the ground.

DEAR MR CAMDESSUS: THAILAND AND THE IMF[1]

The Asian crisis of 1997 was a new kind of crisis. It bore some resemblance to the Mexican crisis three years earlier. But it became apparent that it was different in two important ways. First, the major problem was a buildup of foreign debt by private corporations, and the disastrous prospect of headlong capital flight. Second, the location was not on the American continent but in Asia. This second fact was important in many ways. The IMF and World Bank embarked on crisis management with a highly ideological view of the nature of the Asian economies, and a mission to transform Asian business and politics. They had limited appreciation of the links among Asian economies and the potential to transform a Thai crisis into a regional and global emergency. They had to wrestle with the fact that Japan was part of the debate on the nature and control of crisis management. In these circumstances, the policies to manage the crisis were soon being made on the hoof against a background of heated international debate about the nature of the crisis, the direction of policy, and the future of the Bretton Woods institutions.

This chapter traces the policy responses to the crisis in Thailand from July 1997 through to the millennium. It identifies three turning points: July–August 1997, May–June 1998, and March–April 1999. These points divide the crisis into three distinct phases. The analysis locates the pressures within the domestic and international context which drove these changes in policy. The emphasis is placed on the domestic context, and the international environment is sketched more lightly. This is partly because the international development of the crisis has been extensively analyzed by

This will be big! Camdessus and Tarrin

others, while the Thai story is less well-known. But this emphasis also reflects our belief that Thailand's relatively open political system ensured that Thai policy makers were responding to local pressures to an extent which is not usually recognized.

In the first phase of the crisis, Thailand's readiness to surrender sovereignty over economic policy allowed the IMF (and its US patrons) to impose an inappropriate macro policy and to launch an ambitious plan for opening the Thai economy up to greater foreign penetration. The resulting drastic contraction of the economy provoked social stress and political disorder which in turn made local leaders reassert more control over policy. In the second phase, they reversed the IMF's macro policy but continued with the programme of financial restructuring because it matched with the Thai policymakers' own belief in the need for such reform. But the attempt to restructure finance at the same time all parties involved were competing to offload the damage of the crisis onto one another led to a major breakdown of the credit system, delay in recovery, and a renewed round of political tensions. In the third phase, the discrediting of IMF policies at the international level provided the opportunity for Japan to take the initiative within the region. This in turn gave local policymakers the space to shift the emphasis of policy towards concerted Keynesian stimulus and a revival of the non-financial economy.

PHASE 1: THE IMF BAILOUT

Political context

The IMF arranged the initial package in July–August 1997 against a background of strong urban protest against the politicians in general, and the Chavalit Yongchaiyudh government in particular, for mismanaging the onset of the crisis (see pp. 120–2). The central bank was in disarray. The cabinet had no economic or financial expertise, and had to draft former finance minister Virabhongse Ramangkura to negotiate with the IMF. The business lobby and the articulate urban middle class tacitly welcomed the IMF as potentially better than the recent record of incompetence in economic management. The economist, Ammar Siamwalla, remarked, "As a Thai, I don't mind if we lose some sovereignty by applying to the IMF, because our authorities do not seem to know what to do with the sovereignty that they have" (*AWSJ*, 24 Jul 1997). In such circumstances, the IMF faced little local resistance.

The formulation and implementation of the initial IMF plan also took place against the background of a fierce neoliberal critique in the international press and among American public intellectuals. This critique blamed the crisis in Thailand (and soon elsewhere in Asia) on excess government interference in the economy, on "crony capitalism," and on an "Asian model" of defective capitalism. This critique set up the solution as further liberalization, and greater penetration by superior quality Western-style capitalism, especially in the sphere of finance. American journalists claimed "the latest crisis marks the triumph of the American economic system of open markets over [Asian] state run economies."[2] On the day after the IMF entry into Thailand, the US deputy treasury secretary, Lawrence Summers, said "countries will only enjoy the benefits of a truly global marketplace if our [financial] firms are given greater access to their markets" (speech at Congressional Leadership Institute, *TN*, 16 Aug 1997).

The initial negotiations with the IMF in August 1997 were cloaked in secrecy. The first LoI, signed on 14 August 1997, was not published in full but a "Summary of Important Measures in the IMF Package Outline in the Letter of Intent" appeared a week later as a Bank of Thailand (BoT) press release, and the IMF posted a short statement a week later. These summaries revealed no data or assumptions. The Thai ministers and officials involved gave the impression that they conceded to all IMF demands. The main Thai negotiator with the IMF, Chaiyawat Wibulswasdi, had been installed as head of the Bank of Thailand for a little over a week, and found himself facing Stanley Fischer, his former professor at MIT.

The absence of opposition enabled the IMF to act very aggressively. Over the next four months, IMF officials castigated the Thai government for failing to comply with conditions, and blamed the crisis on the Thai failure to follow past IMF advice to unpeg the currency and regulate the financial sector. The second LoI in November went far beyond the usual fiscal and monetary conditions to include a major project to transform the economy by legislative changes and a rapid infusion of foreign capital. Basle provisioning rules would force banks to recapitalize. Restrictions on foreign equity in the financial sector were effectively removed. Privatization would begin quickly with sale of government shares in the national airline and Bangchak petroleum company "by mid 1998." A week after this LoI, the American Chamber of Commerce in Bangkok called for removal of all barriers to foreign ownership. In November 1997, the IMF's pressure helped to install a new government heavily weighted with the technocrats who had managed the earlier, aborted phase of financial liberalization (see pp. 22–5, 139–41).

In sum, the urban constituency's loss of faith in the government's ability to manage the economy invited the IMF to adopt an aggressive imperial role, dictating change in the structure of the economy. The IMF contributed to a dominant discourse which blamed the crisis on the failings of Asian-style capitalism. The IMF and Western companies expected the crisis would be overcome by infusions of foreign capital induced by privatization, liberalization, legal reforms, and very low entry prices.

The macro package

The IMF package made available US$17.2 billion to supplement the depleted reserves. Of this amount, US$4 million came from the IMF and the rest mainly from Asian sources.[3]

Stanley Fischer, the IMF's deputy head, later admitted that the IMF diagnosed the Thai problem as "a current account problem led crisis combined with a fixed exchange rate" (*TN*, 5 Mar 1999). The macro plan was adapted from the IMF's long record of bailouts in Latin America. First it raised taxes (VAT from 7 to 10 percent) and slashed government spending by 20 percent to deliver a budget surplus of 1 percent. Second it dictated a tight money policy and high interest rates. The package was designed to treat an economy which was overheating due mainly to government overspending. The package was supposed to work by restraining the government's profligacy through the obligation to deliver a budget surplus, and taking the heat out of the economy by tight money. In the Latin American experience, there would be some initial capital flight, but international confidence would return within six months. The IMF confidently predicted a similar effect in Thailand. It believed that the strict IMF package would itself contribute to stability by restoring confidence, stemming the capital outflows, and halting the currency's slide. The baht depreciation would then stimulate exports to overcome the current account deficit, while the budget surplus would have the added benefit of funding some of the costs of financial restructuring. Even after the crisis had spread to Indonesia and Korea, the IMF still predicted that the capital flow to Thailand would be "low but still positive in 1998" (*BP*, 22 Dec 1997).

The IMF envisioned a mild recession, with GDP growth of 3.5 percent in 1998. The first LoI did not specify how this would be achieved, but it can be derived from the LoI's macroeconomic framework (table 3.1). With currency depreciation, exports would grow 8.6 percent while import growth would shrink to 1.6 percent. As a result of the IMF presence and the correction in the current account balance, international confidence would return and the 1998 capital account would show a net inflow of 1.8 percent of GDP. Overall economic activity would suffer only slightly. Consumption would not decline and gross domestic investment would attain the high level of 35.9 percent of GDP.

But the Thai crisis bore only a superficial resemblance to the Latin American model—namely high levels of short-term debt, and a deteriorating balance of current account. The underlying causes of these symptoms were very different. The Thai government had not been overspending. The budget had been in surplus for many years, and levels of public debt were low. The economy was not overheating in any usual sense but had been decelerating for over a year and had already passed into negative growth in the second quarter of 1997. This was not a standard current account crisis, as the IMF diagnosed, but a capital account crisis. The Thai problem was an economy stagnating towards the low point of a cycle, whose real condition was disguised by massive inflows of foreign lending, a significant part of which was short term, and a large part of which was destined to be unproductive given the underlying state of the economy. In these circumstances, the IMF's recipe of tax increases, government spending cuts, and high interest rates caused a sharp deceleration.

While the IMF assumed its presence in Thailand would contribute to stability, the sequence of implementing the package seemed designed to destabilize. The Thai side wanted the IMF to announce the package before it was revealed that the Thai government had committed almost all the foreign reserves in swap contracts, and had lent US$16 billion to collapsed financial institutions through the Financial Institutions Development Fund (FIDF). However, US treasury secretary Robert Rubin and the IMF insisted these revelations be made prior to the package. The FIDF debt was disclosed on 6 August, the reserve swap on the 14th, and the IMF package on the 24th. The swap revelation induced the hedge funds to call off direct negotiation with the Bank of Thailand about unwinding their confrontation, and instead launch an all-out attack on the currency.[4] The FIDF disclosure ensured that capital flight accelerated immediately. One financier concluded, "It's time to turn the lights out and go home" (*TN*, 4 Dec 1998). By the time the package was announced, the IMF had undermined its own belief that the IMF's presence would be a stabilizing factor.

The IMF paid no attention to local criticism of the package.[5] More surprisingly, it took little heed of the reactions among international financial firms whose restored confidence was critical to the way the package was supposed to work. International financial firms pointed out that they could see nothing in the package which addressed the real causes of the Thai crisis. Indeed the deflationary impact of the macro measures would deepen the problem of stagnation.

Several of these firms voiced doubts whether the IMF credit was adequate. Partly this response was real. Some firms published projections showing that the IMF credit line would not cover the Bank of Thailand's forward commitments (resulting from the currency defence) and the expected outflows.[6] Partly, this response was psychological. The package was one third the size of the 1994 Mexico bailout, signalling a lack of commitment. US deputy treasury secretary Lawrence Summers explained, "Thailand is not on our border." Furthermore, some international financial firms stated they could find nothing in the package which addressed the problem of high private sector debt, and the likelihood of bad loans and low or negative returns on portfolios. Indeed, the high interest rates which the IMF believed would help to restore confidence and restrain capital outflow were read as a signal that the economy would surely face a slump. As a result, the package did not deter capital outflow but stimulated it.

Financial restructuring

The IMF moved rapidly to the second stage of the programme: financial restructuring and privatization.

The largest finance firm, Finance One, had already collapsed in March 1997, and several other firms were suffering from over-ambitious lending to property and other saturated markets. By the time of the float, fifty-eight of the total of ninety-one finance companies had taken loans from the FIDF to balance the outflow of deposits. Most firms saw their balance sheets wrecked after July 2 when the decline of the baht increased their dollar-based liabilities, and the withdrawal of short-term funds accelerated. The FIDF had lent 600 billion baht to banks and finance companies. The first element of the IMF financial package was to staunch this bleeding by suspending fifty-eight financial firms, and cutting off access to the FIDF. Government subsequently closed down fifty-six of the firms, and suspended two small banks which had also become dependent on infusions from the FIDF.

The second part was to overhaul Thailand's protected financial sector. In October 1997, under IMF urging, the Chavalit government opened up the banking sector to 100 percent foreign ownership,[7] and indicated financial institutions would have to meet Basle provisioning standard of 8.5 percent of risk assets. In March 1998, the Democrat government changed the definition of a non-performing loans from six to three months, and set a progressive schedule for meeting full provisioning by the end of year 2000. These provisioning standards, coming on top of the rise in the banks' liabilities caused by the currency collapse, and the steady withdrawal of foreign loans, ensured that the banks would have to raise massive amounts of new capital. Existing managements would face at best dilution and at worst total takeover.

Initially government talked of handling the financial breakdown by placing the good assets of closed companies in a "good bank," and passing the remainder to a "bad bank" for liquidation. At the time of closing the fifty-six finance companies in December, it announced this machinery would be in place by February 1998. Radhanasin Bank was founded to act as the "good bank." But the Democrat government abandoned this scheme in face of the practical difficulties of classifying assets as good or bad. Instead government just closed down unsustainable financial institutions wholesale. A Financial Sector Restructuring Authority (FRA) was set up to auction off the closed companies assets, and Radhanasin Bank was deputed to bid for the "good" assets at these auctions. But then government refused to fund Radhanasin Bank so the scheme for a "good bank" collapsed completely.[8]

As a result, many thousands of companies found their savings and their credit lines frozen. At the same time, many companies, led by the largest conglomerate, the Siam Cement Group, transferred much of their day-to-day business transactions from a credit to a cash basis in order to circumvent the lack of credit and the dangers of non-payment. By early 1998, paralysis had begun to creep through the credit system.

Impact

In August 1997, just after the IMF arrival, prime minister Chavalit Yongchaiyudh told *Time* magazine (25 Aug 1997), "It's starting to pick up already." Just two weeks after taking office in November 1997, prime minister Chuan Leekpai predicted, "we will see a definite turnaround in our economy within six months" (*TN*, 26 Nov 1997). In December, OECD predicted that Thailand would be the worst hit of all countries in the crisis, but would suffer only a 1 percent decline in GDP. In February 1998, the finance minister, Tarrin Nimmanhaeminda, predicted that the economy would turn round within the year and deliver a 2.5 percent year-on-year GDP growth in the final quarter (*TN*, 25 Feb 1998).

Short-term capital had begun to seep away in the second quarter of 1997. After the float and IMF package, this seepage turned into a flood (table 3.1). For the next two years, total private outflows net of FDI ran at the rate of almost a fifth of GDP. In total, these outflows over the next thirty months were roughly equivalent to the total inflows under the same categories back to 1990. High interest rates were ineffectual in restraining this flood. The pace of outflow did not change after interest rates were brought down in mid 1998. The outflows were balanced somewhat by inflows of public sector borrowing and of FDI and portfolio money acquiring cheap assets. But the capital account was in deficit by 899 billion baht over two and a half years. The baht slid from 25.7/US$ prior to the float, to touch 56.9 in January 1998.

Table 3.1: Balance of payments, 1994–99
(billion baht)

	1994	1995	1996	1997 Q1/2	1997 Q3/4	1998 Q1/2	1998 Q3/4	1999 Q1/2	1999 Q3/4	30 months post-float
Current Account	-203	-338	-372	-135	95	310	282	222	205	1,114
Exports	1,411	1,752	1,810	939	1,333	1,422	1,302	1,266	1,422	6,744
Imports	-1,599	-2,049	-2,116	-1,027	-1,196	-1,044	-958	-976	-1,189	-5,363
Other income & transfers	-15	-40	-67	-48	-41	-68	-61	-68	-28	-267
Capital Account	306	545	494	-39	-259	-236	-173	-108	-123	-899
Gov't and monetary auths	-18	1	-1	-65	55	17	178	199	19	467
Private	324	544	495	27	-314	-253	-351	-307	-142	-1,367
Direct investment	22	29	36	21	91	193	92	107	95	578
Portfolio	62	105	90	46	89	3	-5	28	2	117
Loans, etc.	240	409	370	-40	-494	-449	-439	-442	-239	-2,063
Errors & Omissions	2	-28	-67	19	20	-85	-40	-24	0	-128
Balance of Payments	105	180	55	-155	-144	-11	69	91	82	86
GDP, current prices	3,634	4,186	4,608	2,316	2,412	2,321	2,314	2,287	2,402	11,736
As percent of GDP										
Current account	-5.6	-8.1	-8.1	-5.8	3.9	13.3	12.2	9.7	8.5	9.5
Capital account	8.4	13.0	10.7	-1.7	-10.8	-10.2	-7.5	-4.7	-5.1	-7.7
Private capital	8.9	13.0	10.7	1.2	-13.0	-10.9	-15.2	-13.4	-5.9	-11.6
Private net of FDI	8.3	12.3	10.0	0.2	-16.8	-19.2	-19.2	-18.1	-9.9	-16.6

Source: Bank of Thailand

The construction sector had begun to crumble since 1996 (table 3.2). With gathering capital flight, the financial sector began to shrink in early 1997. Following the deflationary impact of the IMF package, government and private expenditure contracted sharply in the last quarter of 1997 and first half of 1998. As demand in the economy disappeared, other sectors fell into the pit. Sales of everyday goods dropped by 10–20 percent. Monthly sales of automobiles fell to a quarter of pre-float levels. Starved of credit and customers, thousands of companies ceased functioning. Manufacturing dropped by a fifth. Capital formation halved. GDP growth shrank from around zero at the time of the float, to an annualized rate of -13 percent a year later.

Table 3.2 Quarterly GDP changes (constant prices)
(% year-on-year real change)

	1997				1998				1999			
	Q1	Q2	Q3	Q4	Q1	Q2	Q3	Q4	Q1	Q2	Q3	Q4
Agriculture	5.2	0.9	-0.6	-2.4	-1.3	-8.0	-2.7	3.4	5.5	7.2	3.5	-1.7
Manufacturing	6.3	3.4	0.8	-3.7	-9.5	-11.8	-12.9	-4.3	3.5	7.5	15.5	14.9
Construction	-31.3	-25.6	-14.1	-37.4	-28.7	-43.9	-43.1	-37.4	-26.7	-11.8	2.8	3.5
Commerce	2.1	-2.2	-1.3	-2.8	-8.7	-16.3	-13.5	-6.7	4.9	6.3	5.1	4.7
Finance	-8.4	-3.7	-21.0	-14.6	-8.6	-22.3	-19.9	-41.1	-41.7	-38.2	-20.0	-19.4
Real Estate	7.8	4.3	3.5	1.7	3.8	-1.6	-4.1	-8.4	-0.9	-1.9	10.3	17.2
Other	4.1	5.6	4.3	5.8	6.1	1.3	4.4	8.4	2.9	1.2	1.8	-0.2
Total	1.4	-0.7	-2.2	-5.1	-7.5	-13.7	-12.8	-6.8	0.2	2.6	7.4	6.5
Private consumption expenditure	8.4	2.9	-5.5	-9.5	-12.3	-17.1	-13.7	-5.4	-2.6	1.7	6.7	8.6
Government expenditure	3.0	-3.0	0.3	-12.1	-8.4	-7.8	9.2	14.0	0.8	11.0	-7.1	9.6
Capital formation	-13.1	-16.2	-17.7	-38.6	-38.7	-49.8	-47.8	-39.3	-27.7	1.1	5.5	12.1

Source: Bank of Thailand

However, this steep crash achieved a kind of stability. As a result of the baht depreciation and the collapse of demand, 1998 imports fell to a little over half their pre-float value in US dollar terms (chart 3.1). Exports were sluggish, but the import collapse delivered a current account surplus which peaked at 13 percent of GDP. The central bank was able to start replenishing the reserves. The currency recovered to stabilize around 38–40/US$ from March 1998 onwards. This stabilization was achieved not by the return of confidence and export growth predicted by the IMF, but by a precipitate collapse of demand. This was recovery by destruction.

The IMF maintained its strategy. The second LoI in November 1997 noted the "slower return of confidence" and "much sharper decline in private investment and consumption than originally anticipated," but proposed "determined implementation" of the programme and predicted "overall growth is still expected to be positive" through 1997–98. The third LoI in February 1998 noted the "much larger-than-anticipated decline in economic activity" but made only a small concession on the 1997/98 budget (no further cuts).

Over the year spanned by the first five LoIs, the IMF's projection for the economy in 1998 slid from mild recession to disaster—from a GDP change of +3.5 percent to a final result of -10.8 percent (table 3.3). This 14.3 point swing was driven by two main changes. First, expectations for the capital account changed from a small inflow to an outflow of 8.8 percent of GDP. Second, calculations of domestic demand slid downwards, with consumption growth dropping from +0.8 percent to -12.3 percent, and import growth from +1.6 percent to -33.4 percent.

Table 3.3: Macroeconomic framework for 1998 in the IMF letters of intent

	LoI-1 8/97	LoI-2 11/97	LoI-3 2/98	LoI-4 5/98	LoI-5 8/98	LoI-6 12/98	Actual
Real GDP Growth (percent)	3.5	0/1	-3/3.5	-4/5.5	-7	-7/8	-10.8
Consumption	0.8	-1.1	-5	-8	-	-	-12.3
Gross Fixed Investment	-0.8	-6.5	-21	-24	-	-	-22.7
Gross Domestic Investment (% of GDP)	35.9	34.3	29.1	28.2	-	-	26
Exports in US$, growth (percent)	8.6	7.9	6.2	1.4	-	-	-6.8
Imports in US$, growth (percent)	1.6	0.2	-7.7	-17.7	-	-	-33.4
Current account balance (% of GDP)	-3	-1.8	3.9	6.9	10	11.5	12.7
Capital account balance (% of GDP	1.8	0.3	-12/14	-14/16	-	-	-8.8
CPI inflation (period average, %)	8	10	11.6	10.5	9.2	8	8.1

Note: The fifth and sixth LoIs contained only abbreviated sets of macro assumptions.

PHASE II: TARRIN'S YEAR

Political context

In November 1997, the cabinet was replaced by a new Democrat-led government which commanded broader urban support. The finance minister, Tarrin Nimmanhaeminda, had been Thailand's leading professional banker, had served in the same post in the 1992–95 cabinet, was an open advocate of financial liberalization, and quickly established the personal confidence of the IMF, Washington, and the financial markets.

Ronald Rubin and Tarrin

While the bargaining position of the Thai government strengthened, that of the IMF weakened. As the crisis spread across Asia and threatened to destabilize financial markets on a global scale, the IMF came under attack from both ends of the American political spectrum. Liberals such as Jeffrey Sachs blamed the IMF for deepening and broadening the crisis. The intellectual and parliamentary right opposed any IMF demand for new funds to aid Asia. Jagdish Bhagwati, one of the high priests of free trade, insisted the arguments for freer international trade could not be used to support freer international finance. With markets crashing, international bankers lost much of their enthusiasm for prying open Asian markets. The neoliberal aggression waned.

In Thailand, the speed and severity of the economy's shrinkage provoked two forms of political reaction which came to a head in the second quarter of 1998. First, non-finance businesses protested at the high interest rates and credit squeeze. At the time of the float Chatri Sophonpanich, head of Bangkok Bank, predicted that two-thirds of Thailand's tycoon families would be wiped out. In early 1998, both Chatri and Dhanin Chiaravanont, head of the CP conglomerate, argued that the high interest rates were accelerating bankruptcies. Other business leaders mounted a broader attack on the IMF programme for concentrating too much on fiscal discipline, external stability, and financial restructuring while paying no attention to the real economy. Some argued that the IMF strategy was designed to decimate local firms and create fire sale conditions for foreign purchasers. They protested at the fast-track programme of privatization in the second LoI as evidence of this fire sale mentality. Some broadened this protest by slating the IMF and its US patron as "imperialist" and "neocolonial" (see pp. 140–3).

This agitation came to a climax in May 1998, while the fourth LoI was under negotiation and when decrees to implement the financial restructuring came before parliament. Some businessmen and academics proposed Thailand should declare a debt moratorium to give domestic firms a breathing space to recover. Ministers lobbied leading businessmen to drop the proposal. Soon after, the commerce minister, Supachai Panitchapakdi, broke ranks and sided with the business lobby on the issue of interest rates and liquidity. Chatri of Bangkok Bank announced that he had survived to this point because of prudent preparation, but if the tight money policy continued he (and by implication just about everybody else) would be finished.

The second source of protest was workers and farmers. Around a million lost their jobs in the construction sector alone, and probably the same number again in other sectors. Because of the large and constant movement of people and remittances between city and villages, this impact was rapidly felt in the countryside. Farmers' organizations came together on a call for agricultural debt relief. Political activists argued that the strategy of the IMF and government was saving the rich at the expense of the poor. They backed the calls for a debt moratorium, for rural debt relief, and for tax reforms to ensure the eventual costs of the bailout would be borne by the rich. These agitations climaxed in May–June 1998 as the government struggled to pass legislation required under the IMF strategy (see pp. 165–9).

With growing evidence of the IMF failure, and with growing pressure from business nationalism and populism, criticism of the IMF strategy spread even to some staunch supporters of liberalization. Leading conservative economists in Thailand argued that the IMF's programme of restructuring the economy went far beyond its mandate. When Robert Rubin visited Bangkok in July to restate the need to adhere to the IMF programme, two leading establishment economists used the occasion to voice their dissent. Virabhongse Ramangkura, a former finance minister who had been appointed as link man with the IMF in late 1997, said, "I doubt the US has a true understanding of the local economy" (*TN*, 1 Jul 1998). Supachai, the commerce minister, said "The IMF was wrong and we had to warn them that we would face a severe recession" (*TN*, 3 Jul 1998).[9]

Modifying the macro package

Against the background of rapid economic contraction, rising social stress, and growing political pressure, the Thai government fought a pitched battle with the IMF over the crisis strategy.

The Democrat government maintained the façade of being the "good pupil" of the IMF because that pleased the international financial markets. But behind the scenes there was a major struggle to overturn the IMF's stringent macro conditions. Tarrin's deputy, Phisit Lee-ahtam, admitted "it took a lot of effort to persuade the international institutions" to accept the Thai version of the fourth LoI (at FCCT on 11 November 1998). Given Phisit's soft-spoken politeness, this phrase indicates a big fight. Chuan later reported "we had warned that the high interest rate would be a catalyst for economic casualties," and each LoI was adopted after "hard bargaining" (*TN*, 21 Jan 1999). Tarrin later said that it took six months of argument to turn the IMF.[10]

The fourth LoI (May 1998) showed the first signs of this harder bargaining by the Thai side. Prior to its announcement, Tarrin began holding regular consultations with groups of businessmen, academics, and the press to build a local consensus of support. The LoI began by noting the improvements in the exchange rate and reserves, but went on to stress that "conditions in the real economy are still deteriorating" with "more pronounced weakness in private consumption and investment demand, and continued liquidity shortages." The priority was "to minimize further decline and bring about early recovery." The major policy change was to allow a public sector deficit of 3 percent of GDP in 1997/98. The fifth LoI extended this to a 3 percent deficit for 1998/99, with an additional 1.5 percent to finance interest costs from the financial bailout, and targeted use of the deficit "to maximize the impact on the real economy and on the social safety net." The sixth LoI in December raised the deficit to 5 percent plus 1.5 percent for interest costs. Deflationary stringency had been reversed into a policy of mild Keynesian stimulus.[11]

Monetary policy was changed in parallel. In May 1998, Chatumongol Sonakul was appointed governor of the Bank of Thailand and announced his priority to loosen monetary policy and bring down interest rates. In early June, Bank of Thailand officials publicly criticized the IMF for blocking their attempts to reduce interest rates. Three weeks later, Rubin visited Bangkok and publicly opposed any change in the high interest rate policy. This advice was quickly flouted. In July the Bank of Thailand began to reduce the overnight repurchase rate, which fell from 22 percent to 9.5 percent by the end of August, and further to 2.6 percent by the end of the year (chart 3.1).

The government also stepped quietly back from the fire sale of public corporations to raise revenue. The fifth LoI argued that "market opening policies which aim at increasing the role of the private sector in Thailand's economy, need to be implemented with great care, and based on an overall social consensus." It pushed back the time scale for privatization, and retreated to a policy statement which differed little from those proposed (but never implemented) by Thai governments over the previous decade. Tarrin said, "privatization success is not an integral part of the recovery process."[12]

Tarrin had abandoned hope in any recovery arriving through the IMF's vision of export growth and restored capital inflows. Instead, he sought "greater domestic demand through an increased fiscal deficit, and greater liquidity through a cautious reduction in interest rates and a gradual increase in monetary growth" (*TN*, 6 Jun 1998).

Full ahead on finance

While the Democrat government opposed the IMF's macro plan, it fell in with the scheme for overhauling the financial system. Tarrin had earlier compiled a financial sector master plan which was shelved after the Democrats lost power in 1995. He believed Thailand's protected banking cartel needed to be exposed to international competition and stricter regulation. To that extent he fell in with the IMF strategy.

Yet Tarrin differed from the neoliberal agenda of financial restructuring on two points. First, neoliberals had promoted the idea that American stock-based capitalism was superior to the Asian bank-based variant, and hence the Asian economies needed to make a rapid transition. Tarrin understood that this could not be achieved so quickly. In mid 1998, he stated that the banks would have to be the instrument for leading the capital market out of the crisis. Second, he wished to prevent a wholesale foreign buyout of the financial sector, as had happened in some Latin American crises. Tarrin took advice from the IMF and from J. P. Morgan on the design of a bank restructuring plan. But the final scheme was his own work.

The package announced on 14 August 1998 imagined a banking sector divided between foreign, local, and government control. The foreign segment was new. Since bank ownership restrictions were effectively removed in October 1997, two medium-sized banks had already been bought over—Thai Danu by the Development Bank of Singapore (DBS), and Bank of Asia by Dutch ABN Amro. Nakhon Thon also began negotiating a private sale to Standard Chartered, but government seized the bank and completed the sale. Four other small banks which had already been closed were taken under central bank control for eventual sale to foreign interests. In 1998, one of these, Laemthong, was sold to Singapore's United Overseas Bank.[13] In sum, seven of the existing fifteen banks were sold or slated for sale to foreign buyers. However, these seven amounted to only 13 percent of the commercial banking sector (measured as share of deposits, pre-crisis; see table on p. 222).

The state segment was enlarged. One small bank and thirteen finance companies were merged into the state-owned Krung Thai Bank, converting it instantly into the largest Thai bank.[14] At the same time, government talked about reviving some specialized state financial institutions which dated from the 1960s development era but which had been dormant for some years. This enlarged state banking sector would be used to channel government-to-government loan funds into the economy to free up the credit market and stimulate a recovery.

The local segment was reduced to the four large Thai commercial banks (Bangkok, Thai Farmers, Siam Commercial, Ayudhya) which Tarrin implicitly hoped would survive. However Tarrin wished to avoid the costs and the political backlash which would arise from any injection of government funds into these banks. The 14 August 1998 banking package contained an array of carrots and sticks. It offered government help with recapitalization to meet the Basle rules on condition that the banks restructured loans with their debtors and raised some capital on their own. If they failed, the government would step in, write down their capital, and revise their management. Tarrin also set up machinery for government to encourage and oversee debt negotiations between banks and their customers. Tarrin commented: "we never wanted to sell the banks cheap" (*TN*, 18 Aug 1998).

Financial seizure

With the neutralization of the IMF's fiscal and monetary stringency, the economy levelled out from its free fall dive. The stock market hit its lowest point (207) on the last day of August 1998. Manufacturing bottomed in the third quarter. Exports began to recover in the last quarter of 1998. The GDP shrinkage slowed in the final quarter of 1998 and flattened out in the first of 1999. Private consumption expenditure turned shakily upwards in mid 1999. The outflow of loan capital continued, but the balance of payments was held up by the countervailing inflow of acquisition capital and the current account surplus.

However, the financial system continued to crumble. Only the Siam Commercial Bank—majority-owned by the Crown Property Bureau—applied for infusion of government capital under the August 14 scheme. The families in control of the other local commercial banks saw the conditions attached to the package as a poison pill. Rather than take the government money and risk losing control, they struggled to stay afloat by raising new capital privately on the one hand, and downsizing their businesses on the other. In the second quarter of 1998, Bangkok Bank and Thai Farmers Bank were successful in raising 40 and 33 billion baht of new capital respectively in the international market, taking the overseas share of their capital base to 49 percent in both cases. The Bank of Ayudhya group sold other assets (its cement company) in order to maintain its strong controlling interest on the bank. In early 1999, after local interest rates had fallen, Thai Farmers Bank launched a hybrid share issue (SLIPS/CAPS)—essentially allowing depositors to convert their holdings into equity. The other banks followed suit.

At the same time, the banks attempted to reduce their loan portfolios. Total loans by banks and finance companies fell from 6.2 trillion baht in January 1998 to 5.4 trillion a year later and 4.8 trillion in August 1999.[15]

The government's hope that the state-owned banks would provide some stimulatory counterweight to the commercial banks was not realized. Many of the assets transferred to Krung Thai from closed banks and finance companies were non-performing. Government rejigged the management of

Krung Thai by bringing in some of the most high-profile technocrats of recent years. The idea seemed to be that clean professional managers could succeed where relation-tied family bankers could not. But many of these technocrats lacked banking experience. The loan portfolio deteriorated, and by early 1999 Krung Thai topped the ranking for the proportion of non-performing loans. Government was obliged to inject 77 billion baht of new capital in December 1998, and another 108 billion in September 1999. Within months of appointment, many of the technocrats on the board were competing to *avoid* promotion to the managing directorship. In August 1999, the former head of the stock exchange was brought in to the job. In September, Tarrin sacked the chairman and entire board. The replacement directors again lacked much banking experience. An audit report leaked to the press suggested non-performing loans were higher than reported and the bank's working procedures were unusually shoddy. The enlarged Krung Thai had turned out not to be Tarrin's instrument for easing the credit market, but a deadweight on progress and a lightning rod for criticism.[16]

Sharing the damage

The problems of the financial system were discussed in terms of recapitalization, NPLs, and debt restructuring. But in effect, the financial sector had become the arena in which all parties competed to offload the damage caused by the crisis onto one another. The economic slowdown, capital outflow, and baht depreciation had severely reduced the real value of all assets. The problem now was how the loss representing the difference between the old and new value would be distributed between banks, debtor companies, and the government representing the taxpayer.

The problem was immense because the shrinkage had been so steep, and because the damage was largely localized in Thailand. At the outset of the crisis, the private sector's foreign debt was around US$70 billion. With the collapse of the currency, the baht value of this debt increased by half, swelling total debt in baht terms by around 15 percent.[17] As part of the initial negotiations over the bailout, the IMF insisted the Chavalit government pass a decree guaranteeing the debts and deposits of all financial institutions. Reportedly this was at the insistence of the World Bank whose IFC arm was heavily exposed to Thai finance companies including Finance One.[18] This allowed foreign creditors who had lent to the Thai market through financial intermediaries to withdraw loans and other short term instruments, to the tune of 2,063 billion baht (see table 3.1). Only those foreign creditors who had lent directly to Thai firms were stuck. In early 1999, their total exposure was calculated at 815 billion baht, while debts to Thai creditors amounted to 5,735 billion baht.

Further, the government's guarantee ensured that a significant portion of the debt was already socialized. The FIDF had lent over 1,000 billion baht, including over 600 billion to financial firms which had been closed. The Financial Sector Restructuring Authority's (FRA's) sales of these companies' assets realized only 146.8 billion baht, and 32 billion of this total was bought by the government's own AMC meaning the net realization was just 115 billion. Estimates of the total FIDF debt which would be socialized climbed to 1,300 billion baht.

The August 14 banking package was supposed to provide a framework for banks and debtors to settle the allocation of the remaining loss by negotiation over debt restructuring. Theoretically, the package incentivized banks to negotiate restructuring deals with their clients, so that they could then qualify for inputs of government capital to enable them to meet the progressively higher provisioning targets. Reality was otherwise. With the economy thrown into reverse, many companies could not service their debts. Through early 1998, the NPLs in the financial system roughly doubled. In June 1998 when government first forced the banks to reveal the full extent of their 3-month NPLs, the proportion was 36 percent of all loans in the financial system. Other debtors were reluctant to negotiate. They preferred to delay "until the economy recovers" when their bargaining position would improve. In protest at the high interest rates imposed under the initial IMF policy, the steel magnate Sawat Horrungruang advised his fellow debtors to adopt the "Three Don'ts": don't pay interest, don't negotiate, don't run away. Even after interest rates fell, this slogan was adopted by debtors as a strategy to minimize their loss. Non-repayment became "a scheme to counter the threat of extinction" (Suthep 1999, 24).

In late 1998, under IMF pressure, the FRA began to sell assets of the financial companies under the FIDF. The auctions were held at the low point of the crisis, and the FRA partially restricted Thai firms from participating for fear they would conspire to buy up their own assets at a discount. As a result the returns were only around 25 percent of the assets' estimated value. This allowed some foreign buyers to realize an instant 100 percent profit by selling the assets back to their owners at around 50 percent

Chart 3.1: Main economic indicators, 1996–99

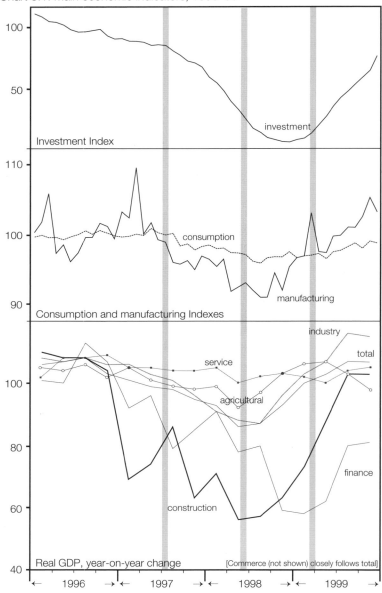

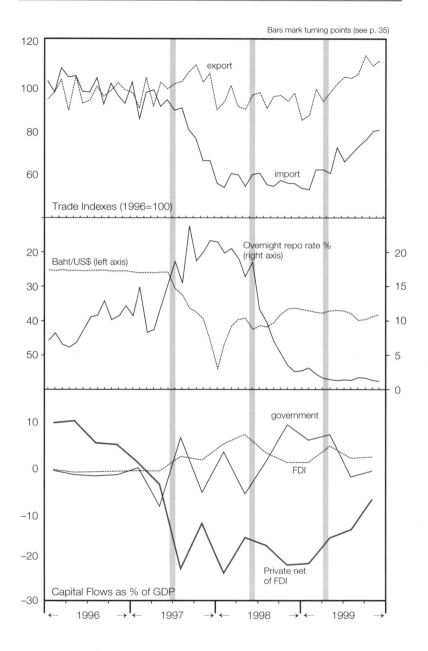

Bars mark turning points (see p. 35)

Trade Indexes (1996=100)

Baht/US$ (left axis)

export

import

Overnight repo rate % (right axis)

government

FDI

Private net of FDI

Capital Flows as % of GDP

← 1996 →|← 1997 →|← 1998 →|← 1999 →

of the estimated value. This in turn sent a signal to other debtors that they might aim at a "haircut" of half their debt's value. Non-payment snow-balled. Over late 1998, the proportion of NPLs rose from 36 to 47 percent of all loans, with increasing amounts coming through deliberate non-payment, quickly termed "strategic NPLs." In early 1999, a banker fumed, "Over the past three months, Thai businessmen suddenly and joyfully have discovered that there are no legal sanctions and they can get away with it" (Chulakorn Singhakowin in *TN*, 6 Mar 1999). In the old personal system of credit, default was impossible because it prejudiced any chance of future credit. But default now became widespread and socially acceptable. Defaulters "found themselves in the very good company of the ex-high and the ex-mighty" (Suthep 1999, 22). Bankers began to talk in horrified terms of a "non-payment culture." With government taking no action to protect firms in the real economy or to stem capital outflow, creditors looked on non-payment as "the corporate equivalent of Mahathir-style currency controls" (Suthep 1999, 28).

The allocation of the losses became a three-cornered battle between Tarrin, the bankers, and the creditor firms. On one side, Tarrin became locked in conflict with the remaining Thai bankers. Through late 1998, he grew frustrated that they would not participate in the August 14 programme, and would not help him to increase liquidity in the economy. Instead they reduced their lending volume, and widened the interest rate spread to cover the revenue loss from NPLs. In November he burst out, "I find this kind of practice unacceptable. If they go on like this, they . . . may survive in the short run but will perish in the long run. If the banks do not accept fundamental responsibility, we need to get tough on them" (*BP*, 7 Nov 1998). The prime minister called for the banks to cut interest rates. Tarrin was rumoured to be threatening the banks with nationalization. In February 1999, a Goldman Sachs report cited Tarrin calling Bangkok Bank the biggest threat to the banking system. Tarrin made a public denial and launched a libel suit. In the same month, Tarrin was rumoured to have told one banker, "I will take your banks if you don't recapitalize and start to extend new loans" (*TN*, 8 Feb 1999).

Chatri Sophonpanich, head of Bangkok Bank, responded that "Under the current circumstances, downsizing is not unusual as our priority is survival" (*BP*, 28 Nov 1998).

Tarrin's ability to coerce the commercial banks was limited. The threat of nationalization was not so credible given the emerging disaster in Krung Thai, the government's main bank. Undermining another financial institution would increase the proportion of the loss borne by the state and taxpayer. In August 1999, Thai Farmers Bank made this limitation perfectly clear. It announced that it was abandoning its finance company, Phatra Thanakit, whose debts would hence fall on the FIDF. The Bank of Thailand was obliged to negotiate a compromise in which both government and Thai Farmers Bank injected extra capital to pay off Phatra's depositors.

On the other side, Tarrin was locked in growing conflict with corporate debtors who were reluctant to restructure debts and who preferred instead to delay in hope of an economic upturn. This tension came to a head in the first quarter of 1999 when the government needed to pass eleven bills promised in the fifth LoI, including major changes in bankruptcy law and procedure. Several major debtors mounted a strong defence from their position as members of the senate. They insisted they had been led into a "trap" baited by foreign loans to enable foreign owners to acquire their companies cheap (see pp. 167–8). They argued in particular for the exclusion from the bankruptcy act of the personal guarantees which had been common in the personalized credit system. Tarrin responded that the foreign angle was exaggerated given that 88 percent of outstanding commercial credit was owed to Thai institutions. He also insisted that "the financial system will break down" if the bills failed to pass (*TN*, 11 Mar 1999). The head of SET (Stock Exchange of Thailand) endorsed this by predicting that the market would become "bottomless" if the senate threw out the legislation (*BP*, 12 Mar 1999).

The bankruptcy bills were finally passed in an atmosphere of high emotion. But the continued deterioration of the financial system and the attendant political conflicts caused the government to delay or abandon many parts of the ambitious programme of financial restructuring set out in the fourth and fifth LoIs. The programme of legislation was still stuck in parliament when the deadline was reached at year end. The schedule for selling off the banks slipped back by at least six months. The proposed new acts to regulate the banking system and to recast the central bank were delayed further.

PHASE III: A MORE JAPANESE APPROACH

Political context

The transition from 1998 into 1999 saw another surge of political discontent. The rural protests reappeared. At the end of 1998, much of the social strain of unemployment was transferred from city to countryside as unemployed migrant workers returned to their villages. The strain was intensified by the international downward trend in crop prices. Early 1999 saw a renewed campaign for a rural debt moratorium, and Latin American-style land invasions by landless villagers and newly unemployed workers (see pp. 144–8).

Business antagonism intensified and became more entwined with formal parliamentary politics. A new party was formed (Thai Rak Thai) with a programme designed to appeal to local businessmen's resentment that their interests were being sacrificed. Outside parliament, this phase of protest saw a renewed series of demonstrations against privatization, and a nationalist campaign against "selling the country." The US campaign to block Supachai Panitchapakdi's bid for the headship of the WTO occasioned an unusually open display of anti-Americanism.

The spreading seizure in the financial system undermined support for Tarrin's finance-led approach to overcoming the crisis. Interest rates fell, but banks continued to reduce their loan portfolios so credit remained tight. Once the impact of the currency depreciation had worked through, the collapse of demand reduced inflation to zero, sparking fears of collapse into a deflationary spiral. In January 1999, the Chamber of Commerce called for government to ease the new bank provisioning rules to enable banks to extend more credit. The TDRI think-tank backed the proposal. Even local mainstream economists began to question the wisdom of attempting drastic financial restructuring in the teeth of such a deep crisis. Supachai again broke ranks by proposing that government should nationalize the NPLs to liberate the banking system, and should weaken the currency to promote exports.

Government insisted that the slow pace of recovery stemmed from the slow pace of loan restructuring between bankers and their clients. The IMF endorsed this view by shouting at the Thai government to accelerate restructuring. But bankers replied that they would not increase their loan activity until they saw some sign of an upturn in the economy signalling that lending could be fruitful. Kosit Panpiemras, a technocrat turned banker, called for a stronger fiscal stimulus. Other conservative economists who were normally advocates of restraint (such as Virabhongse Ramangkura) endorsed such a policy change. By March 1999, even the IMF's Stanley Fischer admitted that "some demand expansion from fiscal policy will help" to improve the environment for debt restructuring (*BP*, 2 Mar 1999).

The Democrats began to distance themselves further from the IMF. In November, Chuan insisted that "the IMF cannot order us about as it wishes," and Tarrin added "we are not following IMF orders" (*TN*, 24 Nov 1998). Another minister said he had had "to explain to the IMF officials that we have to tackle problems in all dimensions—social, economic and political" (*BP*, 11 Nov 1998).

Japan takes the initiative

While locally the IMF's insistence that strict financial restructuring was a prerequisite for recovery came under steadily fiercer attack, in parallel the IMF's management of the crisis came under attack in the international arena. In August 1998, Paul Krugman charged that "Plan A had failed," and Mahathir's announcement of capital controls drew many supporters. In the fourth quarter, the World Bank launched a critical attack on the IMF's policies, with Joseph Stiglitz sermonizing that "pain for its own sake is not a virtue." Against this background, the Japanese also began to criticize the IMF and remind everyone that in late 1997 the US had scotched Japan's plan for an Asian Monetary Fund and an alternative approach to the crisis. In late 1998 and early 1999, Eisuke Sakakibara, Japan's deputy finance minister, was unusually vocal. He criticized the IMF for being "too ambitious" over financial restructuring, and criticized the US more generally for bullying countries into financial liberalization. In April 1999, the Japanese again floated the idea of an Asian Monetary Fund.

In late 1998, it became clear that the developed countries were unlikely to reach agreement on any restructuring of the international financial system which would reduce the dangers and difficulties for smaller and weaker economies. On the eve of the G7 meeting expected to confirm this failure, Japan announced the US$30 billion Miyazawa Scheme for promoting recovery in crisis-hit Asia. The announcement effectively took the initiative in crisis policy away from the US and the IMF. Apparently surprised by the Japanese announcement, the US gave the scheme an initial grudging acceptance. Then in November, the US revealed its own plan to pump money into the Asian economies by backing Asian governments to issue bonds for funding a stronger stimulus. This plan was interpreted as a US attempt to "hijack" the Miyazawa Scheme and retain US control. The Japanese finance ministry responded frostily that "Japan will use the $30 billion aid based on its own policy initiative," and it would be "improper" to allow the US to have any role in how the scheme was administered (*TN*, 13 Nov 1998). Subsequently the World Bank was allowed to become a minor partner in projects under the Miyazawa Scheme so that the initiative did not appear exclusively Japanese. But the initiative in managing the crisis at a regional level had shifted.

Immediately upon the Miyazawa announcement, Tarrin stated it was "exactly what we need" (*TN*, 5 Oct 1998). A month later, he was the first Asian minister to visit Tokyo to discuss details.

The initial announcement of the Miyazawa Scheme envisaged that the US$30 billion might be used in many different ways including corporate debt restructuring, trade financing, additional currency support, social expenditure, job creation, or whatever. However, the Thailand scheme announced in March 1999 had a very definite focus. It would pump money into the economy with the twin aims of providing a fiscal stimulus and alleviating social stress.

The Miyazawa plan for Thailand was announced along with a revised macroeconomic package on 31 March 1999. The announcement eclipsed the seventh LoI which was completed a week earlier and which, apart from alluding to the Miyazawa scheme, consisted of formulaic phrases ("we are pleased to inform that considerable progress continues to be made").[19] The macro package announced in parallel with the Miyazawa plan reduced VAT from 10 to 7 percent, and made cuts in energy prices—these measures finally reversing out all of the IMF's initial programme. The package went further by eliminating the VAT-substitute imposed on small businesses unable to administer the full tax, and made cuts in corporate and income taxes aimed to relieve small businesses and salary earners. These measures increased the budget deficit for 1999/2000 from 5 to 6 percent of GDP plus an additional 1.5 percent for financial restructuring. The Miyazawa Scheme contributed an additional 53 billion baht for stimulus spending. The sum of the macro and Miyazawa packages would deliver a stimulus equivalent to 2.6 percent of GDP.

The Miyazawa package was designed to pump money into the local economies on grounds this would bring about the most rapid multiplier effect through increased consumption.[20] Of the total, 25 billion baht was earmarked for job creation projects, 10 billion for projects to improve the quality of life, and 9 billion for projects contributing to improved public administration. In essence, the design and execution of the scheme was a repeat of the *ngoen phan* or "tambon scheme" launched in 1975 to combat a crisis of similar severity though very different origins.

A few weeks later, Tarrin announced there was no further need to draw on IMF credit and no need for further LoIs. Supachai repeated that "there is no need to commit to the IMF policies and we can terminate if we want" (*BP*, 18 Aug 1999). The eighth LoI was delayed until September 1999, was reduced further to a half-page, and contained the announcement that "we do not expect to make further drawing from the official financial package."

The introduction of the Miyazawa plan signalled a greater Japanese influence on policy making in other, less public forms. On a broad scale, Japanese voices such as Sakakibara became more insistent that the Asian crises could not be treated only as financial breakdowns requiring a financial solution without reference to the real economy. Even more broadly, the Japanese insisted that Asian developing economies needed a guiding hand rather then relying on the unremitting market liberalism of the US model (Suehiro 1999, 2000). These directions aligned with the frustrations of real-sector businessmen within Thailand.

In early 1999, two Japanese-influenced initiatives were announced for increasing the level of government planning in the real economy. The ADB fostered a medium-term plan for the agricultural sector which introduced zoning into different crop areas to facilitate the input of new technologies and streamlining of marketing. The Ministry of Industry announced a sectoral-based industrial plan developed with MITI assistance. The plan drew on Japan's experience with technical institutes and advisory services to upgrade small and medium enterprises. The plan had been under development for some time, but had been delayed by disagreement between the Thai and Japanese sides on the list of target sectors, but also by the Democrat-led government's total focus on financial policy. The plan had been accelerated after Chuan met the MITI minister in November 1998, shortly after the Miyazawa announcement.

In August 1999, the government announced a further stimulus package which focused on the real sector. The package included the sectoral advisory centres which were part of the MITI-influenced industrial plan. It also included deferrals of corporate tax; sweeping reductions in tariffs on capital goods and raw materials, especially those required by the food-processing, textile, and engineering industries; a recovery fund to serve as an alternative source of finance for small and medium firms; and extra funds for both home buyers and developers to begin easing the real estate market. This was followed in October by announcement of a much larger Equity Fund of US$500 million with contributions from the Finance Ministry, IFC, and the Lombard Fund of the US.

In November, government announced a revision in investment promotion rules (*TN*, 2 Nov 1999). The IMF had earlier suggested that the BoI and the investment promotion machinery in general should be abolished, and the Western business lobby in Bangkok had repeated that suggestion. Instead, government revised the rules to increase the promotional concessions, and make them conditional on firms spending on training, R&D, and technical upgrading to ISO standards. BoI also announced it was preparing "rescue plans" for five specific sectors (petrochemicals, pulp and paper, textiles, steel, ceramics) including proposals for tariff protection, mergers, and funding. In early 2000, some government agencies suggested government should boost the electronics sector by investing in a wafer fabrication plant (Alphatech) whose collapse at the start of the crisis had been interpreted as a symbol of excessive and careless investment.

At the same time as stimulating demand and starting to boost the real economy, the Democrat government retracted marginally from the programme of financial restructuring. First, it tried again to tempt the banks into the August 14 programme. It abolished a restriction which barred banks which had raised SLIPS/CAPS from applying for tier-1 capital assistance. It tried to remove the bank managements' fear of annihilation by a new provision allowing the original shareholders to buy back any government stake at a future date. Second, the government made several technical adjustments to ease the banks' difficulties in meeting the provisioning requirements, including allowing banks to declassify a loan as non-performing as soon as a restructuring deal was signed. The Thai Military Bank now applied for help under the scheme, and the Bank of Ayudhya considered following suit.

Fragile recovery

Following the passage of the bankruptcy bill and announcement of the Miyazawa Scheme in March 1999, Siam Commercial Bank raised 65 billion in capital, with half from the international market and half from the August 14 scheme (tier 1). These three events prompted a sustained effort to talk up the Thai economy. Tarrin predicted a turn-around within "four to five months" following the Miyazawa stimulus. In April, the IMF announced that the Asian crisis was over, contradicting the more cautious assessment by Stanley Fischer during his Bangkok visit six weeks earlier. A month later Fischer joined the chorus by proclaiming that "spring is in the air" (*TN*, 5 May 1999). In July, Joseph Stiglitz of the World Bank agreed that the crisis was "over" or at least "bottomed out."

From mid 1999, the signs of recovery became more convincing. The Miyazawa Scheme was estimated to have contributed 0.6 percent to the year's GDP growth. Partly as a result of exporter-specific schemes to circumvent the credit crunch, both manufacturing and exports strengthened through 1999.[21] Predictions of GDP growth were revised upwards from an original 0–1 percent to a final result of over 4 percent. As debtors had always insisted, debt restructuring deals were easier to negotiate once there was some prospect of underlying growth in the real economy. Sawat Horrungruang retracted his motto of the Three Don'ts and agreed to a restructuring deal. The proportion of NPLs started to fall slowly in the fourth quarter, and to fall faster in early 2000. By the end of January they had dropped from the high of 47 percent to around 38 percent. Government announced there would be a ninth and final LoI and that the IMF programme would end in August 2000. It also cut the planned borrowing from the World Bank for reform programmes from US$1.2 billion to 100–200 million, and from the ADB from US$500 to 100 million.

CONCLUSION

In February 2000, Michel Camdessus praised Thailand's recovery and claimed the credit for the IMF. With Gallic flair, he announced that Thailand has "graduated from the IMF University *summa cum laude*. . . .

graduation means victory. . . . the job is done." These statements marked his resignation as managing director of the IMF. Institutions do not easily admit their failures, and the IMF had only very partially and very grudgingly conceded any error in its handling of the Asian crisis. But the departure of Camdessus was probably more than coincidental.

In mid 1997, the steepness of the crash, and the urban public's loss of confidence in political management of the economy, had removed any opposition to an IMF entry and encouraged the IMF to adopt an imperial role. The IMF applied an off-the-shelf macroeconomic solution which was spectacularly ill-suited to Thailand and other Asian crisis economies. It also expanded its programme beyond the usual macroeconomic conditions to include plans for restructuring the economy and significantly increasing the role of foreign capital. Western businessmen, political leaders, and commentators imagined the crisis would result in the "creative destruction" of much of domestic capital, admission of foreign capital at bargain prices, and transformation of the state, moving away from the Asian "develop-mental model" in which the state takes a responsibility to promote the domestic economy, to a "regulatory model" in which the state provides a safe environment for international capital.

Some of this agenda was implemented in the early months of the crisis. Several restrictions on foreign ownership and business activity were removed. The legal framework of the finance industry was overhauled, and plans laid to transform the role of the central bank—a key issue for the regulatory model.

But the IMF macroeconomic package, designed to chastise a profligate government, was totally inappropriate for a crisis brought on by excessive money flows to the private sector. While the IMF strategy assumed a rapid return of investor confidence, the deflationary implications of the package only spurred capital flight. By May 1998, the macroeconomy had begun to stabilize—not in the way the IMF had intended, but because the collapse of demand reduced imports and delivered a current account surplus which replenished the reserves and hardened the currency. From this point onwards, the macroeconomic tutelage of the IMF became irrelevant. The problem now for Thailand's economic managers was how to pull the economy out of a headlong dive, and how to prevent the vicious downturn provoking social disorder.

Between May and August 1998, a series of changes altered the overall direction of policy. Fiscal and monetary stringency gave way to mild Keynesian stimulus. Plans to liberalize and internationalize the financial sector were rolled back in favour of a balance between foreign, state, and private-domestic ownership. The possibility that the Asian bank-based model of the capital market would be replaced by a Western stock-based model was removed when government resolved to preserve a significant proportion of the domestic banking sector. Both private and public assets were afforded some protection against a fire sale.

Both Tarrin and the IMF argued that financial restructuring was a prerequisite for restoring growth in the real economy. The IMF was committed to creating a financial structure in which Western firms would feel more comfortable. Tarrin and the Democrats believed that Thailand needed to move beyond its protected and relationship-based financial sector. But this attempted restructuring was entwined with the difficult business of allocating the damage caused by the bursting of the bubble and the collapse of asset values. This allocation was especially problematic as most of the damage was confined within the local economy. Both debtors and creditors attempted to minimize their share of damage by withdrawing from credit relationships—the banks by running down their loan activity, firms by switching to cash transactions and neglecting interest payments. The creeping collapse of the financial system blunted the attempt at macro stimulus.

The reassertion of a Japanese role in late 1998 followed heavy international criticism of the IMF, and a debate within Japan which showed that Japanese firms still saw Southeast Asia as a source of future growth, and that both firms and policymakers were uneasy about the rapid increase in Western influence and penetration. The prospect of a deflationary spiral and growing political disorder meant that the Democrats eagerly responded to the Japanese initiative. The IMF's role was eclipsed. The Miyazawa initiative not only led to a more concerted fiscal stimulus, but also to a new set of policies aimed to work on the real sector through Japanese-style government guidance.

The policy changes introduced between mid 1998 and end 1999 were driven by factors in the local political environment—the fear of severe social stress and social disorder on the one hand, and increasing business protests on the other. These political pressures reminded the government of two earlier long-term objectives of Thai economic policy, namely, the promotion of domestic capital, and the protection of social cohesion. The Democrats moderated their initial enthusiasm for liberalization when faced with the potential social costs, and with the possibility that they would become estranged from local business to the profit of their political opponents.

The course of policy making through the crisis shows the difficulty of enforcing the neoliberal policy agenda in a country where a relatively democratic political system ensures economic policy is sensitive to the local political economy. It also illustrates the tension between US and Japanese conceptions of their own national self-interest in Asia, and the way this tension provides some space for local independence in policy making.

The lesson of course is that countries should do everything to avoid capital account crises of this nature, but that if such a crisis occurs they should do everything to prevent the IMF interpreting it as an old fashioned current account crisis and applying an irrelevant and counterproductive remedy. As others have noted (Akyüz and Cornford 1999), the best way to counter a capital account crisis is through measures which work directly on the capital account, not through roundabout and slow-acting fiscal and monetary devices. The capital market reacts very rapidly. The headlong flight of capital from Thailand after the float converted a mild crisis into a disaster. The crisis would have been much less deep, and the damage to most parties (including foreign capital) would have been less if that flight had been stemmed by temporary capital controls. The contrasting cases of Korea and Malaysia illustrate this.

The renewed signs of dynamism in the Thai economy in early 2000 were not proof of the IMF's success. The IMF's package was designed to bring a recovery through a rise in exports and a reversal of capital outflows. But thirty months later, the capital outflows had not relented, and export recovery was still weak. The package did not work. Indeed it added to the damage inflicted on the Thai economy and people in 1998. The signs of revival showed a basic dynamism which had been turned into a savage reversal by incompetence, ideology, and opportunism.

NOTES

1. Thailand's policy commitments with the IMF were set out in three-monthly "letters of intent." Each was co-signed by the finance minister and governor of the Bank of Thailand, and addressed to the managing director of the IMF with the opening: Dear Mr Camdessus.

2. James Flanagan of *LA Times* (*TN*, 5 Nov 1997).

3. US$4 billion from Japan, US$2 billion each from Korea and Taiwan, and US$1 billion each from Australia and China.

4. Thanong Khanthong (*TN*, 4 Dec 1998) attributes Washington's policy to Rubin's wish to aid Wall Street friends who were playing poker against the Bank of Thailand.

5. People who met the IMF officials at this stage commented that they did not appear to have a receive mode.

6. These analyses were presented at sessions of the Economist conferences in Bangkok both shortly before and shortly after the float.

7. Previously the maximum foreign share had been 25 percent. The new rule included the qualification that the 100 percent ownership would be allowed for ten years, after which any capital expansion would have to include a domestic proportion. But this qualification was seen as cosmetic.

8. Radhanasin Bank was used to take over a small bank, Laemthong, which was then sold to Singapore's UOB. Government set up the Asset Management Corporation (AMC) to bid for good assets at the auction of the finance companies' assets, but the AMC was also underfunded.

9. Supachai also openly dissented from the neoliberal position on financial deregulation, saying "movements of money and capital . . . cannot be left entirely to market forces without incurring tremendous risks" (*TN*, 16 June 1998).

10. Tarrin was very careful not to show public disagreement with the IMF. This comment came only in November 1999, in an interview with Suthichai Yoon on Channel 9's "Nation News Talk," at a time when Tarrin was under severe political pressure.

11. Exactly who was pushing who here is not clear. The IMF claimed they began to press for expansionary fiscal policy from the time of the third LoI but the Thai government resisted because of a traditional terror of budget deficits. The Thai side gave the impression they were fighting the IMF to allow both fiscal expansion and lower interest rates.

12. Said at FCCT in early 1998. Thanks to Ted Bardacke for this quote.

13. Under the August 14 package, Laemthong was taken over by Radhanasin, the bank originally set up to serve as a "good bank." Radhanasin was then sold to UOB.

14. Krung Thai also took over the small amount of good assets from the Bangkok Bank of Commerce, which was closed down.

15. These figures include local commercial banks, foreign banks, and finance companies. The Bank of Thailand's figures for total loans are slightly higher (e.g.

TN, 19 Oct 1999), probably because they include state institutions like IFCT, GSB, GHB.

16. Tarrin's management of the Krung Thai problem was complicated by the fact that the managing director until mid 1998 had been his younger brother, Sirin, who was later charged with malpractice in Krung Thai lending.

17. On the eve of the float, foreign loans accounted for 22 percent of the liabilities of the commercial banks. The depreciation of the currency promptly increased the baht value of these liabilities by about 700 billion baht. By the end of 1999, the banks had had to repay two-thirds of these foreign loans. See table 4.9 of the Bank of Thailand's Databank at www.bot.or.th.

18. This was the interpretation of Thanong Khanthong (*TN*, 6 Aug 1998).

19. In early March, on the eve of the announcement of the Miyazawa funding, Stanley Fischer of the IMF visited Bangkok. His main agenda seems to have been to forestall any backsliding on the programme of financial restructuring. He attended a seminar to allow businessmen and academics to criticize the IMF. Dr Viphandh Roengpithya of the Federation of Thai Industries drew attention to the devastation of firms in the real economy: "Your policies have been similar to killing a cow to get more milk" (*TN*, 7 Mar 1999).

20. Tarrin explained the thinking in *BP*, 1 Apr 1999.

21. Firms also increasingly resorted to bond placements to circumvent the seizure in the banking system.

SOCIAL IMPACT, SOCIAL SAFETY NET, SOCIAL BAILOUT

Across the world since the early 1980s, adjustment programmes administered by the IMF and World Bank have been criticized for placing the burden on the poor. Fiscal and monetary stringency restores economic stability by reducing demand, destroying jobs, lowering incomes. This issue became more sensitive in the 1990s as the nature of financial crises changed. In earlier Latin American crises of the 1980s, the IMF could lay the blame on the profligacy of the national government. But since the late 1980s, crises have been linked to the liberalization policies which the World Bank and IMF have urged countries to adopt. The international institutions bear some of the responsibility. More importantly, they appreciate that the social (and political) fallout from these crises threatens to undermine the attractiveness of their liberalization agenda.

Hence one striking feature of the Asian crisis has been the meteoric rise in importance of the concept of "social safety nets." The vocabulary is not new. It has been part of internal World Bank discussions since the late 1980s. But during the Asian crisis, the idea of social safety nets became a main tenet of the "Post Washington Consensus"—a recasting of the neoliberal agenda with more attention to the social and political issues thrown up by market liberalization.[1] Indonesia played an important part in raising sensitivity to the social aspect of crisis. In early 1998, Indonesia was wracked by food shortages, racial riots, and a sharp increase in both poverty and political violence. Thailand suffered much less. But Thailand also played a role in this process for two reasons—because there was a strong local lobby demanding social action to cushion the crisis, and because

Thailand provided an arena for field-testing experimental social programmes.

The idea of social safety nets figures on at least two levels—as part of the actual management of the crisis, and as part of a debate in the neoliberal camp. The two cannot be separated. Thailand and the other crisis countries became the arena where new social strategies were implemented. Any assessment of the result becomes part of the political debate. Not surprisingly, the analysis of the impact of the crisis, and of the efficacy of social cushioning, has been highly politicized.

This chapter looks at the social impact of the crisis—both as fact and as discourse. The first section looks at the development of the idea of social safety nets in debates within the international organizations. The following sections cover the growth of concern over the social impact of the Thai crisis; the main policies developed to cushion distress; the importance of unemployment as a measure of the the social damage; and a periodization of the social impact of the crisis. The concluding section looks at the first attempts to assess the overall effects on society, and draw conclusions for the future.

THE INTERNATIONAL DEBATE ON SOCIAL POLICY

Through the 1980s, the World Bank and IMF were criticized for supporting macroeconomic policies which increased poverty. In particular, the conditions attached to the World Bank's structural adjustment loans in the wake of the oil crises, and to IMF programmes for relieving debt crises, were criticized for creating economic shocks which were felt most heavily by the poor. These criticisms were voiced first by radical academics, but later also by mainstream thinkers, and by influential lobbies within international organizations.[2] UNICEF lobbied the World Bank to change its strategies. In 1990, UNDP began publishing its *Human Development Report* which advocated a social approach to development broader than the narrow focus of the bank and IMF on economic stability and growth. The World Bank and IMF also came to realize that more countries were inclined to refuse or resist programmes of structural change because of the adverse social impact.

Around 1990, the World Bank and IMF began to respond to these criticisms. In 1990, the World Bank's annual *World Development Report* adopted the theme of poverty for the first time. In 1992, the IMF admitted, "Mistakes have been made. . . . One of the results . . . is a greater emphasis on social aspects of adjustment and the explicit incorporation of affordable safety nets in an increasing number of instances" (IMF 1992). Two years later, the IMF recognized that "some policy measures may have important distributional implications, that such distributional effects can undermine public support for the reforms, and that the design of Fund supported reform programmes should evaluate and seek to mitigate the short term adverse effects of policy measures on vulnerable groups" (IMF 1994, 120). In other words, the IMF had to recognize that the social impact of its policies could create political consequences which undermined its economic plans; and hence some attention to social policies was politically wise (IMF 1995b). A World Bank expert made the thinking very clear: "safety nets can provide an environment in which economic reform is more politically sustainable" (Graham 1994).

This new orientation was first put to the test in the restructuring of Eastern Europe following the collapse of the Eastern Bloc in 1989. The new transition states of Eastern Europe became a laboratory where the details of this new social policy making were elaborated, debated, and tested (Deacon 1997). The World Bank recruited many new social policy experts from Europe. This led to a fierce policy debate within international organizations operating in Eastern Europe. One side backed a US concept of minimal social provision designed to protect only the most vulnerable in society. To achieve this ideal required drastically scaling back the elaborate social provisions inherited from the former socialist regimes. Many World Bank and IMF loans came with conditions requiring such scaling back. The other side backed a European concept of universal rights to social welfare which required much more limited rationalization of existing systems.

In parallel, these two major approaches were debated through a series of international conferences climaxing at the Social Summit in Copenhagen in 1995. The Europeanists had to admit that the ideal of universal social welfare was in retreat because globalized capital markets punished countries which spent too heavily on social welfare. Yet they continued to argue that a welfare state created a more efficient and sustainable capitalism. The

Americanists were chastened by the spectre of East European states voting communism back into power through the ballot box, in part because of the massive social dislocation in the transition from one economic system to another. They were prepared to expand the scope of social safety nets, while still resisting any concept of welfare by right.

During this debate, the American-minimalist approach took on the title of "social safety net" to distinguish it from "social welfare." This approach had three main ideas. First, the state should provide only for people who were poor because of market failures. Second, methods had to be devised to identify and target such people. In European social policy jargon, this identification process was shorthanded as "means testing." Third, the provision should be limited to basic essentials.[3]

By the mid 1990s, the World Bank and IMF had adopted social policy. Moreover, as a result of their experience in Eastern Europe, they had a new and subtle appreciation of the dynamics of economic change, political change, social policies, and crises. Reflecting on the difficulty of persuading local elites to accept economic reforms, a World Bank theorist (Graham 1994) recognized that social policies had a strategic significance and that times of dislocation were times of opportunity:

> . . . reaching the poor and vulnerable with safety nets tends to be more difficult in closed-party systems where entrenched interest groups have a monopoly on state benefits. In contrast, dramatic political change or rapid implementation of economic reform undermines the influence of such groups and therefore can provide unique political opportunities to redirect resources to the poor. . . . The poor . . . may gain a new stake in the ongoing process of economic and public sector reform through organizing to solicit the state for safety net benefits.

In other words, social policies did not only help to minimize resistance to policies of economic reform but also might help build a coalition of support for these policies in the teeth of opposition from established elites. The conditions in which such a strategy might be possible were created by a dislocating crisis.

SOCIAL SAFETY NETS IN THE THAI CRISIS

In Thailand, sensitivity about the social impact of the crisis was present from the very beginning. In the first letter of intent agreed with the IMF in August 1997, one of the "medium-term" objectives of the programme was stated as follows:

> The government will pursue the policy of alleviating poverty and ensure that the adjustment program does not have undue adverse short-term effects on the poorest sections of society. Budget allocation to education, health and essential infrastructure investment will be maintained. (LoI-1, August 1997)

But the specific measures proposed were half-hearted. Most were undertakings not to make things worse—such as by cutting social spending and raising prices of public services. But in view of the very steep and rapid downturn of the economy over the next few months, the second LoI gave this task more urgency:

> Given the sharper-than-expected impact on the domestic economy of the adjustment process, the government is determined to accelerate the implementation of plans to protect the weaker sections of society. Thus, we expect the Asian Development Bank to move speedily and announce a social support program by early 1998. (LoI-2, November 1997)

But before this programme had appeared, the issue of the crisis impact had risen to the forefront of public debate. Government faced a chorus of journalists, academics, public intellectuals, and NGO workers warning that, on past experience, the crisis would weigh heaviest on the poor. A rural NGO leader said, "It is unfair to make the poor pay for measures to solve economic problems caused by a minority." Several NGOs conducted surveys and issued reports to demonstrate that the crisis hit the poor. The king gave encouragement to this lobby through his speech in December 1997 suggesting that "Being a tiger is not important. What is important is to have enough to eat and to live; and to have an economy which provides enough to eat and live." In early 1998, Prawase Wasi (*BP*, 13 Jun 1998) became the most distinctive voice in this chorus, telling the cabinet:

I believe the problems of the poor will become more serious within a few months. They have become dissatisfied with the government for not having a "heart" for the poor. A remedial action must be taken immediately otherwise the problems will grow beyond control.

In May, the former student leader, Thirayuth Boonmee, brought the issue to a head by challenging parliament to reject measures to restructure the financial industry unless there was a countervailing tax package to ensure the ultimate cost was not borne by the mass of the people. Thirayuth did not pose the issue as rich vs. poor, but that was how it was adopted in public debate.[4] Opposition politicians also discovered an interest in "the poor." This sudden and intense controversy brought a response from prominent conservatives concerned to defuse the issue. Former premier Anand Panyarachun said, "I don't want to see the country being divided into left and right or rich and poor" and recalled the polarization of the cold war. The combined effect of the king's speech, NGO reports, the Thirayuth intervention, and the warnings of establishment figures like Anand and Prawase was that the government was obliged to make policy with one eye on the issue of the poor.

Later in 1998, the World Bank added its voice to this warning chorus. In its paper on *East Asia: The Road to Recovery*, the World Bank (1998, 3) pictured societies unravelling:

> East Asia's economic and social structures are under strain, and decades of unparalleled social progress are under threat. . . . The poor are being severely hurt during the crisis as demand for their labor falls, prices for essential commodities rise, social services are cut, and crop failures occur in countries experiencing drought. . . . Widespread economic hardships are tearing at the fabric of society: There are food riots and ethnic tensions in Indonesia, farmers are protesting in Thailand, and workers are expressing their discontent in Korea. These signs of social stress are not only politically worrisome but the increased tensions at the household and community level are equally damaging, especially for women and children. Children are being pulled out of school and put to work; food is being rationed within the household, and women and girls are frequently the first to sacrifice their portions; and violence, street children, and prostitution are all on the increase. This is the human crisis.

This emphasis on the social aspect of the crisis formed a major part of the World Bank's criticism of the IMF in the fourth quarter of 1998. The social aspect of the IMF's Thailand programme evolved against this background of debate. The concept of a social safety net made its first appearance in the third LoI in February 1998.

> We have stepped up efforts, in collaboration with the World Bank, the Asian Development Bank (AsDB) and the Overseas Economic Cooperation Fund (OECF) to strengthen the social safety net, the need for which has become acute in the wake of rising unemployment and falling real wages. (LoI-3, February 1998)

Each subsequent LoI over the next year reiterated the promise that this net was being strengthened.

> . . . we have developed concrete measures to strengthen the social safety net and increase well-targeted public works programs, and have allocated an additional 0.5 percent of GDP in the 1997/98 budget for this purpose. (LoI-4, May 1998)

> . . . additional measures have been taken to cushion the impact of the recession. We have augmented and better targeted the social safety net, while avoiding entrenching new costly schemes that could introduce distortions into the labour market. Infrastructure spending is to be increased to support priority areas in rural and urban sectors in order to augment broader agricultural production and industrial restructuring. We will accelerate the social investment program targeted at addressing many dimensions of unemployment. (LoI-5, August 1998)

> . . . we have taken additional measures to augment the social safety net. . . . These measures remain consistent with our approach to support priority areas in rural and urban sectors, through carefully designed and targeted expenditure programs, while avoiding the kind of benefits schemes that could distort Thailand's labor market. (LoI-6, December 1998)

> . . . this package [Miyazawa] is aimed at strengthening the social safety net for

those most affected, especially the rural poor, and boosting domestic demand, through labor-intensive investment projects. (LoI-7, March 1999)

In early 1999, a Japanese academic compared the IMF programmes in Korea, Thailand, and Indonesia. He dubbed the Thai version a "social bailout."[5] He meant that social concern played a larger part in dictating the overall balance of crisis policy making in Thailand than in the other countries. This had come about for several reasons. The World Bank and the ADB had seized the opportunity to activate their new concern for social policy. The ADB had lent Thailand US$500 million under what the World Bank described as "the largest social program loan ever provided" by the ADB (World Bank Thailand 1999, 17). But also, public lobbying in Thailand had made it impossible for the Thai government and the IMF to ignore the social consequences of crisis policies.

SOCIAL SAFETY NETS IN PRACTICE—I: THE THAI GOVERNMENT

In the first six months of the crisis, the measures taken to alleviate the social impact were limited to minimizing the consequences of fiscal stringency. The budget cuts required to meet the IMF's demand for a fiscal surplus would not fall on social expenditure. Subsidies would not be removed from services such as bus and train fares which were used largely by the poor. The first LoI also undertook to "expand enrolment in secondary and vocational education. . . . develop training program for retrenched workers. . . . [and] provide relief to the urban and rural poor," but these were vague promises with no specific plans attached.

The policy to tailor the cuts in the 1997/98 budget to social objectives was only partially successful. The expenditure budget was reduced from an original 982 billion baht to 800 billion, a cut of 18.5 percent. The reduction in the allocation for education, health, and social services was 18.2 percent, in other words roughly proportionate to the total (Ammar and Orapin 1998, 19).

However, by the end of 1997, the alarming deceleration in the economy forced a rethink. From this point on, the policies for social cushioning had two parts. First, the Thai government would target its budget spending to social issues. Second, the World Bank and ADB would develop a major social safety net programme.

In early 1998, the government developed three main strategies for managing the social impact. First it extended an existing (1996) scheme of student loans to keep children in school. Second, it set out to cushion unemployment, largely through public works programmes to generate jobs. Third, it put some extra budget into rural health care. These schemes were expanded in mid 1998, when the fifth LoI set the budget deficit for 1998/99 as 3 percent of GDP. The student loan scheme was extended to a target of 650,000 students at a cost of 20 billion baht.[6]

The sixth LoI in December 1998 widened the 1998/99 budget deficit to 5 percent of GDP, with the increase "focused on maximizing the impact on demand and on the social safety net." The main innovation was to fund the creation of 200,000 temporary (two year) jobs in the public sector, many of them earmarked for new graduates about to fall on the job market. In addition, more funds were put behind skill training, the student loan programme, and other forms of indirect subsidy of education (e.g. school lunches).

The largest of these government efforts was the plan to combat the expected wave of unemployment. The plan, adopted in January 1998, included repatriating 300,000 foreign workers (mainly Burmese); exporting an additional 210,000 workers to work overseas; and creating 53,000 jobs in industry and 350,000 in the rural sector. A year later government claimed to have achieved these targets.[7] But these claims have to be moderated.

The repatriation of Burmese workers was opposed by both local employers and human rights activists. Many of those who were pushed back over the Burma border quickly returned. The government announced a second wave of repatriations in 1999, but then delayed action several times in the face of employers' resistance. Eventually the attempted repatriation began in the third quarter amidst deteriorating Thai-Burmese diplomatic relations following the Burmese embassy siege in Bangkok. Some 50,000 Burmese workers were pushed across the border, but many quickly returned, and the project was quietly abandoned.[8] Government admitted the "majority" crossed back into Thailand (*BP*, 12 Feb and 1 Mar 2000).

The claims on the numbers employed in rural job creation fail to record the length of employment, which in many cases was very short. NGOs complained that the schemes often benefited contractors more than the jobless. Many of the truly poor had difficulty learning about the schemes available. The central bureaucracy was often reluctant to engage in this kind of activity. This problem dogged even the schemes launched under the banner of the self-sufficiency strategy advocated in the king's December 1997 speech. The Interior Ministry made a public show of espousing the strategy and assigning a 67 billion baht budget for 1999/2001. However, in practice the ministry's officials were not trained or orientated to such activity. The ministry's role of "control" could not so simply be turned into "care."[9]

Of all the government schemes, the most public and controversial became the student loans programme. The controversy focused first on the extent of the need for such a programme. Some NGOs published figures suggesting that around 500,000 had dropped out of school. These figures were based on an unstructured survey of a sample of schools through the NGO network. The Education Ministry produced its own survey which claimed the figure was closer to 50,000. The National Education Commission predicted 300,000 would drop out in 1999 because of financial difficulty. Some researchers claimed the government's labour and socioeconomic surveys showed that enrolment had gone up rather than down. Using this same survey data, the World Bank concluded that "predictions of . . . significant declines in school enrolments and increases in dropouts *to date* have not been realized" (World Bank Thailand 1999, 13).

But the World Bank's own figures showed that while the numbers attending pre-school and primary levels continued to increase, the numbers dropping out at the transitions to secondary and higher vocational levels had risen. The report also noted that data from school surveys and household surveys did not match. Asked to comment on the confusion, a leading educational economist, Sirilaksana Khoman, pointed out that the Education Ministry had only a hazy idea of the number of schools under its care, so expecting the ministry to count students was very challenging.[10] The ADB produced a report confirming that the official figures showed the number of dropouts in 1998/99 was 165,821 higher than two years earlier, with the increases at the higher education levels (see table 4.1). A UNESCO survey showed that most dropped out because they could not afford to continue and needed to earn some money.

The second controversy over the education scheme concerned implementation. In mid 1999, the Auditor General's office conducted a random check on the administration of the scheme. It found that officials "didn't do their job properly in trying to locate poor schoolchildren" but concentrated on disbursing the budget allocation to "meet the deadlines set by their superiors" (*TN*, 23 Aug 1999). Two months later, a UNESCO review of the scheme came to the same conclusion. The loans were distributed through "a top-down allocation mechanism that has been superimposed on the organizational and administrative structure of the educational system." The loans were allocated to institutions on a "fair shares" basis with no reference to poverty incidence, and then distributed to meet numerical targets (*TN*, 25 Oct 1999). A parallel scholarship scheme funded by ADB met a similar fate. A review committee concluded that 80 percent of the students would have remained in school without the scholarships.

Table 4.1: Number of school dropouts, 1996–99

	1996/97	1997/98	1998/99	Change 96/7–98/9
Total school-age population (6–17)	13,495,000	13,398,000	13,301,000	-194,000
Dropouts during the year				
In primary	174,600	154,100	159,363	-15,237
Between primary and secondary	94,100	82,100	110,300	16,200
In lower secondary	74,200	86,000	101,277	27,077
Between lower secondary and above	50,100	105,700	137,700	87,600
In upper secondary	47,700	49,191	51,508	3,808
In vocational	69,700	69,800	116,073	46,373
Total	510,400	546,891	676,221	165,821

Source: Brimble and Suwannarat, from Reports of the National Education Commission

The government's experience with its social cushioning schemes suggested a simple conclusion. Maintaining or extending a simple programme such as employment-generating public works was no problem. But expecting the bureaucracy to identify the poor, develop programmes to respond to their needs, and implement them effectively was much more difficult. The Thai government had not been developed for such purposes. Neither could it be transformed quickly by a combination of need and hope.

SOCIAL SAFETY NETS IN PRACTICE—II: INTERNATIONAL INSTITUTIONS AND SIP/SIF

The second LoI imagined the major ADB social safety net programme would be announced "by early 1998." This timetable proved very optimistic.

In line with the international agencies' heightened attention to "civil society," the team designing the programme met with Thai academics and NGOs. The NGOs urged them, "Don't give money to the government and bureaucracies" (*TN*, 1 Feb 1998). It would result only in leakage, delay, and other bureaucratic habits. The ADB team felt unable to meet this demand, but tried to be innovative in ways which would reduce the usual bureaucratic problems. Part of the total programme budget (the Social Investment Programme, SIP) would be allocated through the government machinery, and would be earmarked largely for job creation schemes whose results could be fairly well monitored. But the larger chunk of the total programme budget (the Social Investment Fund, SIF) would be allocated to projects proposed by local groups. The funds for these projects would be distributed through the Government Savings Bank (GSB) rather than through line agencies which might have established habits in using such funds. The GSB had never before been used for such a scheme.[11] The machinery for approving local projects was staffed with representatives of NGOs and independent technocrats rather than line officials. Individual projects would also be screened by civic forums from their specific area.

Designing such new machinery took time. The SIF programme was finally launched in August 1998, over a year after the crisis had begun. Making the new machinery work took even longer. The guidelines defining acceptable applicants and acceptable schemes were narrow. Few local groups had the expertise to prepare the project proposals required. The programme offered funding for projects of community welfare, conservation activities, skill development, or community economy. Such schemes offered little or no immediate benefit to cushion the impact of the crisis. Few communities saw the point of applying. Most of the projects submitted to SIF in the early rounds were requests for working capital from small businesses, particularly from construction contractors. Very few applications fitted the rubric. Of the 836 projects screened by the end of 1998, only twelve qualified for approval. In March 1999, the rubric was extended to include projects of emergency community welfare for the needy. Such projects had an immediate benefit and applications increased.

Still by June 1999, only one hundred projects had been passed. Total approvals under both the SIP and SIF schemes had risen to US$16 million, only 5 percent of the total available funds. Disbursement was also slow, because the GSB had to devise and learn new procedures. A World Bank official explained that the government-based SIP had progressed slowly because of bank rules to ensure honesty and transparency, but also because of "enormous inertia resulting from the general lack of a sense of urgency among tens of thousands of officials." The official admitted the bank would have to "restart the project" (*TN*, 23 Jul 1999). The crisis was now two years old. The bank itself had already pronounced that the crisis was over.[12]

The SIP/SIF and the ADB's education schemes were based on the principles that had evolved in the internal debate of the international organizations. The truly poor had to be identified and targeted. Civil society groups and local communities should be involved. But there was still a major problem. Either the existing governmental machinery had to be used—with the risks of leakage, delay, or perfunctory implementation. Or new machinery had to be designed which took time and involved a high risk of failure. There was a large input of expert and expensive manpower (particularly within the World Bank and ADB) into designing these schemes. Yet their contribution to cushioning the crisis was limited.[13]

By late 1998, the government came to rely on a shotgun approach to both fiscal stimulus and social cushioning. In the plan to utilize the funds from the Miyazawa scheme announced in March 1999, the government abandoned all pretence of careful targeting, elaborate bureaucratic procedures, and innovative channels. By this time there was a real sense of urgency borne of fear that the crisis would take a further lurch downwards into a great depression-like spiral. Government based the Miyazawa scheme on a twenty-five-year-old model of crisis spending[14] which disbursed funds through local government bodies despite the fact that these bodies were often very new and supposedly prone to corruption by the locally powerful. Government relied only on a high level of publicity to ensure some degree of transparency. There were scattered reports of corruption and misuse, but these were meagre in relation to the size of the funds involved. Most of the funds were spent within the target of nine months.[15]

By late 1998, the IMF was openly blaming the failure to implement social safety nets on the Thai government. In reality, the IMF had a vision of the political utility of social safety nets, but had no conception of the difficulties of establishing them in a country where the government did not have the relevant experience or commitment. The IMF assumed it would be possible in the same way that economists like to assume conditions which have little relevance to the real world.

UNEMPLOYMENT AS A MEASURE OF SOCIAL IMPACT

The statistic most often used to measure the impact of the crisis was unemployment. This of course reflected the recent history of advanced economies where the unemployment rate has become the most eloquent single reading on an economy's equity.

The Thai government surveys the labour market through sample surveys. The *Labour Force Surveys* (LFS) are conducted two to four times a year, while *Socioeconomic Surveys* (SES) with additional information on household income and expenditure are usually conducted every two years.[16] The unemployment statistic in advanced countries is calculated largely from numbers of people applying for social welfare. The unemployment figure in Thailand is taken from a periodic sample survey. This difference highlights the very different meaning of the figure in the two environments. In the absence of social welfare, many people *cannot* be unemployed and survive.

The use of the unemployment rate as a measure of social impact assumes that there are two main states of existence: either paid employment, or unemployment with social welfare support. The Thai labour market diverges a long way from this model. Only around 40 percent of the 32 million people in the labour force are paid employees. Around 30 percent are own-account workers, mostly farmers but also many small family business owners. Around 20 percent (these percentages vary across the year, see below) are unpaid family workers, meaning they are working on a family farm or family business. Moreover, there is a constant movement between these categories which is still dictated by the agricultural season and the associated movements of migration.

Many people shift between different types of employment over the course of one year. Table 4.2 shows these movements for a sample year. In the on-

Table 4.2: Labour flexibility, 1993

	February '000	August '000	February %	August %	Aug–Feb '000	Aug–Feb %
					—Difference—	
Total labour force	31,636	32,845			1,209	
(household work)	3,525	2,594			-931	
Employed	29,207	32,153	92.3	97.9	2,946	5.6
Unemployed	1,193	494	3.8	1.5	-699	-2.3
Seasonally Inactive	1,236	198	3.9	0.6	-1,038	-3.3
employers	629	632	2.0	1.9	3	-0.1
government employees	2,166	2,182	6.8	6.6	16	-0.2
employees	9,748	8,857	30.8	27.0	-892	-3.8
own-account workers	8,972	9,450	28.4	28.8	478	0.4
unpaid family workers	7,691	11,032	24.3	33.6	3,341	9.3
employed in agriculture	14,294	18,245	45.2	55.5	3,950	10.4
employed outside agriculture	14,913	13,908	47.1	42.3	-1,005	-4.8

Source: *Labour Force Survey 1993*, February and August rounds. Percentages are based on total labour force

season (August), agriculture employs an extra four to five million people, equivalent to 10–15 percent of the labour force. About half a million of these are own-account workers (farmers), and the rest are unpaid family labour. Outside the season, about two-thirds of these (2.5–3 million people) describe themselves as unemployed, seasonally inactive, or engaged on household work. The others (1–2 million) go to work elsewhere. Many migrate to work as agricultural wage labour in such activities as sugarcane cutting and cassava planting. Others go to the towns and cities. In the off-season, the proportion working outside agriculture may rise by as much as 2.5 million people. In recent (pre-crisis) years, the biggest rises in off-season employment were in construction (about 0.8 million), and manufacturing (0.5 million).

In addition, there has been a longer-term shift from agriculture to non-agriculture, from village to city. This shift is rather more complex than a simple rural-urban migration. For several decades, large and increasing numbers of people have shuttled back and forth between village and city. Many are the seasonal migrants described above. Others are young people who go to the city for a few years as much as a rite of passage—in search of experience and modernity—as a search for employment. In between these two extremes, there are people who go to the city for one or a handful of years because of bad rains, family circumstances, debt, or a host of other reasons. Over the boom years, more people were drawn into these rural-urban flows, the time spent in the city lengthened, and increasing numbers made a more permanent shift away from agriculture into urban employment. As a result, over the twelve pre-crisis years from 1984 to 1996, employment (peak season) in agriculture shrank by 2 million, while employment outside agriculture grew by 8 million, especially in manufacturing, commerce, and construction (table 4.3). The pre-crisis urban workforce included a lot of new recruits.

Table 4.3: Labour force changes, 1984–96

	1984 mil	1996 mil	1984 %	1996 %	Change 96/84 mil
Labour force	26.6	32.8	100.0	100.0	6.1
Employed	26.0	32.2	97.7	98.4	6.2
Agriculture	18.1	16.1	68.1	49.2	-2.0
Manufacturing	2.0	4.3	7.5	13.2	2.3
Construction	0.5	2.2	2.0	6.6	1.6
Commerce	2.2	4.3	8.3	13.3	2.1
Transport	0.5	1.0	1.9	2.9	0.4
Services	2.4	4.1	8.9	12.5	1.7
Other	0.3	0.2	1.0	0.6	0.0
Total Non-agriculture	7.9	16.1	29.6	49.2	8.2

Source: *Labour Force Surveys*, August rounds

This long-term shift also involves income transfers. Migrants in the city send home remittances to their village families, and take back savings on their return trips. Wage earnings and remittances account for around a quarter of all rural incomes, with the proportion rising higher among the lower income groups.[17] Longer-term migrants keep up these remittances—and often finance the family purchase of house or land—partly out of a sense of gratitude and responsibility for their families, but also as an investment in social security. Without such payments, migrants might lose their claim to inheritance of family land, or their right to return to the village household. In the absence of any urban social security system, such an investment is highly significant.

In previous crises of the urban economy in Thailand, much of the impact had fallen on the rural sector as rural migrants returned to their village homes. This mechanism eased the threat of severe social stress or political disorder, at the expense of raising the numbers below the poverty line. At the onset of this crisis, many speculated how the impact would fall on this occasion in view of the increased urbanization of the previous decade.

The Thailand Development Research Institute (TDRI) produced two predictions. First, it surmised that the impact would be largely urban. It suggested that "farmers in general appear to have benefited directly from the currency depreciation" (Ammar and Orapin 1998, 12) because the fall in the currency resulted in a sharp rise in the baht prices for most of the crops which the farmers had to sell. In addition, "by not benefiting from any major [government] transfer programs or subsidies that target the poor (such as food subsidies) during normal times, there was relatively little for them to lose through the fiscal cutbacks during the hard times" (Ammar and Orapin 1998, 20). These conclusions of course ignored the close connections between the urban and rural labour markets through migration and remittances. This was surprising since TDRI had done much of the best analysis on this aspect of the labour market.[18]

Second, a TDRI researcher argued that the rural sector would be unable to counterweight the urban collapse during this crisis (Nipon 1999). The drain of labour from agriculture during the boom years had resulted in reductions of cultivated area, introduction of labour-saving machinery (especially for harvesting), and shifts to less labour-intensive cropping regimes (especially perennial tree crops). It would be impossible to reverse these changes quickly. Besides, many migrants had left the village at a young age, or been away for a long time, and hence had neither the skill nor inclination to resume agricultural work. This analysis was obviously correct to a large extent. However, it was exclusively economic, and neglected the *social* importance of agriculture and the rural household.

In sum, the use of the employment rate as a measure of social distress reflected the preconceptions of advanced economies with relatively stable employment patterns and with social welfare systems. By contrast, Thailand had almost no social security provisions and a highly mobile labour market. For those who lost their jobs, there were three main survival options: find any other employment; fall back on savings; or revert to the traditional social safety net provided by family and community. Only the second of these would affect the unemployment rate—those returning home would most likely be redefined as unpaid family labour or outside the labour force.

So what happened? How was the impact allocated? Here we attempt an account based both on the available survey statistics, but also on some more casual and impressionistic observations. The impact is best divided into two phases.

CUSHIONING PHASE I: JULY 1997 TO LATE 1998

Over the first twelve to eighteen months of the crisis, the main impact was felt in the urban economy which decelerated very rapidly in the second half of 1997 and the first half of 1998. By February 1998, there were 0.9 million fewer people working in construction than at the same time in the previous year. The numbers of lay-offs in other sectors is more difficult to judge. Some 25,000 lost their jobs with the collapse of the finance companies, and many more were disemployed from real estate and other finance-related businesses. In July, the Board of Investment (BoI) reported that 82,000 had been laid off from promoted companies in food, textiles, plastics, automotive, and service industries. The Labour Ministry reported that 330,000 had been laid off from industrial jobs between January and July.

But these counts were undoubtedly imperfect. They came before a surge in lay-offs just ahead of 19 August when an amendment in the labour law increased the levels of severance pay. The official counts also were biassed towards large enterprises, while Kakwani showed that the main employment impact came among smaller firms. He found that by February 1998, the crisis had reduced wage employment in small firms with 6–10 workers by a quarter. By August, the impact had spread on to firms of 11–100 workers, where the crisis had reduced employment by around a third. By contrast, large firms suffered a much smaller (7 percent) impact on employment (NESDB, *Indicators*, 2 (4), October 1998, 12).[19] By a conservative estimate, the total number of lay-offs in urban Thailand between the float and the end of 1998 was 2 million and may have been higher.

Some of these could not find another job. In the first post-crisis reading in February 1998, unemployment had risen by 0.8 million over the same period of 1996, to reach 4.6 percent of the labour force (table 4.4). The figure eased slightly in the peak agricultural season, but rose over 5 percent in early 1999, with slightly over a million more unemployed than in 1996. But to understand the impact of the crisis, we need to look beyond this figure.

Table 4.4: Unemployment, 1995–99

	Feb '000	May '000	Aug '000	Nov '000	Feb %	May %	Aug %	Nov %
1995	723.5		375.1		2.3		1.1	
1996	641.3	659.6	353.9		2.0	2.0	1.1	
1997	697.8		292.5		2.2		0.9	
1998	1,479.3	1,612.9	1,137.9	1,463.0	4.6	5.0	3.4	4.5
1999	1,715.7	1,758.5	985.7	1,070.3	5.2	5.3	3.0	3.3
2000	1,418.0				4.3			
Change from 1996								
1998	838.0	953.3	784.0		2.6	3.0	2.3	
1999	1074.4	1098.9	631.8		3.2	3.3	1.9	

Source: Labour Force Surveys

According to the labour law, employers must pay severance pay. The maximum amount, payable to a worker employed for over three years, was six months pay, adjusted to ten months from August 1998 onwards. But this applied only to workers in the formal sector. Government surveys showed that around three-quarters of those laid off got no compensation at all (Sauwalak and Chettha 2000, 13–4).

In 1997–98, the urban disemployed appear to have adopted three survival strategies. First, many accepted whatever employment they could find, even at a considerable loss of income and deterioration in work environment. Surveys of laid-off women factory workers indicated that around half found work in sweatshops, usually at a fraction of their earlier wage, generally with irregular income (from piecework), no security of employment, and poor working conditions.[20] Second, many chose to survive on their savings rather than accept such employment. By August 1998, the numbers recorded as unemployed in urban areas had risen by 0.3 million over the same time in the previous year. Third, many started their own small businesses, particularly vending or petty services. Surveys of laid-off workers found that around a quarter took this option. In the February 1998 labour survey, employment in manufacturing remained constant over the previous year, while employment in commerce and services increased by 0.1 and 0.3 million respectively. These numbers disguise a much larger shift—with numbers in formal-sector employment falling, and those in informal activities rising (Sauwalak and Chettha 2000, 31).

By casual observation, the number of petty vendors and service businesses in Bangkok increased very rapidly in late 1997 and early 1998. The small service businesses which expanded included all kinds of repair work, foot massage, car washes, laundries, and trash recycling. Even more strikingly, in the city centre and key suburban areas, large areas of pavement were newly taken over by vendors. The most popular choice was food vending as the investment required was small and the market relatively assured. Among food vending, the most popular speciality was *luk chin ping*, grilled meatballs. The capital investment could be as little as a simple grill made from scrap metal. The daily investment amounted only to charcoal and the meatballs sold in small quantities at early-morning markets. While this vending explosion was most visible in Bangkok, it could also be seen in major provincial towns and, by late 1998, along many of the main highways. This expansion was possible because crisis-hit consumers were happy to move downmarket.[21] For many the meatball was the true social safety net.

In other ways, the social impact was lessened by sharing. Some firms chose to retain all or most of their workforce, but to require their employees to accept shorter hours and lower pay. In February 1998, the numbers working less than 20 hours a week stood at 3 million, almost double the figure recorded a year earlier. In Bangkok alone, the numbers underemployed in this way rose by ten times to 0.7 million, or over a sixth of the whole city workforce. In upcountry urban areas there was a similar effect (see chart 4.1). In addition, there were many smaller efforts to manage the crisis by sharing the strain. Some families appear to have amalgamated. The average household size in Bangkok increased from 2.9 to 3.35 between 1996 and 1998. In Bangkok and the urban area as a whole, increased money transfers between families helped to alleviate the slide into poverty (World Bank Thailand 2000, 18).

Chart 4.1: Un/Under-employment, 1996–99

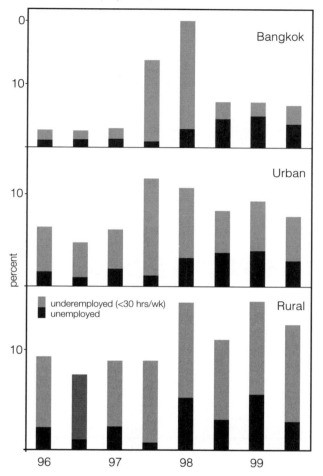

As a result of these shifts to informal-sector employment, reductions in hours, and sharing strategies, average earnings were reduced. In Bangkok, at the eye of the crisis, the fall was 10.1 percent (see chart 4.2). In sum, the unemployment rate shifted only a relatively small amount. But the total of the unemployed and underemployed amounted to a fifth of the city workforce. And city incomes dropped by a tenth in real terms.

Chart 4.2: Real monthly wages, 1996–99

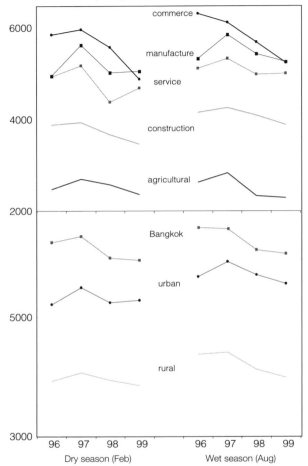

A survey on workers still employed in Bangkok's industrial suburbs found that household income declined by 19 percent because of cuts in food allowances, bonuses, and overtime payments. Many households also found that supplies of rice, usually sent from their villages, dwindled because the villages were also in difficulty and many had returned to share in the family rice bowl. They adjusted to this reduced income by sending less money back to their village homes; cutting their expenditure on social activities (weddings, temple merit making); taking kids out of school or sending them back to the village; taking up vending or other means to generate some extra cash; defaulting on their loans; and hunting and gathering for food such as vegetables and fish in the suburban canals (*Matichon Sutsapda*, 11 Apr 2000, 31).

At this stage of the crisis, the impact was largely confined to the urban areas—Bangkok and major provincial centres which had some manufacturing, finance, and construction business. The impact on rural areas was more mixed. Many farmers enjoyed a windfall profit at the end 1997 harvest. The yield was generally good as baht prices surged because of the currency devaluation and international price rises caused by El Nino's impact elsewhere in Asia. Rice prices were strong, while only rubber prices were poor because of a world glut.

Most rural-urban migrants chose not to go home at this stage. Akin Rabibhadana asked a northeastern villager why more were not coming back. He was told, "They don't want to create difficulty for their relatives."[22] However, there was still some transmission of the crisis impact into the rural areas. From casual observation, the numbers leaving the villages for short-term cash-seeking trips in the off-season of mid 1998 were reduced, and many who went on such trips came back empty-handed. Besides, remittance from disemployed relatives in the city declined, and returns from ancillary businesses which depended on urban market demand were reduced. Some rural-made goods continued to fare well because their low price proved attractive in a falling urban market. But others suffered because of the general collapse of demand or the disintegration of the transport and marketing networks on which they depended (Nathan, Kelkar, and Nongluck, 1998).

As a result of these conflicting forces, the overall impact on the rural sector in early-mid 1998 was mixed. Average earnings fell, but only by 3.2 percent in real terms. Moreover, the *Socioeconomic Survey* (SES) conducted in 1998 showed that this fall was very unevenly distributed. The upper levels (i.e. higher income deciles) of rural society tended to prosper, as they had land and crop income. The exception was the south where rubber prices slumped. But among the lower strata of rural society, the impact was severe. Poor households suffered from the collapse of remittances, the lack of wage-earning opportunities, and the rise in food prices. The impact was concentrated in the northeast which was the poorest region and contributed the largest number of migrants to Bangkok (NESDB, *Indicators* 3 (1), 4, tables 9 and 12).

CUSHIONING PHASE II: LATE 1998 ONWARDS

The initial impact was cushioned within urban society by drawing down savings, falling back on the informal sector, and sharing the strain. In the last quarter of 1998, this phase came to an end. Urban employment continued to shrink. By February 1999, numbers employed in construction had dropped by another half million, and those in manufacture by 0.1 million. These falls were partly compensated by rising employment in commerce (0.1 million) and services (0.2). But by now many found they could no longer survive in the city on their savings or on the proceeds of part-time work. By February 1999, the large numbers working short-time had almost completely disappeared in Bangkok, and dwindled in the provincial towns (see chart 4.1).

Similarly, the expansion in vending and petty services passed the critical point where expanding supply overshot dwindling demand. In late 1998, the ranks of vendors and petty service operators cluttering the pavements of Bangkok visibly declined. Many were dislodged by official clean-up campaigns connected with the staging of the Asian Games in December 1998. Underlying economic logic ensured the change was permanent rather than temporary. By mid 1999, surveys found long-established vendors in provincial towns returning to their villages because the collapse in demand made their business uneconomical.

For many migrants who had earlier refused to transfer the burden back to their village-based family, the harvest at the end of 1998 provided an opportunity to return home to "help" and then simply stay. By February 1999, the burden of unemployment had been transferred away from Bangkok, especially to the northeastern region, the major source of rural-urban migrants. Open unemployment in the northeast was 8.8 percent (compared to 5.2 percent in Bangkok). Among northeasterners aged 15–29, the major source of migrants, 18 percent of males and 15 percent of females were out of work (ADB 1999, annex table 3.6).

By February 1999, the numbers employed in agriculture were 0.9 million higher than a year earlier. By May, this figure had risen to 1.9 million. Two changes contributed to this figure. First, possibly over a million had returned home. Second, 0.6 million people who would normally be inactive at this season were working, mostly as unpaid family workers in agriculture. The strain of the crisis had been transferred back to the villages, and village households were mobilizing their spare labour resources to meet this strain. The back flow and price fall had resulted in a large fall in rural incomes. According to Kakwani's adjusted figures, real earnings from the farm had fallen 15.2 percent over the year up to February 1999 (table 4.5). The transfer of the crisis impact from city to village had political repercussions. Through 1999, government faced a string of rural protests over debt relief, over access to land for those returned from the city, and over subsidies for low crop prices (see pp. 143–8).

Table 4.5: Real incomes by origin, 1997–99

(February)	Wage	Earners in Business	Farm	Total
1997	8232	6516	1633	5395
1998	7978	5504	1575	5038
1999	7674	5153	1336	4624
% change 97–98	-3.1	-15.5	-3.6	-6.6
% change 98–99	-3.8	-6.4	-15.2	-8.2

NESDB, *Indicators* 3 (3), July 1999, 26

While almost 2 million attempted to survive by a return to agriculture, as TDRI predicted, many could not or would not be reabsorbed. Many treated the village as a welfare cushion—making constant forays into the city in search of employment, and returning to the village when their resources were exhausted. By August 1999, people were drifting back from agriculture to other jobs.

Looking at the unemployment rate (table 4.4) suggests that the crisis at its peak added about a million people to the ranks of the unemployed, and that the situation had eased by early 1999. But this way of reading the data underestimates the scale and the duration of the problem. Only a portion of those who lost work defined themselves as "unemployed." In Bangkok,

Chart 4.3: Unemployment, underemployment, non-participation 1996–99

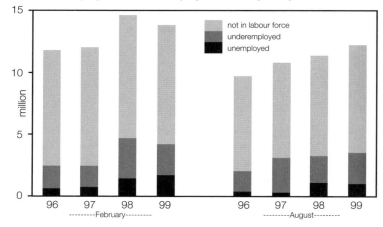

for instance, 4–5 percent of all people of working age disappeared from the ranks of the fully employed, but only about half of these defined themselves as "unemployed." The others were studying, working in the household, or working short hours. Moreover, the situation had not eased in 1999. Fewer were unemployed, but more were disappearing from the labour force (chart 4.3). The same was true in the rural areas, only more so. Across the country, the numbers unemployed, underemployed, or outside the labour force (but not studying) grew by 2 to 2.5 million between 1996 and 1999.

IMPACT SUMMARY

The simplest measure of the scale of the crisis is the effect on the economy as a whole. Per capita real GDP (chart 4.4) fell almost a fifth from its quarterly high (Q4 1996) to its quarterly low (Q3 1998). But both peak and trough were momentary. On a moving annual basis the fall was around 14 percent. This measurement accords closely with the 14.5 percent fall in real income over 1997–99 calculated by Kakwani (see table 4.6). At the bottom, the level of per capita GDP was around the same as early 1994— just before the final phase of the bubble. By the end of 1999, per capita real GDP was moving back towards the level of early-mid 1995. In rough terms, the crisis set incomes back by around four to five years.

Chart 4.4: Real per capita GDP, 1993–99

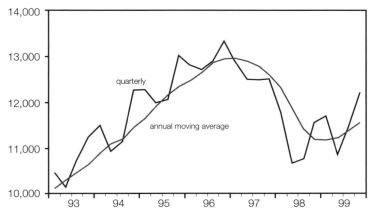

Of course this income drop was not evenly distributed. Attempts to map the impact across different social groups reached three main conclusions (ADB 1999; World Bank Thailand 1999; Sauwalak and Chettha 1999, 2000). First, the crisis hit hardest at the top and bottom of the income scale, while the middle ranks suffered less. The top echelon suffered from business bankruptcies, asset collapse, and shrinkage of white-collar employment. The lower echelons suffered from the shrinkage of jobs and earnings. Second, the poorly educated young (especially teenagers, also 20s) seemed the hardest hit. Many dropped out of school. Large numbers failed to find jobs. Third, by 1999 the worst impact was in the rural northeast, the major source of city migrants.

Even at the onset of the crisis, large numbers of people immediately began to drop down below the poverty line (table 4.6). The *Socioeconomic Survey* found that by mid 1998, the crisis had pushed an additional 1.1 million people below the poverty line, including an additional 0.6 million into the ranks of the ultra-poor. Almost all this increase was found in the rural areas among those who were landless or held less than five rai of land, especially in the northeast (always the poorest and most vulnerable region) and the south (affected by the rubber price drop). Over the nine months following this survey, the economy slid much further down. There are no data yet on the poverty impact in the worst period of the crisis, and estimates vary widely.[23] But the available data on employment and incomes suggest a

95

further worsening in the northeast. Ultimately, the crisis struck at the weakest.

Table 4.6: Poverty incidence 1988–98
(percent)

	Total	Urban	Semi-urban	Rural	Centre	North	North east	South	Greater Bangkok	<5 rai land
1988	32.6	8.0	21.8	40.3	26.6	32.0	48.4	32.5	6.1	67.7
1990	27.2	6.9	18.2	33.8	22.3	23.2	43.1	27.6	3.5	52.9
1992	23.2	3.6	12.7	29.7	13.3	22.6	39.9	19.7	1.9	41.2
1994	16.3	2.4	9.6	21.2	9.2	13.2	28.6	17.3	0.9	28.9
1996	11.4	1.6	5.8	14.9	6.3	11.2	19.4	11.5	0.6	37.2
1998	12.9	1.5	7.2	17.2	7.7	9.0	23.2	14.8	0.6	41.9

NESDB, *Indicators* 3 (1), January 1999

Signs of the human strain are fragmentary but compelling (World Bank Thailand 2000; Sauwalak and Chettha 2000). The numbers of children abandoned at hospitals or admitted to orphanages increased above the trend. A health survey found striking increases in malnutrition and underweight children, especially in the northeast. The incidence of suicide and mental health problems increased. Theft and other property crimes turned sharply upwards. The numbers in jail doubled over two years, and the numbers in remand homes for young offenders almost tripled, leading to massive overcrowding and a wave of protests in early 2000. The major contributor to these startling increases was amphetamines.

The trend of increase in amphetamine use originated before the crisis.[24] But the years 1998–99 saw an explosion. In 1998, the police reckoned that the consumption of methamphetamine doubled. In 1998, the Office of the Narcotics Control Board reckoned 1.4 percent of students used drugs. A year later the Board revised the estimate up to 12.4 percent, or almost half a million people (Nualnoi, Noppanun, and Lewis 2000, 34–5). By late 1999, the Thai authorities had mapped over forty drug production centres across the northern borders in Burma and Laos. The army was engaged in a low-level war with the cross-border traders. Seizures of a million or more amphetamine pills had become almost weekly events, and the total annual supply for 2000 was projected as 400 million pills. The total of convicted people in jail had doubled from 65,336 in 1996 to 128,825 in October 1999. Three-quarters of this increase came from drug offenders.

The crisis may have contributed to this drug explosion in three ways. First, stress and desperation helped to widen the market. The unemployed were a disproportionately high percentage of users. Second, unemployment helped the dealers to create a pervasive retailing network. A Chulalongkorn University survey found that the distribution system worked through a pyramid selling scheme involving large numbers of people. Dealers encouraged existing customers to become sub-dealers—an offer which appealed to unemployed or low income earners looking for ways to fund their own consumption and earn extra income (Nualnoi, Noppanun, and Lewis 2000). Third, the loss of other forms of income made drugs an attractive business for illegal businessmen, and for officials who normally expected to enhance their income through ancillary businesses. In one report, a regional police bureau announced it was monitoring 777 officials suspected of involvement in drug trading, including 433 policemen and 160 village heads or their assistants (*BP*, 29 Jul 1999). This problem was so extensive that government made television commercials designed to shame and intimidate officials who became involved in the amphetamine trade.

POST MORTEMS

In mid 1999, the ADB published a report stating, "The effects of the regional economic crisis in Thailand have been exaggerated and have at worst returned most Thais to 1996 levels of income and welfare." It found that only 41 percent of households had suffered a loss of welfare, while the remaining 59 percent had become better off. It suggested that much of the distress had been psychological: "Many Thais were convinced that their situation must have deteriorated, even if there was no concrete manifestation of it" (ADB 1999, 10, 1; *BP*, 19 Jun 1999; *TN*, 2 Jul 1999).

The report was based on a comparison between the *Socioeconomic Surveys* of 1996 and 1998. The findings were not surprising. The data came from samples interviewed between February and July. The midpoint of the sample range was thus April-May. The survey asked respondents to estimate their income and expenditure over the previous six months. The midpoint of this estimate was thus around the start of the survey year. Hence this analysis was a comparison between conditions at the start of 1998 and those at the start of 1996. Between these two dates, there were eighteen months of bubble economy and six months of crisis. On the one hand, the period of the bubble saw more trickledown of wealth than ever before. The price distortions and tight labour markets in this period temporarily reversed the long-term trend towards worsening distribution. On the other hand, the worst period of the crisis had yet to come. Between the two survey dates, per capita GDP had fallen only about 1 percent. The rapid shrinkage of the economy came in the first three quarters of 1998, when per capita GDP fell another 13 percent. The sense of distress was not a psychological aberration. Rather it was not captured by this analysis because of timing.

In fact, the ADB report (compiled by two highly respected researchers)[25] included much other data and many caveats about timing. But the publicity surrounding the issue of the report was designed to give the impression that the impact had been exaggerated. By this time, the ADB and other international institutions were pronouncing that the Asian crisis was over. The ADB launched a website to vaunt the recovery. The ADB had contributed expertise to alleviating the social impact of the crisis. There was an obvious temptation to claim some credit and consign the crisis impact to the past.

At the same time, the ADB report set out a future agenda for social policy. It pointed out the need for better targeting of vulnerable groups, better sources of information, and better monitoring through community participation. It concluded that "the formal social safety net has been conclusively shown to be wholly inadequate for the needs of a modern society," and that "the public sector needs to have much better ability to rapidly implement targeted support programs in the face of a crisis" (ADB 1999, 10: 3). It criticized the Thai government's tendency to rely on family and community to cushion the impact of economic dislocation. Early in the crisis, Chuan Leekpai argued that the family was Thailand's social safety net, and government should not do anything which would cause this function to atrophy. Later, Anand Panyarachun (CERN 1999, 34) expressed a similar sentiment:

> A social safety net has to be devised on its own merits, in accordance with the history, tradition and culture of that particular land. . . . Our approach to the whole social security system is different from what is being practised in the

West. . . . We in Thailand believe that we must steer clear of the invisible hand of the market, the interventionist hand of the state, and the heavy hand of socialism. We cherish our family tradition [and] have long relied on the family social safety net.

Officials of the IMF and ADB publicly criticized this reliance on the family. The ADB's post mortem (ADB 1999, 10: 2) admitted the crisis impact had been "tempered by a number of practical and sometimes innovative coping mechanisms," but warned that,

> Although Asians arguably have stronger family ties than Europeans or North Americans, this belief can be overstated and can lead to complacency on the part of government and society alike. . . . The informal social safety nets . . . must be seen as a temporary solution to a fundamental societal problem. If stretched too far the "nylon" net may break, with obvious social consequences.

An IMF post mortem criticized the government's "lack of preparedness" and sermonized: "Governments should have the capacity already set up to identify those groups and regions where poverty is particularly a problem, as well as to understand the factors and dynamics responsible for the persistence of such poverty" (Heller, 1999).

In January 2000, the World Bank's Thailand office published an issue of its *Social Monitor* which adopted a sharply different view. Reviewing the social impact of the crisis, it concluded:

> Family based coping mechanisms remain effective, and any new social protection initiatives should reinforce the priceless Thai values of self reliance and family cohesion. (World Bank Thailand 2000, 7)

The report made only a passing reference to the expensive World Bank/ ADB schemes; praised efforts by the family, local communities, and Thai government agencies to cushion the crisis; noted that there had been "a conspicuous absence of civil conflict in Thailand during the crisis, unlike the experience of other Asian countries"; and burnt incense before some major social concepts popular with the NGO movement—man and nature, local knowledge, community, reciprocity, diversity, holism. Then it enveloped all of these into a framework of "social capital."[26] Thailand had survived the crisis, the bank suggested (2000, 8), because of the large stock of social capital represented by the family and local community:

> The Thai approach to social capital can be described as more holistic than linear. Social capital for Thailand is a complex matrix of connected institutions, values, spirit, philosophy, achievements and resources, at the centre of which sits the Thai family, receiving enrichment from education and religion, from the community and friends, and sharing its knowledge and resources with other families and institutions, and contributing to Thai governance, history, culture and natural resources.[27]

However, the bank carefully went on to suggest that the severity of the crisis had rendered this social capital inadequate at the margins. The *Social Monitor* showed that statistics of thefts, drug-related arrests, mental depression, suicides, and abandoned children had all risen above trend over the years 1998–99. It concluded that "the social safety net was inadequate to protect all people living at the margin, and some of them resorted to desperate measures to alleviate this increased hardship." The implication, similar to that of the ADB post mortem, was that there remained a role for the international organizations in helping to improve social provisions. But these provisions should build on the foundation of family and community, and should work through community organization rather than the government bureaucracy.

CONCLUSION

By the time of the Asia crisis, there was a consensus in the international institutions and the US policy making establishment that crisis policies needed a social component—not just for humanitarian reasons but because of political realism. Larry Summers (1999b) said:

> It is arguable that reform would not be politically sustainable in these situations without an assurance that the pain of adjustment will not fall only [sic!] on the poor.

At the outset, the IMF acknowledged the need for a social response to the crisis, but in a half-hearted fashion. By early 1998, the severity of the crisis made social policy a more urgent priority, and the clamour from Thai public opinion pushed the issue to the fore. From this point forward, Thailand's approach was a "social bailout" as much as a financial rescue.

Within two years, the crisis set Thai income levels back by around four to five years. In the first phase, the impact was confined largely to the urban areas. The social safety net schemes designed by the World Bank and ADB were still in the design stage. The Thai government's schemes were directed mostly to the rural area, and were not targeted at vulnerable groups in the city and provincial towns. Those who lost their jobs survived by drawing out savings, accepting work with lower pay and shorter hours, dropping into the informal sector, and sharing hardship. But these strategies were only effective in the short term. Savings were ultimately exhausted. Survival in the city was difficult on low earnings. Demand for the vending and service products of the informal sector at first increased as consumers adjusted downwards, but ultimately faltered when expanding supply exceeded declining demand.

Some of the impact was already transmitted into the rural area by the decline of remittances and the collapse of markets for rural-made ancillary products and short-term wage labour. But from late 1998 onwards, the crisis entered a second phase in which the major impact was rural. Large numbers went back from city to village. This was not a one-time sudden movement and was hardly visible. Many people shuttle back and forth between city and village all the time. Now more people shortened their trips to the city or gave them up completely. Some returned home and either stayed longer or never left.

To some extent this move to the countryside was cushioned by the government's job creation schemes, and by the Miyazawa funds. But the most important cushion was the readiness of family and community to reabsorb people. TDRI predicted there was little chance that agriculture would expand in proportion to this extra labour. Yet the dry season of 1999 found almost 2 million more people trying to make a living from agriculture than in the same period of the previous year. A third of these were family members who would normally be idle at this time. The rural household was drawing on its reserves to carry the strain. Besides, the rural community could act as a social cushion with food, shelter, and mental support. A rural trader commented that the returning migrants might have lost their income but had regained the "warmth" of family and village. Yet this phase transferred the greatest strain to the most vulnerable region—the rural northeast—and especially to the landless or land-poor, and the young, whose economic survival depended heavily on migration to tap the fringes of the urban job market.

The cushioning approach spearheaded by the ADB and supported by the World Bank was built around the idea of a "social safety net," with this jargon's comforting image of a sure rescue from certain disaster. The scheme was built on two main principles. First, the poor and vulnerable groups could be identified and "targeted." Second, help could be delivered through community organizations with the twin benefits of precluding too large a role for the bureaucracy, and contributing to community strength. The result would be a cost-efficient and semi-privatized delivery of short-term social protection.

But this ideal proved impossible to realize. The information was not available for targeting. The bureaucracy could not be kept out of the scheme. Community organizations were poorly developed. Some of the schemes missed their targets. Others were just starting when the crisis eased. The Thai government adopted a more realistic approach. It first concentrated on classic forms of employment-generating public works expenditure. Then when the crisis became desperate, it resurrected a twenty-five-year-old scheme for hurling Japanese cash into the villages with its eyes closed.

The World Bank and ADB approached the Asia crisis with the lessons from the debate and practice of social policy in post-communist Eastern Europe. But in Eastern Europe they had been creating a social safety net by shredding a much more solid fabric of social protection. In Thailand they had to knit a net out of nothing. Their approach ignored the sociopolitical realities of a country which historically had an over-centralized state whose major function has been social control, and whose infrastructure for social welfare was minimal. The international institutions were reduced to blaming their failure on the Thai government. Such blame may well be justified. But the learning for the international institutions is that they cannot expect an over-centralized, control-oriented, and often corrupt bureaucracy to start acting as an agency of social care.

The ADB's initial post mortem on the crisis hoped for changes in government capability which would enable its original strategy of social safety nets to work. The World Bank adopted a more subtle strategy. After initially criticizing the Thai government for relying on family and community to cushion the crisis, it later welcomed this approach with enthusiasm. The central principles of the minimalist idea of "social safety nets," as it emerged from the European debate, were that the scheme must be economical, welfare should not be available by right, relief must only be afforded to those failed by the markets, and systems needed to be devised for identifying and targeting the poor. The Thai experiment showed that the targeting exercise was difficult, despite large investments in improving data sources and developing new delivery systems. However, the experiment also showed that reliance on the "social capital" of family and community could deliver on the other principles. It was cost-effective, conveyed no permanent rights to welfare, and was reasonably efficient at targeting. The objectives of the strategy of minimalist social safety nets, the World Bank tentatively concluded, could be achieved by selective support for traditional systems for cushioning distress.

The Asian crisis provided an opportunity for the international institutions to field-test their ideas for managing the social transition to a more liberalized market economy. The failures of many of their initial ideas, and the relative success of traditional forms of social cushioning, changed the nature of the debate. Moreover, as the World Bank and IMF discovered in Eastern Europe, espousing the cause of the poor is a strategy for building a moral and political base from which to override opposition to reform. This bears no small resemblance to the classic stance of dictators who claim their legitimacy from the support of the poor, the mass, the silent majority. After the criticism of the international organizations during the Asian crisis, the World Bank began to lay much more emphasis on its role in social policy and announced its new commitment to "The Quality of Growth." The ADB made poverty reduction its "overarching objective" and announced it would banish poverty from the region by 2025. In his retirement statements, Michel Camdessus declared that the IMF and other international institutions were the "best friend of the poor" and that "poverty reduction is at the heart of our programmes."

The poor might not recognize the IMF as their best friend. Financial crises handled by IMF methods still hit the poor, the rural, the landless, the young.

NOTES

1. "The lexicon of this new policy paradigm underlying this new consensus includes *civil society, institution building, safety nets,* and, especially *governance* to be added to the conventional Washington terminology of open markets, deregulation, and liberalization and structural adjustment" (Jayasuriya 1999).

2. This section depends heavily on the superb account in Deacon (1997).

3. A major IMF policy statement in 1995 indicated such safety nets might include "targeted subsidies, cash compensation in lieu of subsidies, improved distribution of essentials such as medicine, temporary price controls for essential commodities, severance pay and retraining for retrenched public sector employees, employment through public works, and adaptation of permanent social security arrangements to protect the poorest" (IMF 1995a, 15).

4. See the press generally between 19 and 30 May 1998.

5. Professor Akira Suehiro speaking at the Oriental Hotel, Bangkok on 26 March 1999.

6. The number of students receiving loans increased from 148,444 in 1996 to 435,426 in 1997 and 675,614 in 1998.

7. It claimed to have repatriated 305,778 workers resulting in 268,259 jobs for Thai nationals; employed 477,404 people on rural job creation projects; sent 154,295 people to work overseas; and helped 300,000 others with new jobs in industry and services (*BP*, 3 Jan 1999).

8. Television news showed boatmen assigned to ferry Burmese workers across the Moei river. They drove round the first bend then killed the engine and offered their passengers a free disembarkation on the Burmese bank, or a small fee for the Thai bank.

9. This assessment of the ministry's reaction to the king's project is based on private communication by someone deeply involved.

10. Said at the Thailand Update conference at the Australian National University, Canberra, April 1999.

11. Paiboon Wattanasiritham, who had earlier resigned from a banking career to involve himself in NGO work, had become head of the GSB.

12. After that point, the machinery began to work. By the end of 1999, SIF had received 8,293 applications, and approved 1,626 at a budget of 1,607 million baht (World Bank Thailand, 2000, 20–1).

13. By early 2000, the World Bank stopped emphasizing SIF as an anti-crisis strategy, and reimagined it as a more long-term strategy for building community organizations (see World Bank Thailand 2000, 25).

14. For a description of the earlier model in 1975, see Morell and Chai-Anan (1981, 123–31). Morell and Chai-Anan concluded that this scheme was more significant politically than economically. The party which devised it (Social Action) doubled its seats at the following election after campaigning on a platform of extending the scheme.

15. At the initial planning meeting with the World Bank, political scientist Suchit Bunbongkarn warned against using the new local government bodies because they were "weak, corrupt and ineffective" (*TN*, 1 Feb 1998). But in its post mortem, the Budget Bureau praised these bodies (the TAOs) for being faster and more efficient at spending the funds. "The participation of people is the key factor for the success of these projects," reported a senior Bureau official (*TN*, 20 Jan 2000).

16. These surveys normally took the National Statistical Office (NSO) two to four years to process. The World Bank and ADB needed more relevant data for the design of social safety net programmes, and also for prosecuting their campaign for more social elements in the crisis management effort. These agencies donated money and expertise to NSO to accelerate the production of these two key reports. By late 1998, NSO was able to process the top-line results within four to six months. It made available incomplete datasets from the 1998 *Socioeconomic Survey* to enable a quick reading on the social impact. ADB also sponsored a statistician, N. Kakwani, to work with the National Economic and Social Development Board (NESDB) on improving the interpretation of the labour, education, health, and other social statistics. The NESDB began a newsletter to publish these analyses. The World Bank launched a *Social Monitor* to track the crisis.

17. In *Agricultural Statistics of Thailand 1995/96*, off-farm earnings from wages, salaries, and overseas work contributed 26 percent of total farm income nationwide, and 37 percent in the northeast.

18. TDRI researchers later recognized the mechanisms transferring the crisis impact to the rural sector (Chalongphob, Flatters, and Sauwalak 1999).

19. Note that Kakwani computes a "crisis index," which is the residual after removing seasonal and long-term trend effects. Since the long-term trend was positive (4.5 percent for employment), Kakwani's figures overstate the actual increase. For the statistical approach, see Kakwani (1998).

20. These surveys were conducted by the Friends of Women and the Arom Phromphangan Foundation. See for instance Banthit (1997). The issue of the gender impact of the crisis is complex. We do not treat this issue here, not because it is unimportant, but because it is too big.

21. This observation is highly impressionistic, and it cannot be confirmed by *Labour Force Survey* figures. The numbers of own-account workers in commerce and services did not increase, but this might reflect the net result of increases in these informal-sector businesses balanced by declines among formal businesses.

22. Related to us across a lunch table in mid 1998.

23. Kakwani (NESDB, *Indicators* 3 (1), January 1999) calculated that poverty incidence had an elasticity of 1.38 to GDP growth. Warr (1998a) calculated that an estimated GDP shrinkage by 7.5 percent in 1998 would increase poverty by only 1.08 percent of population.

24. The turning point seems to have been in 1995–6, when the defeat of the drug warlord Khun Sa by the Burmese government army created a shortage and price rise for heroin.

25. Amara Pongsapich and Peter Brimble.

26. The report then tried to formalize this social capital into a stocks and flows model. Each religion has its own forms of worship.

27. The World Bank topped this display of cultural sensitivity a few weeks later when the bank's president, James Wolfensohn, spoke in Bangkok during Unctad X, praising the king's model of a "sufficiency economy" (*TN*, 17 Feb 2000).

REFORM, GOVERNANCE, SCANDAL

On 31 August 1997, when the Thai government signed the first letter of intent with the IMF, the ex-premier Anand Panyarachun commented, "There is nowhere else in this world where people have lost all faith in their own government and prefer their financial and monetary affairs to be managed by the IMF" (*BP*, 5 Aug 1997). On 27 September, parliament passed an ambitious new constitution which had earlier been opposed by almost every power centre in Thai society. On 5 November, the prime minister (Chavalit Yongchaiyudh) resigned in the face of media criticism and urban street protests. On the following day, Chuan Leekpai told his new cabinet, "Politicians are being watched by everyone—the people, the opposition, the media and private organizations. . . . Things are not as they were, and I will not protect any Cabinet member who is found to be dishonest" (*TN*, 7 Nov 1998).

Over just ten weeks, Thailand experienced an unprecedented alienation of sovereignty over economic policy, passage of an ambitious constitution which aimed to transform politics, and a cabinet change driven by urban protest rather than electoral success. Running through Anand's comment on the government, the movement to pass the constitution, the agitation against Chavalit, and Chuan's fears of being "watched," there is a single theme—a wave of urban pressure to exert greater control over the politics of the nation.

This special intensity of Thai politics in the late 1990s was not simply a response to the stimulus of the economic crisis. The rate of change had been quickening since (at least) the mid 1980s, driven by two main developments: first, the gradual disintegration of the remnants of the old dictatorial state which opened the way for new groups, new demands, and new types of organization to invade the political arena; second, the rapid industrialization from the mid 1980s which made large changes in the social structure, in the demands on the state apparatus, and in the relationship between Thailand and the outside world (Hewison 1993; Pasuk and Baker 1997). Party organization and leadership changed rapidly with a total of seven different premiers over a decade. Political and semi-political organizations multiplied. In the early 1990s, before the crisis hit, Bangkok had witnessed a coup, an urban uprising, and the biggest rural protests since the mid 1970s.

Out of these changes came a debate on how to reform politics to bring them into line with changes in economy and society. This debate developed from the early 1990s, and came to a climax at the onset of the crisis. The 1997 constitution is important not only because of its content, but also because of the groupings which came together to press for constitutional reform, because of the nature of their campaign, and because of their subsequent ambitions.

This chapter looks at the politics of the crisis from the angle of political reform—the new constitution, its passage, and the aftermath. The following chapter focuses on party politics, and offers some pointers to the future.

THE POLITICS OF DISILLUSION

Through the 1980s, the shortcomings of Thai politics were often attributed to the country's "semi-democracy" under which many of the institutions and procedures of representative democracy coexisted with much of the culture and practice of military rule. Hence May 1992, when street demonstrations brought down a coup regime, was a watershed. After the incident destroyed the political aspirations of the military, many reformists were optimistic. Thirayuth Boonmee, the 1973 student leader turned "social critic," wrote a book claiming this moment as a "turning point" on a scale which occurs only once a century. With the military now out of the way, Thirayuth (1993, 56) foresaw a period of benign change under the leadership of the middle class working through the institutions of formal democracy:

> This will lead to a transfer of power and legitimacy from the state to society
> . . . from the bureaucrat group to businessmen, technocrats, and the middle
> class. Society will change from a closed society to an open society, from
> conservative thinking to a much broader perspective, from narrow
> nationalism to greater acceptance of internationalism and regionalism, from
> centralization to decentralization.

This phase of optimism was relatively short-lived. The protesters in 1991–92 had set out an agenda of reform designed to prevent a recurrence of military rule. This agenda included changes in the constitution, liberalization of the media, decentralization of government, and controls on the corruption which had provided the excuse for the military coup in 1991. Thirayuth stressed that his optimistic vision depended on a pro-gramme of reform in these areas. But the cabinet headed by the Democrat Party installed in December 1992 proved half-hearted about such reform. It grudgingly began a process of constitutional revision which resulted in only minor changes—such as lowering the voting age from 21 to 18. The demand to release the electronic media from virtual monopoly control by government and military ran into fierce resistance. The promise to license several new TV channels was delayed and whittled back to a single new licence. Over decentralization, the Ministry of the Interior watered down plans for tambon councils (*O Bo To*), and squashed proposals to abolish the colonial-style system of provincial governors. On corruption, Prime Minister Chuan Leekpai presented a clean image, but the cabinet launched no initiative to combat corruption among politicians or bureaucrats, and scandals soon emerged around Democrats in their electoral heartland in the south over logging concessions, and profiteering under a land distribution scheme (*So Po Ko 4-01*).

Political scientists and commentators began to argue that the problem lay in the political system which cultivated politicians who had little interest in legislation and a large interest in making money. "Semi-democracy" had been supplanted by "money politics." They raised the issue whether democracy and capitalism were compatible or, more exactly, whether *early* democracy and *early* capitalism were compatible. As long as the capitalist spirit of acquisition was not restrained by a strong civil society, would the freedoms allowed by democracy always be exploited to concentrate power and wealth in the hands of the few? The growing popularity of the term *chao pho* (godfather) to describe provincial businessmen-politicians reflected this sentiment.

In an influential essay, the political scientist Anek Laothamatas (1995) confronted this growing concern. Thai cabinets, he argued, were set up by the rural population which dominated the electoral vote. They were then felled by urban public opinion exercised through the media and personal networks. The result was growing frustration on both sides. The problem arose, Anek argued, because democracy was founded on a peasant electorate. The rural voter was a captive of the local patronage system (*rabop uppatham*) and inevitably gave his vote to a local boss. Hence the rural majority was not directly represented in parliament and its interests were never reflected in the policy agenda. This exclusion fed rural disinterest in politics which in turn confirmed rural exclusion. Provincial politicians were relatively free of any sanctions imposed by the electorate. As long as they funnelled some budget patronage back to their constituency, they could exploit their political status as a commercial asset.[1]

For the short term, Anek sought solutions through institutional adjustments—the inclusion of rural issues on the policy agendas of political parties, and stronger sanctions to combat corruption. For the longer term, Anek looked to social change. He was haunted by Barrington Moore's (1967) proposition that large peasant societies are incompatible with democracy and must collapse either towards revolution or fascism. The *rabop uppatham*, he feared, had been one of the key foundations of Thailand's earlier military dictatorship and could serve as the foundation of more subtle forms of fascism in the future. The long-term project, Anek argued (1995, 91–2), must be to undermine the *rabop uppatham* by modernizing the peasantry out of existence by a mixture of prosperity and education:

> . . . we must first destroy patronage relations to release the "little people" of the village from the unequal, unfree association with the "big people" or "patrons," so they become "individuals" like the people of the city and other modern classes. . . . then they can join together in free associations as "civil society," which from the angle of liberalism is an unavoidable condition of democratization, because only such a "civil society" can deal with the state and truly control and reform the bureaucracy.

While Anek laid out the problem, two different groups began to push for versions of a solution.

The first group developed among establishment figures in bureaucracy and business. Amon Chantharasombun was a lawyer, member of an establishment bureaucratic family, and formerly secretary-general of the Council of State in the 1980s. In the early 1990s he began working on proposals for constitutional reform along with the conservative political scientist, Chai-Anan Samudavanija (1995). These proposals were published in mid 1994 and hotly debated (Amon 1994). Amon argued that parliament had become too powerful, and had subtracted too much authority from the senior bureaucracy. Besides, parliamentary democracy was unstable and inefficient, as indicated by the succession of squabbling coalitions and the poor record on legislation. Amon's solution was to have a much more elaborate constitution which would limit the power of parliament and would impose checks and balances by separating the executive, legislative, and judicial powers.

The second group jelled among NGOs and activists. In 1991–92, the NGO groups which united to oppose the coup regime had found common cause in the need for better legal defence of human rights and community rights, and for reforms to erase the old military-bureaucratic dominance. In 1992–93 these groups pushed—without success—for a charter of rights in the Democrat government's limited constitutional reforms. In early 1994 Chalat Worachat, who had conducted a hunger strike against the military leaders in 1992, began another hunger strike to demand action on the constitution. The government conceded establishment of a committee to make initial proposals on the direction and the procedure. Dr Prawase Wasi was chosen as its head (CDD, 1995). By virtue of his long years of activism, his writings, his royal connections, and his Magsaysay award, Prawase was a de facto leader of the NGO movement. Earlier, he had taken little direct interest in the formal political process. Now he was drawn in by the NGO movement's growing interest in using a constitution to define human and community rights so they could be legally defended—largely against the depredations of the state.

The point is this. Debate on the need for major reforms emerged in 1992–94, during the tenure of the Chuan I government, and before the rise of Banharn. Moreover, there was not just one discourse on reform, but many—reflecting different social backgrounds and political agendas. The two most prominent agendas were sharply diverse. First, an establishment coalition wanted to shore up the bureaucratic polity to limit the expanding power of provincial business-politicians. Second, an activist coalition wanted a charter of rights and an array of reforms (decentralization, liberalization of the media, freedom of information) to shift power away from the state and towards the community and individual.

BANHARN, CHAVALIT, AND THE CONVERSION OF BUSINESS

Up to this point, the Bangkok business community showed little interest in political reform. Over the next two years, this changed. Provincial-based parties captured control of the cabinet at the time when massive financial inflows precipitated the economy first into a bubble and then into a bust.

At elections in July 1995, Banharn Silpa-archa became premier by log-rolling many of the provincial businessmen-politicians into an alliance. He was sensitive enough to the growing concern over political reform to make constitutional amendment a plank of his electoral campaign, and to endorse the reform process once in power. But this did little to allay urban antagonism. Banharn faced a hostile media from a first tussle with the TV anchorman, Chirmsak Pinthong, on the eve of the elections, through to media frenzy over the two censure debates which forced his resignation fifteen months later. Anek's proposition—that urban people were frustrated at their inability to make governments and vented this frustration by breaking governments through media pressure—was illustrated in fine detail. But this much was only the continuation of an established pattern. The innovation of the Banharn era lay in giving this urban concern over politics an economic dimension.

The Banharn premiership (July 1995 to November 1996) coincided with the first signs that Thailand's boom was over. In the first quarter of 1996, export growth faltered from its 20+ percent average to 7 percent. The banker Olarn Chaiprawat, who had foretold the "golden age" in 1984, pronounced "our luck is running out" (*TN*, 13 June 1996). Over the remainder of the year, export growth disappeared. But the Banharn term also coincided with the bubble. Net private capital inflow in 1995 soared to 544 billion baht, almost 70 percent above the previous year, and dropped back only slightly in 1996 (see p. 24). Direct investment increased after a four-year decline, and large amounts went into property projects. The economy was giving off mixed signals. Those sensitive to the real economy (Japanese firms, big Thai banks, some Thai conglomerates) began to talk the language of crisis. But those connected to the pumped-up financial market were flush with cash and optimism. Many international stock brokers and merchant banks had recently set up in Bangkok. Their analysts' reports and pre-dictions were a novelty in the local context and conveyed a spurious authority. The press gave them great prominence. Until the crash of the Bangkok Bank of Commerce (BBC) in mid 1996, they mostly minimized problems and projected a booming future. Some were still boosting Thailand until the eve of the collapse.

The Banharn cabinet was poorly equipped to manage this fragile situation. The premier revealed his lack of economic knowledge at an early cabinet meeting by failing to understand the Thai term for inflation. Later he proudly trumpeted his own scheme for controlling inflation—increasing the variety and volume of small-denomination notes and coins so that traders could adjust prices in small increments. More importantly, Banharn weakened the role of the two key posts in economic management—the finance minister and the governor of the central bank. For finance minister, Banharn appointed Surakiart Sathirathai, a young, well-connected, and ambitious lawyer with some experience in trade negotiations but no training or track record in economics. Later he replaced him with Bodi Chunnananda, a lacklustre Budget Bureau official who had reputedly helped Banharn to channel budget funds to his Suphanburi constituency. Neither had the ability to diagnose the growing problems in the economy. Neither had a political base and hence both were dependent on Banharn.

The governorship of the central bank had already been compromised by two political sackings over recent years. The current incumbent, Vichit Suphinit, offered no significant resistance to Banharn. In December 1995, Banharn used Vichit to sack the head of the Stock Exchange Commission (Ekkamon Khiriwat), possibly over a personal slight. The incident rattled the technocracy. The Nukul Report (see below) noted later that after this incident "the atmosphere became much gloomier than before. . . . officials of the central bank were shocked . . . and subsequently were reluctant to air their opinions" (Nukul 1998, para 64). Banharn found it increasingly difficult to find good candidates for key technocrat posts. When the head of the Stock Exchange quit, Banharn scraped around to find an obscure businessman as replacement. When Vichit was forced to quit the Bank of Thailand governorship over the BBC affair, several potential candidates refused, forcing Banharn to allow the post to pass by seniority to an uninspired candidate.

Moreover, the problems of the technocracy stemmed not only from political interference but also from social pressure and financial temptation. The boom had exaggerated the gap between the salaries (and the excitement) in the public and private sectors. Technocrats were tempted away to executive jobs in the private sector, blurring any dividing line between businessmen and regulators. Vichit Suphinit was found to be involved in share dealings which were not technically illegal but certainly appeared unethical for a central bank governor.[2] His failure to act over the BBC scandal could hardly be separated from the fact that he and BBC's chief executive were old central bank colleagues who still socialized together.[3]

After the BBC crash in May 1996, business opinion became openly critical of economic management. Businessmen and officials complained that "politicians increasingly interfere with the day-to-day operations of the Bank of Thailand" (*TN*, 18 Jun 1996). The association of stock market investors called on the government to resign. The Bankers Association demanded the "depoliticization" of economic management. A senior technocrat urged that macro-management "is so urgent and technical it cannot be left to the politicians" (Phisit Pakkasem in *TN*, 31 Aug 1996). Anand Panyarachun, the unofficial political head of Bangkok's modern business, pronounced that the Banharn government was "shameless," and took up the cause of reforming the constitution.

Over the course of the Banharn premiership, the arguments for reform crafted by the likes of Anek, Amon, and Prawase were supplemented by a simpler proposition: Thailand's rurally weighted electorate could not be trusted to deliver a government which knew how to manage Thailand's increasingly sophisticated, globalized, and delicate urban economy.

The pattern was now set. The transition from Banharn to Chavalit in November 1996 made no effective difference. Many MPs slid effortlessly from one coalition to the next (chart 6.1). The level of economic expertise was only marginally better. Chavalit announced a "dream team" of technocrats, but all save one refused the posts. The banker who became finance minister (Amnuay Wirawan) had no political base, and resigned when his measures were blocked by business interests. Another central bank governor quit, and again the post was filled by seniority as other candidates refused. Another key technocrat (Chatumongol Sonakul, permanent secretary at the Finance Ministry) was eased out for being too independent. The finance ministership was shuffled around minor banking figures.

The fall of the Chavalit government, and the passage of the constitution, were closely linked not only in time but also in motivation. Both were driven by urban opinion expressed through the press, street demonstrations, and the modern business lobby. Several business leaders came out to support the passage of the constitution before most of the political leaders capitulated. Many of the same leaders used the press to signal that Chavalit should resign.[4] In both cases, the head of Thailand's largest conglomerate, Dhanin Chiaravanont of Charoen Pokphand (CP), overcame his usual reluctance to display any political involvement.

THE DECLINE OF THE TECHNOCRACY

One last part of the diagnosis of political failure emerged in early 1998. The new Chuan II government commissioned an investigation into the official actions which had led to the crisis. The report is important not only for what it says but because it became a surprise bestseller (Nukul 1998). The commission was chaired by the former central bank governor, Nukul Prachuabmoh. However the pen-prints found all over the report point to the economist, Ammar Siamwalla. Shortly after the baht float, Ammar published an analysis of the bust which highlighted the role of capital flows, but also pointed specifically to failures in the Bank of Thailand over the BBC affair and over the battle with the hedge funds (Ammar 1997). The Nukul Report extended this latter critique along two main themes. First, the Bank of Thailand had failed to adjust to globalization. It had clung to old truths of Thai macro-management (the dollar peg) and had rejected advice from the IMF and Thai economists. Its senior executives were ill-equipped to oversee modern global currency management. The poker game with the hedge funds had been left to junior officials who had limited appreciation of the true stakes involved. The bank's management structure and style belonged to the simpler, cosier world of the 1980s.

Second, the quality of technocratic management of the economy had

115

collapsed, partly because the best people had left for the private sector, and partly because political pressures had transformed the relations among the central bank hierarchy from collegial cooperation to mutual competition.[5] The Nukul Report highlighted the failings of Roengchai Marakanond, whom Banharn had picked as governor of the central bank because better candidates refused. Ammar (1997) concluded, "With a non-functioning technocracy, political leadership becomes an essential backstop. It is here that our parliamentary system has failed us badly."

THE CHARTER'S THREE AGENDAS

The 1997 constitution has been variously described as a breakthrough for liberal democracy and as a reactionary plot. The head of the drafting assembly called it a "people's constitution" on account of the high degree of public participation in its creation. Critics have suggested this participation was mostly show and that the core ideas were those of Amon Chanthara-sombun and the conservative pressure group (Connors 1999; McCargo 1998). A third, ingenious interpretation suggests the conservative members of the drafting assembly backed the most radical provisions in the belief this would ensure the draft would be rejected; but this strategy backfired because of a wave of popular support generated by the crisis.

It is better to see the charter as a subtle compromise between two main agendas: on the one hand, the NGO and liberal lobbies' interest in rights, decentralization, liberalization of the media, and similar reforms; and on the other hand, the conservative lobby's concern to break the provincial bosses' domination of parliamentary politics.

The committee set up by the Chuan I government and headed by Prawase Wasi identified three main areas of weakness which demanded reform of the constitution (CDD 1995): the poor performance of parliament and the erosion of its legitimacy because of vote-buying, corruption, and the quality of most politicians; the continued over-centralization of government; and the lack of any true rule of law. Following his electoral pledge to pursue constitutional reform, Banharn set up a committee to lay down a process. Controversy flared. Parliamentarians wanted to control the process. Outside pressure groups wanted to deny them this control. A compromise was negotiated. The Constitution Drafting Assembly (CDA) would be independent of parliament, but chosen by a two-stage process in which parliament controlled the final say. Parliament would have the power only to accept or reject the final draft, not to make amendments. Rejection would trigger a referendum.

The two-stage selection allowed parliament to insert several ex-MPs and other party place-men inside the ninety-nine-member CDA. However, the twenty-three CDA members chosen under "expert" quotas included many academics and lawyers who occupied most of the seats on the smaller drafting committee. Among this group, there were representatives of both the conservative reform pressure group, and of lawyers interested in human rights.

The major innovations of the charter can be grouped under three main headings, and these in turn can be seen to represent the two different reform agendas and supporting constituencies. The first set of provisions included a much more extensive definition of human and civic rights, and also of the duties of the state to enforce and uphold such rights. This set reflected the agenda that had evolved among the NGO movement, democracy activist groups, and human rights groups since the mid 1980s and especially since these groups came closer together during the politics of 1991–92 (Thai NGO Support Project 1995; Naruemon 1998). Further, this reflected a major trend within the discourse of the 1973–76 activist generation. Their interest in democracy interpreted as "representative institutions" had diminished, while their interest in "civil society" had risen.[6] Within the discourse on civil society, the two main poles of interest had become the local community and *rights*.

The draft charter's list of human rights included the right to information; equal gender rights; the rights of criminal suspects (intended to suppress police methods of intimidation); the rights of local communities to be involved in the management of local resources; the right to freedom of broadcast media; and the duties of the state to safeguard the environment. The military objected when this list was extended as far as the right to resist coups. However, the military was less successful in opposing inclusion of a section on the right to freedom of media, and the duty of the state to break up the military's near-monopoly on electronic media. Moreover, the charter imposed on future governments the duty to implement these rights. In effect, this amounted to writing a policy programme into a constitution.

The second set of provisions concerned the mechanics of parliament and other representative bodies. Here the charter's measures reflected the

117

conservative reform agenda evolved between 1991 and 1994. The broad framework followed the proposals outlined in Amon's 1994 book. The discussions at various stages of the CDA changed only the details (Connors 1999).

These measures aimed to change the economics of politics-as-a-business by increasing the costs, increasing the risks, and reducing the rewards. The costs were increased by making it more difficult to secure election by the old methods of patronage and vote buying. This was done by breaking multi-member constituencies down to single-member, establishing an election commission, increasing the penalties for infringing campaign rules, and (most importantly) centralizing vote counting so candidates could not trace how particular villages or wards had voted. The risks were increased and rewards hopefully reduced by strengthening the machinery to monitor and suppress corruption, and by a "separation of powers" under which ministers would have to resign their parliamentary seats. This was intended to disrupt the long-term patronage relationships between ministers and constituencies, and make ministers more careful about being forced out of their jobs.

This change in the economics of parliamentary politics, it was hoped, would reduce participation by those who treated politics as a business, and encourage participation by those currently deterred by the dirty image of politics. Moreover, the constitution also promoted expansion of local government so that the politics of local patronage would be transferred away from parliament, freeing up time and focus for national concerns.

Two other measures directly reengineered parliament to ensure an urban bias. First, the number of MPs elected by local territorial constituencies was maintained at 400 (the last election in 1996 had been 393), while another 100 MPs would be elected by the "party list" system—a national vote on parties, with seats divided proportionate to votes among all parties which secured at least 5 percent of the turnout. Under the previous system, Bangkok had accounted for only thirty-seven seats, less than a tenth of the assembly. The addition of the party list was expected to increase the number of MPs who stood for "national" (i.e. Bangkok) interests. Second, MPs were required to hold at least a B.A. degree or equivalent. Roughly a quarter of all MPs elected in the 1990s would be disqualified by this measure.[7] More broadly put, this measure excluded around 90 percent of the total adult population, over 95 percent in the rural areas, and over 99 percent in the agricultural sector.

The third set of measures in the new constitution created many new judicial and quasi-judicial bodies. As a whole these measures promised to increase the role of judicial processes in society as a whole, and more emphatically in the political system. The demand for these new bodies came from both the liberal and conservative agendas. From the conservative side, the strengthening of the judiciary was part of the "separation of powers" designed to control the power of parliament and increase the role of "good people" who emerged somehow other than by election. From the liberal side, strengthening the judicial framework was important for implementing many of the items defined in the catalogue of people's rights and public duties.

A new constitutional court would have power to rule not only on interpretations of the constitution, but also on whether future legislation conformed to the constitution. An administrative court would handle complaints over bureaucratic malpractice. Other new quasi-judicial bodies included a much-strengthened counter corruption commission, a commission on human rights, election commission, boards to oversee the liberalized media, independent commission to monitor environmental issues, board to audit government agencies, judicial commission, and ombudsmen. The reengineering of the senate also formed part of this third set as the key roles of the reformed senate were to monitor the behaviour of the lower house and to propose candidates for many of these new judicial bodies. After discussing hybrid systems of election and appointment, the CDA made the two-hundred-strong senate totally elective but hedged around with conditions intended (rather optimistically) to make the senators independent of political parties.

PASSAGE AND PARTICIPATION

Besides its content, the 1997 constitution was important for the way it was passed. The four-year campaign to *begin* the process, and in particular the final vituperative battle over *control* of the process, meant that the CDA began in an atmosphere of conflict between politicians and reformers. Public interest was high and 19,335 candidates stood at the first stage of elections for CDA membership. The CDA organized itself as both a drafting body and a campaign centre. It set up a publicity committee to drum up support in parallel to the drafting process. It invited those who had stood and failed in the first-stage elections to man local working committees which organized public scrutiny of the draft proposals. The CDA claimed 600,000 people gave their opinions on the initial round, while over 120,000 attended public hearings on the final proposals and 87,000 responded by questionnaire. Press comment, TV discussions, and radio phone-ins continued throughout. This participation was very largely urban, and was conspicuously more enthusiastic in the provincial towns than in Bangkok.

As the CDA's proposals emerged, many holders of institutional power came out to voice their objections. Several political leaders were openly hostile. Banharn said the drafters had "gone way too far for politicians like me to follow." Snoh Tienthong (interior minister) said the charter was a plot by communists "using the strategy to use towns to surround the jungle" (*TN*, 24 August 1997). Samak Sundaravej (deputy prime minister) argued, "The draft will create division in society and will not change the country for the better, so we should oppose it" (*TN*, 1 July 1997). Chalerm Yubamrung (deputy interior minister) called Anand, head of the drafting committee, "sadistic" and "hysterical" and promised to "lead a crusade" of police and judges against the draft (*TN*, 14 May 1997).

The army chiefs objected to the provisions about opposing coups, and to the liberalization of media. The police chiefs objected to restrictions on police procedures. Senators objected to provisions for election. Judges criticized proposals for new courts. The head of the senate objected to the human rights commission on grounds it would affect business interests and expose rights violations in Thailand to international view. Political parties railed against the requirement for ministers to resign as MPs. Conservatives pronounced that the charter gave "too much liberty" and would result in the break-up of Thailand.[8] Village officers damned proposals which would diminish their role. The Ministry of the Interior objected to decentralization, police reforms, and the transfer of the conduct of elections to an independent election commission.

The CDA process unfolded against a background of political disorder and economic decline. Just prior to the CDA's inauguration, the Banharn government was brought down in a blizzard of corruption allegations, dramatized on television in no-confidence debates attracting unusually high audiences. Through the 240 days of the drafting process, the economy deteriorated through the collapse of Finance One, the flotation of the baht, the arrival of the IMF, and hapless fumbling by the government. Against this background, the CDA gathered support from businessmen and a broader urban middle class spooked by the collapse of the economy. The fate of the economy, the future of Chavalit, and the passage of the constitution became intimately linked. The CDA passed its final draft on the same day (15 August 1997) that the IMF bailout was agreed, and that Chavalit announced a desperate cabinet reshuffle. The CDA orchestrated a campaign to shame parliament into passing the constitution. Activist groups threatened mass demonstrations if the draft was rejected. White-collar employees staged demonstrations in Bangkok's business district demanding a change of government, passage of the constitution, and action on the economy. Middle-class demonstrations sprinkled with socialites took over the space outside Government House usually occupied by protesting farmers. Some with a poor sense of history called on the military to step forward and save both economy and democracy.

White-collar street demo, 1997

The military chiefs were the first of the official power centres to come out and support the passage of the constitution to avoid public disorder at a time of national crisis. They were followed by Dhanin of CP and other business leaders who endorsed a similar argument. The Democrat Party had supported the draft earlier in May, but not without appending objections to some proposals. The core of the provincial political establishment still held out.[9] The interior minister mobilized village officers and revived the village scouts movement (which had orchestrated rural opposition to communism in the 1970s) to organize counter-demonstrations in favour of rejection. Prime Minister Chavalit was caught between pressure from his old military connections, and pressure from his provincial parliamentary supporters. He flipped and flopped. In his most famous outburst, he announced he was "100 percent" without clarifying whether for or against. As the threat of public disorder rose, he appealed to the army chiefs to declare an emergency. When they refused, he called off the organized rural counter-demonstrations and capitulated. The constitution was passed on 27 September with 518 voting for and only two MPs and sixteen senators voting against. Five equally turbulent weeks later, Chavalit resigned.

SAVING THE CONSTITUTION

Thailand's previous two reform constitutions—of 1946 and 1974—had each lasted around eighteen months before they were torn up after a coup. The 1997 constitution faced a different kind of opposition. Implementation of the new parliamentary structure and establishment of the new judicial and quasi-judicial bodies required a raft of enabling bills. The Council of State had the duty to draft (or fine-tune) these bills, and the parliament had the power to pass them. The Council of State represented the old bureaucratic mentality which distrusted democratization, and wished to retain the powers now concentrated in the hands of central officialdom. The Council staged the last stand of bureaucratic paternalism. The parliament—particularly the lower house—tried to water down new rules and new institutions which would limit its own power.

When the three main enabling bills on the political structure (on elections, political parties, and the Election Commission) came up for scrutiny, the lower house rewrote as much of them as it could. One of the constitution drafters complained this was "going back to square one." The senate reversed out most of the lower house's amendments. But the government then deliberately under-funded the Election Commission. One charter writer believed this was a carefully laid plot to ensure this commission would have a short life. The first election would be a disaster, the Election Commission would get the blame, and responsibility would be passed back to the Interior Ministry. Certainly the ministry seemed to hope this was the case. Senior officials began campaigning to retain a large role for the ministry in handling elections.

On the Human Rights Commission, the Council of State drafted a bill which totally ignored the constitution and totally ignored the conclusions of a thorough series of public hearings. Instead of the independent commission envisioned in the charter, the council placed the body under the executive, and packed it with a majority of bureaucrats selected by bureaucrats.

On the commission designed to manage communication frequencies on behalf of the people rather than on behalf of the military, the original draft ignored the constitution's wish for an independent body. It placed the commission under executive control, and packed it with bureaucrats and telecoms interests.

Each one of these attempts to blunt the constitution was met by a howl of protest from the constitution drafters, activists, and NGO groups. By and large, these protests were effective in overcoming this rearguard action. The attempt to rewrite the political bills was conclusively blocked, and parliament eventually passed versions closely in line with the constitution. Government reluctantly increased the funding for the Election Commission. The bill on the Human Rights Commission had to be redrafted twice. The Frequencies Commission was redesigned in a more acceptable form. But then the drafters inserted a clause that required leading broadcasters to be licensed. Another howl of protest sent the bill back for redrafting.

There was another round of resistance at the stage of implementation.

The Freedom of Information Act was first invoked by a lone mother challenging a university school over the transparency of its admission exams. The school officials prevaricated, obstructed, back-pedalled, dissembled. The mother was subject to threats, a lawsuit, and very nearly a disciplinary investigation by her own employer. The official in charge of implementing the act was removed for being too enthusiastic about the principle of freedom of access.

The first effort to activate the constitution's provision to enable 50,000 signatories to initiate a corruption investigation met a similar fate. Again a sole woman fronted the effort. She collected the signatures before an enabling law had been passed specifying a procedure. The officials accepted the petition, but asked her to "verify" the signatures. The potential subject of the enquiry responded by slapping her with a lawsuit.

The new and exceptionally powerful Constitutional Court was blooded with the decision whether the Buriram MP, Newin Chidchob, should lose his parliamentary seat because of a suspended jail sentence for defamation. Six judges ruled the constitution was clear he should be removed. Seven gave a potpourri of reasons why he should not. Newin announced this split decision revealed the "beauty of democracy."

The old Counter Corruption Commission had never once managed to catch a big fish. Its successor, the National Counter Corruption Commission, had much better teeth. But when the personnel of the commission were announced, some doubted that they would know how to gnash them.

Again this resistance at the stage of implementation met a barrage of criticism from the press, academics, and activists. To a large extent, this pressure was effective. The Freedom of Information Act lurched into use. Rulings of the Constitutional Court became more rational (though still usually divided). The National Counter Corruption Commission eventually bared its teeth (see below). The reform of the constitution was activated, passed, and implemented by the pressure of urban opinion orchestrated through the press and activist platforms.

BEYOND THE CONSTITUTION TO GOOD GOVERNANCE

Prior to the CDA, activists from all corners of the political spectrum had debated how to trigger institutional changes in Thai politics from outside the formal parliamentary institutions. The CDA had provided a model. Moreover, the CDA had provided the foundation for an unusual alliance between liberal and conservative activism. After the CDA was dissolved, some of its key members concluded an informal alliance to monitor the parliament's drafting of the many enabling laws. In addition, this reform alliance now took up the torch of "good governance." Anand Panyarachun, prime minister twice in the coup period of 1991–92, emerged in the mid 1990s as the unofficial leader of conservative activism (Prasan 1998). He headed the drafting committee under the CDA. As premier he had made much of the term "transparency" in government. During Banharn's premiership, he spoke publicly several times on corruption, and began to use the modish term, "good governance."

Thirayuth Boonmee used the same term in advocating support for the constitution draft. After the passage of the charter, Thirayuth and Anand agreed together to promote "good governance" to continue the pressure for political and administrative reform. This pairing nicely symbolized the alliance between liberal and conservatism activism. "Good governance" became their flag for continuing the alliance and the strategy of extra-parliamentary pressure pioneered by the CDA.

This project quickly ran into difficulties, beginning with the Thai translation of the term, good governance. Thirayuth proposed *thammarat* (*BP*, 10 Jan 1998; Thirayuth 1998). The first component of the word was the Buddhist concept of dhamma, which conveyed a blend of righteousness, morality, and justice. Some were bothered that this was stronger and more morally forceful than the "good" in good governance. The second component was the Thai word for state, which was a lot narrower and more precise than the deliberately archaic and ambiguous word governance. For many in the liberal and NGO camps, the idea of a "righteous state" perpetuated the paternalism etched into the Thai polity from its absolutist and dictatorial past. No alternative translation gained a significant following, and the controversy tailed away without resolution.

The division underlying this linguistic controversy emerged much more clearly at the next stage. Anand undertook to campaign for good governance among his circles of technocrats and business leaders while Thirayuth worked among NGOs, intellectuals, and activist groups. But this latter constituency wanted a very different interpretation of *thammarat*. The senior community activist, Saneh Chamarik, called *thammarat* elitist and argued it should be reinterpreted to mean grassroots participation. Prawase Wasi redefined *thammarat* as a self-sufficient, community-based economy and society. Kasian Tejapira joked that, "The IMF and World Bank . . . might be very surprised that the Thai people have come up with so many different versions of good governance" (*TN*, 28 Apr 1998). In mid 1998, Thirayuth hosted a conference of NGO and community groups to discuss the issue. The meeting totally rejected the conventional international interpretation of "good governance" (transparency, accountability, and efficiency) on grounds it was a formula for making the state stronger and for making Thailand safer and more accommodating for foreign capital.[10] Among the NGO groups, the idea of *thammarat* was reinterpreted to mean strengthening the local community, reducing the ambit of the state, and inventing new forms of direct democracy (see pp. 201–2).

After the Chuan II government was installed in November 1997, the prime minister commissioned Anand to convene a think-tank to propose long-term measures for strengthening the Thai economy and society. Chuan requested three taskforces covering social and economic reform, but Anand proposed a fourth on the topic of good governance. Members of these taskforces were recruited from Anand's circle of senior technocrats and businessmen with the addition of some academics and others. The good governance panel was assigned to Chatumongol Sonakul, who was temporarily unemployed after resigning from the Finance Ministry, but who would shortly be anointed as governor of the central bank. A year later in December 1998, the good governance panel proposed a large agenda of reforms covering corporate governance, bureaucratic reform, and measures to reduce corruption (TDRI 1999a). Even before these reports, Anand and his group had confronted the likelihood that these taskforce proposals would be shelved given the increasing complexity of the crisis and absorbing focus on short-term survival. The report proposed an independent body, founded by government but independent of it (like the CDA) tasked with monitoring good governance issues and campaigning for the panel's agenda of reforms. Chuan failed to respond.

The issue languished. Specific proposals for administrative reform now passed into the political process, and bogged down in the crowded legislative programme. Besides, as the crisis deepened and lengthened, this conservative group became more concerned about economic survival and social stress, and less focused on good governance. The annual TDRI conference, which at the end of 1998 was devoted to the governance programme, was devoted the following year to the king's concept of a sufficient economy. Anand Panyarachun's enthusiasm for administrative change became tempered by contextual conditions:

The travails of the last two years have taught us some lessons about democracy and free markets. The first is that for an efficient, thriving market system to operate it must be within the framework of a set of rules of the game. . . . But these rules in themselves have to command a broad social acceptance, the process by which they are adopted must be participatory to the broadest extent possible. (Anand 1999, 4)

Constitutional reform has a special place in the modern Thai political tradition. The reform alliance of the mid 1990s came together over the constitution issue, but fell apart when it tried to move beyond. The split that emerged, first over the translation and then over the interpretation of good governance, indicated the true gap between the conservative and liberal reformers. The conservatives interpreted both constitutional reform and good governance as ways to make the state stronger and more effective, and to give "good people" like themselves a greater role. But as the crisis deepened and lengthened, their enthusiasm about forcing the pace of reform was tempered by their fear about the society's capacity to absorb stress and change. The liberals and NGOs were largely interested in the extension of the rights of individual and community at the expense of the over-powerful and over-centralized state descended from absolutism and dictatorship. They needed constitutional reform to catalogue these rights, and to provide a better judicial and political framework for protecting them. But their further reform efforts would be directed towards strengthening civil society organizations rather than reforming bureaucracy and politics.

SCANDALIZATION

The urban pressure which passed the constitution and felled Chavalit, also developed scandalization as a technique for controlling politicians and officials in the absence of better legal remedies. This technique has a history in Thai politics going back to the 1930s. But it came into far greater use in the 1990s, after the media had gained a greater degree of freedom and daring in the events of 1991–92. Activists discovered scandals. Newspapers made them public issues. Opposing politicians then embraced them. By the mid-1990s, the parliamentary no-confidence debate had become a traditional annual event, a political *songkran* during which dirty water was poured over the political leaders, watched by a large and fascinated national audience on live TV.

The passage of the constitution emboldened public political activism. On becoming prime minister in November 1997, as noted at the start of this chapter, Chuan Leekpai recognized that the atmosphere had changed, and public tolerance of misbehaviour had fallen. As he feared, the scandals quickly accumulated.

Salween logging

A senior forestry official burst into Government House with five million baht in an old cardboard box. He claimed the money was an attempted bribe by illegal loggers. He could not think what else to do except give the money to the prime minister on live TV. The media soon detailed how 13,000–20,000 logs had been felled illegally in the Salween forests, shipped through Burma, and brought back to Thailand as legal imports. These reports detailed the payoffs to police, border officials, army men, and forestry officials. They also speculated on the involvement of politicians. In a newspaper interview, the log dealer at the centre of the affair made a virtual confession, boasted of his powerful connections, and showed off the diamond-studded belt holding up his jeans (*TR*, 3 Mar 1998).

The forestry official with the five million baht in a box lost his job. Six forestry officials were disciplined. The police repeatedly said they were about to file a case against the diamond-belted log dealer, but nothing emerged. Meanwhile illegal logging was reported in at least eight other national forests.

The edible fence

The Agriculture Ministry distributed a glossy package of seeds to farmers, and made a TV ad boasting how this project, the "edible fence," would rescue rural Thailand from the economic crisis. Within days, it was leaked that the seeds were overpriced by about ten times. The ad disappeared. The deputy minister had to resign. The Counter Corruption Commission found evidence of massive collusion by lots of officials. Leaks from the probe suggested the scam went right to the top of a certain political party. The Agriculture Ministry launched its own probe. Forty-seven officials were disciplined for minor "negligence." The minister declared the case closed.

Later reports confirmed that the profit from the scam had been around 100 million baht. Attempts to investigate the politicians involved were stifled.

Health Ministry

The deputy minister of health lifted price control on drugs and medical equipment. Provincial hospitals were instructed to buy supplies from specified companies that were charging two to ten times the market price. An association of rural doctors exposed the scandal. The health minister and one of his deputies were forced to resign. The head official of the ministry was suspended. Seven other officials were punished. The press carried detailed accounts of how the scandal had been organized. The Counter Corruption Commission ruled that there was no evidence to proceed with a criminal charge against anyone else involved, either politician or official. But the rural doctors would not give up. They campaigned hard to prevent the scandal being buried. They staged dramatic press conferences, and brought respected old officials out of retirement to back their case. Thirty NGOs came together to use the new constitution's provision to launch a corruption probe with a petition of 50,000 signatures. But this was blocked (see p. 124). Repeated calls for the ex-ministers to be properly investigated were buried by delaying tactics and evasion.

Si Nakharin

In Kanchanaburi, three luxurious villas were found under construction on land which looked suspiciously like forest land. The documents had been issued improperly. The Accelerated Rural Development Department was building a road which happened to go to these houses and nowhere else. The provincial governor's daughter was probably an owner. Senior political figures had been seen at the site.

The scandal started to snowball. Down the road another two to three thousand other plots, supposed to be resettlement areas for displaced local villagers, were owned by military men, Bangkok socialites, rock singers, and relatives of the deputy governor. One housed a shooting range. Another thousand plots were identified at a nearby reservoir with nice lakeside locations and boat jetties. Another area in Ranong was found to be owned by the same people who had been involved in a 1994 land scandal in Phuket. An enormous hill-top house in a national park in Udon Thani was emblazoned with the personal emblem of an ex-minister.

This snowball got too big and dangerous. The army came out to argue that the forestry department was using inaccurate maps. The forestry chief objected but then backed off. Subsequent attempts to reopen the case were sternly resisted by men in uniform.

Rice support

Government provided money for rice millers to buy paddy at guaranteed prices. Some millers simply took the money and revalued stocks of paddy they had bought earlier at much cheaper rates. Others were so impressed by this accounting trick that it was copied all over the northeast. The bookkeeping required collusion by local officials. When the scandal broke, one of these officials fainted under questioning. Chuan said, "We will not let the guilty escape unpunished." No charges were laid.

Nong Ngu Hao airport

A Prime Minister's Office committee ruled that the bidding for the landfill contract for Bangkok's new airport had been rigged, and the pricing vastly inflated. It suggested both politicians and officials had been involved. The contract was worth 6.8 billion baht. Nothing happened.

Other scandals

A host of lesser scandals were exposed in the media. Bidding for an electronic data transmission contract looked suspicious. Computer equipment sold to schools seemed overpriced. The province of the former interior minister had secured an extra MP by shifting ten thousand house registrations across from the adjacent province. A judge found that ballot boxes in Samut Prakan had been stuffed with twenty thousand votes but had to exonerate those who benefitted (including a deputy interior minister) because of a constitutional technicality. Municipal elections in the same province ended chaotically after a TV station filmed ballot-stuffing. Various MPs came under suspicion for having luxury cars which seemed to be smuggled, for being photographed in the company of German gangsters, for having illegally imported machinery for replicating CDs, for having sons who had faked documentation to enter the police service, for having faked their own educational qualifications, and for having loads of possibly illegal timber delivered to houses they possibly owned.

These scandals had three main themes. First, many focused on the tendency of those in power to act as if they were above the law, and immune from prosecution or other forms of legal restraint. Second, most were focused on schemes to make money from the budget or other national resources (forests). Third, often these schemes entailed collusion between politicians who were in a position to change the rules, and officials who could then manipulate the rules for profit.

The outburst of scandals reflected the growing boldness of press and activists after the passage of the constitution, and a diminishing public tolerance in the context of economic crisis. But almost none of the scandals was resolved. The combination of officials and politicians succeeded in burying the cases in investigative committees or other strategies of bureaucratic delay. However in March 2000, in one of its first major decisions, the new National Counter Corruption Commission established under the 1997 constitution ruled that the interior minister, Sanan Kachornprasart, had submitted false documents in his declaration of assets. The minister resigned. This was the first time a minister had been forced out by legal process. And this was not any minister, but the second most powerful post in the cabinet, and the political manager of the ruling coalition. One Thai paper headlined the event as a "revolution."

CONCLUSION: URBAN WAVE

The mid and late 1990s saw a wave of urban political activism to change the structure of politics. This wave secured the passage of the 1997 constitution, and defence of its major innovations in the face of some last-ditch warfare by politicians and conservative bureaucrats. This wave flowed over into projects to continue reform of politics and bureaucracy under the heading of good governance, and into a burst of scandalization of the wrongdoing by bureaucrats and politicians.

This wave originated well before the crisis. It emerged after the lifting of dictatorial controls allowed a thickening of civil society organization, and after the quickening pace of economic change intensified conflict over resources and over access to political power and influence. This growth of organization spread widely through society, but it was activists from the urban middle and upper classes who first seized on the opportunity to mobilize and direct public opinion to force the pace of change. The onset of the crisis contributed to this rising wave by creating an atmosphere of panic, and by recruiting temporary support amongst businessmen and white-collar workers who normally stayed aloof from direct political involvement.

The liberal and conservative strains in urban activism came together in an alliance of convenience. But their agendas were sharply different. The liberal strand was interested in undermining old monopolies (on the media, on information), destroying vestiges of dictatorial power, and opening up opportunities for greater access to decision making. The conservative strand was focused more on restricting the freedoms of the MPs elected by the rural electorate. These two strands cooperated to pass the constitution, to defend it against a die-hard rearguard action, and to oppose the abuse of power through scandalization. But the attempt to continue this alliance to pursue further political and administrative change under the fuzzy flag of governance exposed the difference between the two agendas. The conservative strand envisioned a strong state under the influence of good people delivering national leadership. The liberal strand wanted to roll back the state to provide more space for individual and community. Despite this divergence, the liberal and conservative alliance for reform had transformed the framework of politics.

NOTES

1. Bowornsak Uwanno, a law academic who took a large role in drafting the constitution, explicitly referred to Anek and this argument to explain the thinking behind the drafting of the 1997 constitution (see "Political culture vs CDA charter," *BP*, 26 Sep 1997).

2. When Vichit Suphinit was assigned by the central bank as a director of Siam City Bank, he acquired several thousand shares in a subsidiary finance company at par value. He later chaired the meeting of the Securities Exchange Commission which approved the subsidiary's listing on the stock market (*TN*, 27 Jun 1996; *Bangkok Post Mid Year Economic Review 1996*, 35).

3. Bangkok Bank of Commerce owned a motor yacht which fell into the hands of the Financial Sector Restructuring Authority. The logbook showed that Vichit had used the yacht very often. Thanks to Gordon Fairclough for this titbit.

4. In September, the Chamber of Commerce called on Chavalit to resign. The Chamber's spokesman, Thammanun Duangmani said: "The proposal is aimed at restoring confidence immediately. . . . The call . . . . has nothing to do with politics,

but is simply the frank and straightforward opinion . . . of the businessmen. They are non-partisans" (*TN*, 11 Sep 1997). Anand Panyarachun had called for Chavalit's resignation a month earlier on grounds both of his government's economic incompetence, and his personal prevarication over support for the constitution (*TN*, 7 Aug 1997). In October, the Federation of Thai Industries, and a key member of the Board of Trade, called for Chavalit to quit (*TN*, 14 Oct 1997).

5. "This situation [a decline in working unity] arose because the bank lacked good leaders with knowledge, ability, and experience. There was no fairness in administration and hierarchy, no moral integrity. Good leadership is difficult. The internal division arose as a result. . . . Besides, in the latter period, politics interfered with the Bank of Thailand more than in the past. This may have arisen because senior executives of the bank wanted to please politicians for the sake of their own job security" (Nukul 1998, paras 428–9).

6. In a book written by veterans of 1973 to commemorate the event's 25th anniversary, not one of the chapters carried the word "democracy" in its title, and not one discussed parliament, parties, and other representative institutions. Instead the authors focused on social movements, ideology, community, civil society, and the politics of everyday life (Phitthaya, 1998e).

7. However, help was at hand. Ramkhamhaeng University promptly laid on fast-track degree programmes phased to suit the parliamentary calendar.

8. "If we vote for this draft, that will mean we want to see provinces have their own flags and the only Thai national flag left will be on the Government House" (Senator Kohlak Charoenrak, *TN*, 25 Aug 1997).

9. The Democrat Party formally backed the draft earlier in May, but simultaneously criticized several points and urged the CDA to make revisions (*BP*, 23 May 1997).

10. Thammarat workshop held at Chulalongkorn University, 25–26 July 1998.

OLD POLITICS, NEW POLITICS

In the early 1990s, all the major parties were coalitions of provincial businessmen-politicians. Collectively they stood for their own business interests, and for the diversion of a greater share of the national budget to provincial spending. Over the course of the decade and the crisis, this pattern was modified. The personnel of parliamentary politics changed. More importantly, the context of parliamentary politics changed. New forces invaded the political arena. These forces were driven by the globalization of the Thai economy, and by the stresses within Thai society, accentuated by the cycle of boom and bust.

PROLOGUE: THE PASSING OF THE *CHAO PHO*?

On the eve of elections in July 1995, the Thammasat academic and TV host Chirmsak Pinthong asked Banharn Silpa-archa to name his prospective cabinet. Banharn refused angrily, and after becoming premier closed down the programme as "uncontrollable" (*TN*, 14 Feb 1996). Chirmsak's question hinted at Banharn's lack of a credible economic team, but also at the looming contest for the Interior Ministry. For the provincial bosses, the Interior Ministry was critically powerful because it controlled the provincial administration, the conduct of elections, and the police. Banharn had secured his election victory in advance by log-rolling all the major provincial barons and their followers into his Chat Thai Party. However, at least three of these barons hoped to become interior minister and each of the three believed that Banharn had promised the post to him.

One was the unchallenged godfather of the fishing port which had grown into one of Bangkok's industrial suburbs. His original wealth was rumoured to have come from smuggling and gambling. He founded a network of gas stations in the early 1990s when oil smuggling was booming. He became an investor in casino developments across the Thai-Burmese border. The US leaked information that he was suspected of drug dealing. A judge later ruled that twenty thousand votes had been stuffed into the ballot boxes in his constituency. The second of the barons was unquestioned godfather of the far north. His aspiration to become prime minister had earlier been blocked by US leaks about involvement in the drug trade. The third was unquestioned godfather of the eastern border. His main legitimate business was trucking. His barony included the border crossings where gems, timber, arms, and various smuggled goods passed between Thailand and areas still controlled by the remnants of the Khmer Rouge.

By revealing his choice as interior minister, Banharn would have attracted fierce urban criticism for putting the care of law and order under one of these three. He would also have started a baronial war.

Banharn's success in log-rolling the great provincial bosses in 1995 was the apogee of *chao pho* (godfather) politics. Over the next few years, there was a generational shift in party political leadership. By keeping the Interior Ministry for himself, Banharn delayed rather than doused the baronial war. A year later, his Chat Thai Party was torn apart. Many MPs defected to Chavalit but then were unhinged by Chavalit's fall and the subsequent disintegration of his New Aspiration Party. Some of the barons were defeated at the 1995 elections, while others withdrew before the 1996 polls. Others were beached by the party splits which attended the fall of Banharn in October 1996 and of Chavalit in November 1997. Montri Pongpanit, who had steered the Social Action Party through membership of every elected coalition government since 1988, resigned the party leadership after half the members revolted against him. Over the next couple of years, the party disintegrated. The death in May 1998 of Chatichai Choonhavan, the first party leader to rise to the premiership by log-rolling the provincial barons into a coalition in 1988, symbolized the passing of a political era.

The eclipse—full or partial—of so many of the major provincial barons reflected a larger shift of political generations. Around a third of the total seats changed hands at the 1996 elections, mostly passing to new first-time MPs. Many of the barons wanted to make their baronies hereditary and were training their children to succeed them in electoral seats. The system of multi-member constituencies facilitated this. Banharn brought in his daughter on a joint ticket, and was planning the same for his son. Many others did the same.[1] However even these hereditary shifts constituted a change in the old *chao pho* model. The fathers had clawed their way up from humble origins by understanding the laws of primitive capitalism. The sons and daughters started their political careers with US degrees, inherited money, and the personal networks gained through elite educational careers.

Beyond these dynastic successions, many of the new provincial MPs elected in 1992, 1995, and 1996 represented a new type which reflected the increase in prosperity and sophistication of urban provincial centres. They were children of successful but not necessarily prominent businessmen. Often they had gone from education into a professional career as teachers, doctors, or lawyers. Several had participated in the student movements of the 1970s. Some had been involved in local activism before standing for parliament. In short, the *chao pho* generation of provincial political leaders was a product of the pioneer provincial economy of the Vietnam war era. Their successors were products of the more mature and sophisticated provincial urban expansion of the 1980s and 1990s.

In 1998–99, this generational shift spread towards party leadership. In the Social Action and Chat Phatthana parties, the leadership passed to younger figures.[2] The two largest parties, Democrat and New Aspiration, appointed younger, successor figures as deputy leader and general secretary respectively.[3] Parties which resisted this process (Chat Thai and Prachakon Thai) seemed to atrophy with age. A thinning layer of older politicians still dominated party leadership, and commanded the respect due to their seniority. But this layer was becoming more brittle, more fragile.

THE DEMOCRAT PARTY I: FROM THE PROVINCES TO BANGKOK

The Democrat Party was transformed through the middle and late 1990s. At the start of the decade, the Democrat Party was one of many provincially-oriented parties whose particular character derived from its heartland in the southern region. At the close of the decade, the Democrats stood for globalization, financial liberalization, and the maintenance of Thailand's open economy.

The Democrats are Thailand's oldest party with roots going back to a royalist faction in the immediate postwar era. In the brief opening up of parliamentary politics in the 1970s, the remnants of this Bangkok-based conservative group were joined by a small handful of southern politicians. During the 1980s, the party developed these two bases of support. Its Bangkok wing expanded through recruitment of business politicians, and support from bureaucrats and small businessmen. In the south, the Democrats became the predominant party in the region (Noranit 1987).[4]

In the late 1980s and early 1990s, provincial figures came to dominate all the major parties by the simple arithmetic of electoral demographics. Southerners came to dominate the Democrat Party. Many Bangkok Democrats resisted this provincialization and defected. Others lost at the polls when the Bangkok electorate became fascinated with the soldier-monk-politician, Chamlong Srimuang (McCargo, 1997). The southerner, Chuan Leekpai, rose to leadership of the party. After Chuan became prime minister at the end of 1992, southerners predominated among the Democrat ministers.[5]

The pendulum began to swing back during the Chuan I government (1992–95). On one side, several southern Democrats were embroiled in scandals over land, logging, and contract corruption which brought the government down. On the other, the Democrats began to develop a new Bangkok base which reflected the rapid modernization of the city in the boom. On appointment as prime minister in 1992, Chuan recruited a cadre of technocrats to manage the increasingly complex and open economy. Supachai Panitchapakdi, who had joined the party earlier after a career in the central and commercial banks, became commerce minister. Tarrin Nimmanhaeminda, the young head of the establishment Siam Commercial Bank, was recruited as finance minister. This duo gave the Democrat Party unparalleled expertise in the economic management whose political importance would rise steeply through the mid 1990s.

After the May 1992 incident, the political career of Chamlong Srimuang declined, and the Democrats regained some initiative in Bangkok. Many of their new recruits were young professionals attracted by the image of technocrat modernism radiating from the Democrats' economic team. After the party's southern barons were damaged by the scandals which brought the government down in May 1995, Chuan exploited the potential of this new Bangkok wing. In the no-confidence debates against Banharn, Chuan kept many of the Democrat old guard sitting on the benches, and allowed the new young Democrats to hold the floor and enthrall the large urban television audience. These young, smart, articulate, clever speakers presented a stark contrast to the old provincial boss politicians whom Bangkokians saw as the threat to Thailand's democracy and economic success.

Chart 6.1: The 1996 election log-roll

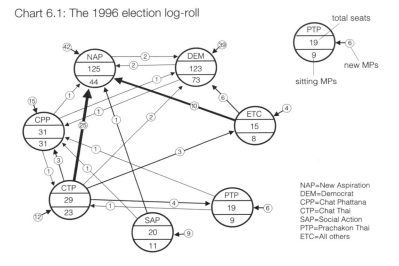

In the November 1996 elections following Banharn's fall, the Democrat Party increased its share of the thirty-seven Bangkok seats from seven to twenty-nine. However, on a national scale Chavalit repeated Banharn's success in log-rolling the provincial factions (chart 6.1) to secure the largest number of seats (125 to 123) and hence the right to form a coalition. In opposition, Chuan used two strategies. First, he again paraded his youngblood team to hound the scandals which emerged over the budgets for education and rural road construction. Second, he paraded the Tarrin-Supachai duo to criticize the Chavalit government's inept handling of the economy. The Democrats had been reengineered to reflect a growing urban demand for economic expertise and cleaner government.

Table 6.1: Election results, 1986–96

	1986	1988	1992a	1992b	1995	1996
Democrat	100	48	44	79	86	123
Chat Thai	63	87	74	77	92	39
Social Action	51	54	31	22	22	20
Prachakon Thai	24	31	7	3	18	18
Palang Tham		14	41	47	23	1
New Aspiration	-		72	51	57	125
Chat Phatthana	-	-		60	53	52
Samakkhitham	-	-	79	-	-	-
Others	109	123	12	21	40	15
Total	347	357	360	360	391	393

As the Chavalit cabinet disintegrated through September and October 1997, the Democrat Party came under great internal strain. The Bangkok wing was pressed by financial backers and constituents to step forward, supplant Chavalit, and take management of the collapsing economy. The southern wing argued intensely against such a move on grounds it would invite failure and popular antagonism. They proposed the Democrats should allow the Chavalit government to suffer further, and should assume power only after an election had increased the Democrats' parliamentary seats. The southerners also feared the Bangkok wing of the party would dominate any government formed against the background of urban agitation. These fears were overtaken by events. On 3 November, Chavalit announced he would resign and open the way for an alternative coalition. According to various accounts, Chavalit was pushed to this decision by the IMF, the army, or leading businessmen including Dhanin. While the Chat Phatthana Party tried to resurrect Chavalit's coalition under new leadership (Chatichai), two parties (Prachakon Thai and Social Action) split, and the defections were just enough to give the Democrats the advantage.

The southerners' fears were confirmed. In the new Chuan II cabinet, the Bangkok duo of Tarrin and Supachai, along with their personal nominees, dominated the key economic portfolios, while members of Chuan's youth team, mainly from Bangkok, were promoted to the middle-ranked ministries.[6] Suthep Theuksuban, the unofficial leader of the southern wing, had to be accommodated in the Communications Ministry, and another southern party financier was given a deputy ministership in finance. But other senior southerners had to be content with minor posts. Chuan II had been installed on a wave of urban Bangkok sentiment, and this was reflected in the cabinet selection.

Moreover, a further transformation was about to happen. At the press conference following official receipt of the royal command, Chuan sat flanked by Tarrin and Supachai, with other party members and coalition allies ranged behind. This tableau nicely signalled that the economy was the government's main concern, and the economic team its spearhead. Moreover, while the others were arrayed in the official white uniforms customary on such occasions, Tarrin and Supachai stood out starkly in dark business suits—the uniform of *international* business.

THE DEMOCRAT PARTY II: FROM BANGKOK TO THE WORLD

Supachai, Chuan, and Tarrin begin the Chuan II administration

Over the following year, the Democrats became identified as the party of the IMF programme and hence as the party of the neoliberal agenda for transforming Thailand's economy in general and its financial structure in particular. The way in which the government was installed—on a wave of urban sentiment spurred by the shock of the crisis—and the disarray of the opposition, afforded the government an unusually long honeymoon. To give the coalition a parliamentary majority, Chuan was obliged to include some of the least attractive detritus from the party splits and defections of the previous two years. Chuan lectured them not to provide press and opposition with opportunities to raise corruption scandals. This was only partially successful, but the scandals did not threaten the government as a whole. Nor was Chuan subject to the usual blackmail by coalition partners which in recent years had resulted in coalition reshuffles at roughly nine-month intervals.[7]

As finance minister and chief architect of the government's economic policy, Tarrin profited from this general immunity to criticism, and also from the credibility he established with both the foreign business community and the IMF. For over a year, until the opposition targeted him in the no-confidence debate of January 1999, Tarrin was relatively safe from local criticism.

At the same time, he and the Democrat-led government as a whole were exposed to strong outside pressures. The desire of the World Bank and IMF to restructure Thailand's financial system led logically to a need to restructure the political institutions which frame financial markets. Many outside institutions started politically oriented projects in Thailand. USAID returned to Thailand in 1998 after a long absence. Its agenda of activity had nothing to do with economic aid, but was wholly focused on projects connected with political and governmental reform. The World Bank launched a number of projects on institutional reform of the financial sector, including both the commercial banks and the framework of governmental regulation.[8] The ADB launched a project on governance with focus on bureaucratic reform.

Private foundations and lobby organizations were also involved. The Asia Foundation was already sponsoring projects concerning corruption and governance before the crisis.[9] The foundation's Bangkok head wrote a paper in 1998 analyzing the new 1997 constitution and indicating ways it could be used to improve governance (Klein 1998). Some other US lobby organizations appeared in Thailand. The Carnegie Foundation held an international conference in Bangkok in mid 1999 on the politics of the crisis, with the emphasis on institutional reform (CERN 1999).

While there were differences in emphasis, strategy, and detail, the outline agenda of all of these efforts were similar: bureaucratic reform; control of corruption; privatization of state enterprises; changes in the legal system to approximate more to a Western model; and insulation of economic policy from political pressures by increasing the role of the central bank and other supposedly rule-based technocratic institutions.

The Democrats resisted the IMF's stringent macroeconomic programme, but largely fell in with plans for financial restructuring (see pp. 41–2, 49–51). Tarrin himself was circumspect in his public comments on the nature of Thai financial institutions and business in general. But Phisit Lee-ahtam, whom Tarrin handpicked to serve as his deputy minister and mouthpiece, was more explicit. He openly blamed the crisis on the old-fashioned organization, lack of transparency, and outdated methods of family-based Thai banks, and enthusiastically called for more foreign participation (at FCCT, 11 Nov 1998). For Tarrin, the only sticking point in liberalization was land—"something has to be left to the Thais."

At each of the mini-crises over the implementation of the IMF programme—the financial decrees, banking package, debt restructuring, bankruptcy bill, no-confidence debates, and the TPI bankruptcy case—the Democrat leaders reacted against criticism with the same argument. Failure to comply would mean that Thailand would be abandoned by "the markets." The consequences would be an "atom bomb," "death," a "bottomless" pit.

The government grew more remote from the business community in a way which was unique in Thai political history since the late 1950s. The conviction—shared by the IMF and Tarrin—that finance was key to the crisis and its solution, led to almost complete neglect of policies to operate directly on the real economy. The industry (and agriculture) portfolios were allotted to ministers from coalition partners who were not brought into the main policy-making forum. Supachai at commerce fared little better. In May–June 1998 and again in March 1999, he broke Democrat ranks to criticize the financial focus of the recovery effort and the neglect of the real economy. Leading entrepreneurs in the real economy petitioned at regular intervals for more attention, but without success. After the issue of the 14 August 1998 banking package, Tarrin's relations with the bankers also deteriorated as they resisted his carrot-and-stick approach to recapitalization and debt restructuring (see pp. 52–7).

From a largely provincial-based party in the early 1990s, the Democrat Party had been transformed in 1997 into the spearhead of urban aspirations to regain control over the cabinet and the economy, and then in 1998 into the local arm of the IMF programme to transform the Thai economy through a programme of financial restructuring and associated legal and administrative reforms. Through this transition, the party retained strong urban support. But from mid 1998 onwards, the Democrats in general and Tarrin in particular were subject to growing criticism from entrepreneurs and bankers who felt the government had abdicated its duty to protect domestic capital (see pp. 165–7). Through 1999, the Democrats tried to distance themselves from the IMF. But their alignment in the critical year of 1998 would leave a mark.

SOCIAL DIVISION AND RURAL PROTEST

While the IMF's presence changed the Democrats, the social fallout from the crisis began to change their political opponents.

The boom years increased the gap between Thailand's rich and poor, urban and rural. The economic gap widened as most of the material gains were concentrated among the urban upper and middle classes, and began to trickle down to other groups only as labour markets tightened in the last few years before the crash. The political gap widened as urban political participation increased, while rural participation was hindered by structures and mentalities left over from the cold war. The social gap widened as Bangkok enthusiastically embraced everything modern (Pasuk and Baker 1998).

The number of local protests increased from sixty-one in 1982 to 170 in 1990 and 988 in 1994 (Praphat 1998, 27, 30, 39). Most were rural. Around a third were about the control and use of resources of land, forest, and water. New organizations sprung up including NGOs, local community associations, farmers' groups, and people's networks. In 1996, groups under the umbrella organization of the Assembly of the Poor camped outside Government House for ninety-nine days, negotiated with the Chavalit government on a list of 121 demands, and secured agreements to pay 4.65 billion baht of compensation (mostly for disruption by dam projects), resolutions on land policy, and a moratorium on certain dam projects (Praphat 1998; Prudhisan 1998). The scale of this protest and of the concessions was unprecedented.

143

The transition from Chavalit to Chuan in late 1997 blocked this rural political emergence. Chavalit had agreed to negotiate with farmers' groups and had accepted the principle that some rural issues could only be settled outside the framework of law and procedure because it was biased against the poor. Chuan retreated behind the barricades of law and bureaucracy. He insisted that laws must be upheld and officials must be in charge. When rural protesters arrived outside Government House in early 1998, Chuan's personal secretary called the leaders "parasites" and "opportunists," and claimed, "politics and interest groups are major hindrances to easing their [the poor's] plight" (*BP*, 4 Mar 1998). While the Democrats might promote democracy in urban Thailand, they believed the rural area must remain under paternal rule.

Chuan snubbed the Assembly of the Poor's attempts to continue negotiation. In early February 1998, farmers' groups rallied in the northeast to discuss another march on Bangkok. The government dispatched a minister to negotiate, but the protesters pronounced it "useless" to talk with someone who lacked the power and will to solve their problems. From April, the government began systematically reversing the concessions which the previous government had made to the Assembly. It revoked the promised dam compensation through a cabinet resolution denying any compensation for projects already completed. It launched court proceedings claiming fraud in the case of Rasi Salai dam where some compensation had already been paid. It revoked three resolutions allowing farmers to remain in areas of "official" forest, and decreed that farmers would have to prove they had occupied such areas before 1941. Local officials were emboldened to restart dam projects which had been frozen. Associated legislation such as the community forestry bill was shifted onto the back-burner (Baker 2000).

This aggression raised the political temperature. Three thousand people affected by the reversal of policy on dams moved to Bangkok and camped outside Government House for the rest of 1998. A protest outside the Agriculture Ministry in April turned into a scuffle with policemen. A month later, protesters fired a bamboo rocket into the Government House compound, and hurled mud at police. Villagers in the north seized the area designated for one of the disputed dam projects. The Assembly of the Poor set up a protest camp at the controversial Pak Mun dam.

Several farmers' organizations from the northeast made a compact to focus protest on the issue of debt. As government prepared decrees to fund the debts of the collapsed finance companies, the farmers' leaders demanded, "If the government can borrow money to help the finance companies, why not for the poor?" (Bamrung Kayotha in *BP*, 25 May 1998). Twenty thousand rallied in Khon Kaen to demand a five-year moratorium on agricultural debt. Government tried to defuse the issue by promising to increase the funds available through the government's agricultural bank, setting up a complaint centre to deter farmers from bringing issues to Bangkok, and devising a system of local-level committees designed to undercut the farmers' organizations. When the farmers' groups threatened a mass rally in Bangkok on 24 June, government set out to split the movement by negotiating with separate leaders. One of the major groups accepted an offer of a one-year moratorium on a case-by-case basis, and the threatened rally collapsed amid accusations of betrayal.

From mid year, when the rains began and the agricultural calendar started, rural protests faded away. At this stage in early-mid 1998, the countryside was still cushioned against the crisis. By year end, the situation had changed. Farming input prices had risen because of the baht depreciation. Selling prices had weakened on international trends. Relatives in the city had stopped sending remittances and started to drift home (see pp. 92–4). On top of all this, the rains were bad.

The debt issue now became more urgent. In early February 1999, ten thousand farmers from the northeast staged a rally at Sanam Luang in Bangkok, while another ten thousand gathered in Khon Kaen and smaller numbers at other provincial capitals. The government agreed to extend the case-by-case moratorium from one to three or five years. The rallies dispersed, but three months later one of the farmers' groups blockaded the Bank of Thailand's northeastern branch to complain that the relief was still insufficient, that the government was working for the IMF rather than the Thai people, and that while the government was racing to process legislation demanded by the IMF, a farmers rehabilitation bill had not progressed over the past year. The rally burnt an effigy of the finance minister.

The land issue became more heated. The Democrats' resolution that settlers on "forest" land would have to prove occupation before 1941 potentially turned some 10 million people into illegal squatters. The government promised to reclassify "forest" by identifying watersheds and other key areas, and legitimating settlement in other areas where the trees had disappeared. However this process would take time, and many settlers felt insecure. In Kanchanaburi, where officials reckoned that sixty thousand people were settled on "forest" land, farmers besieged the provincial office for a week.

Invading Dong Larn

The back flow of unemployed people created increased pressure to find new land. In mid 1998, a thousand families occupied an area of the Dong Larn forest in Khon Kaen. The core of this group was 643 families which had been moved off the land by the army during the 1970s counter-insurgency, and had never received the resettlement land promised in compensation. Some had gone off to work in Bangkok but had now lost their jobs. Their numbers were swollen by relatives and friends who had lost city jobs and returned to the village despite having no land to work. Some told the media that they would prefer a city job, but as no jobs were available they needed land. For six months they negotiated with the local authorities to find them land. Then in frustration they began cutting trees to attract attention. A group of disemployed construction workers started a smaller forest invasion in Phu Phan. Farmers' leaders claimed to have identified areas in seven other forests which they believed could accommodate some four thousand families. The government understood

146

the significance of this event, and staged a grand show of force, dispatching 300 police, 200 border police, 500 rangers, the head of the forestry department, the police chief, and the interior minister to negotiate a settlement in Dong Larn. Clashes between officials and farmers attempting to gain access to land continued sporadically throughout 1999. In early 2000, a group which had lived in the Phu Phan forest during the communist insurgency over twenty years earlier, returned to settle in their old base area complaining that jobs were scarce and government had never delivered on its promise to provide them with land.[10]

Falling international prices sparked another front. Late in 1998, maize farmers in the east blocked roads and demanded government increase the floor buying price. At the end of the year, the annual negotiation between planters and mills over sugarcane prices became even more heated than usual. The crash in rubber prices precipitated the Democrats to launch a 4-billion-baht support scheme for this crop which predominated in their southern heartland. Dairy farmers protesting against milk prices began to march on Bangkok with a herd of cattle. After protests by rice farmers, government reactivated an old price support scheme, even though it was aware the scheme benefitted millers and dealers more than growers. Cassava farmers blocked a major provincial highway, staged a protest in the capital, and threatened to start a bonfire of cassava. Government conceded a small level of price support. When sugar farmers threatened to invade Bangkok with loaded trucks during the Unctad X conference in February 2000, government hastily conceded a price subsidy to head them off. In March, central region rice farmers blocked roads in the Bangkok suburbs and threatened to stage a demonstration in the heart of the capital unless government increased price support.

The Democrat government handled this surge of rural protest with a mixture of repression and selective concessions. By the end of 1998, some rural activists began to question whether farmers' demands would always be blocked unless they exerted more influence in formal parliamentary politics. But other rural leaders shrank from the idea. Some argued that the timing was wrong. Any such move would invite repression and would gain no sympathy from urban opinion in the context of the crisis.[11] The Assembly of the Poor stuck to a strategy of *dao krachai*, scattered stars—protests scattered around peripheral localities rather than in Bangkok where they might have more impact, but also be more inflammatory.

Towards the end of 1999, this issue of political involvement reappeared with a greater sense of urgency. Several farmers' groups discussed plans to form larger organizations to bargain with government. In November, a thousand met to commemorate the Peasant Federation of Thailand, the organization which had pioneered rural protests in the 1970s. A spokesman said (*BP*, 21 Nov 1999):

> . . . we have come to the conclusion that it is necessary for farmers from all over the country to unite as one in order to effectively push for a national policy advantageous to farmers in all four regions. We need a central organization which is strong enough to bargain with the state power.

In February the Assembly of the Poor brought its protests back to the city, staging demonstrations during the Unctad X conference. In March, several rural leaders agreed in principle on forming a "green party" to counter the urban domination of politics.

NEW ASPIRATION AND NEW POPULISM

The growth of local protest, particularly in the poor northeastern region, was reflected in party politics. When General Chavalit Yongchaiyudh quit the army and began building his New Aspiration Party (NAP) in the early 1990s, he recognized the potential of the northeast. The region contained a third of the population and had a tradition of antagonism towards Bangkok. Chavalit recast himself as a son of the region, established a constituency base in one of its remote provinces (Nakhon Phanom), and systematically recruited established northeastern politicians. As prime minister in 1997, he announced visionary plans to transform the northeast through modern agriculture and industry, showed himself more sympathetic towards rural protest than his predecessors, and held a cabinet meeting in the northeast for symbolic effect.

However, this regional and largely rural base was only one part of Chavalit's strategy. He also drew on his military ties, worked closely with provincial barons from all the regions, and built selective links among big business groups, especially in the telecommunications sector. At the time he was premier, Chavalit stated his vision was to make the NAP a centrist "conservative party" on the model of the LDP in Japan. He imagined such a party could embrace all classes—using the rhetoric of *samakkhi* (unity) which had long been part of the Thai military's political ideology.

But as Chavalit came under increased urban pressure to resign in late 1997, he fell back on rural support. His henchmen mobilized village officers and resurrected the village scouts movement. A newspaper appeared, targeted at the northeast and intended to counter the growing antagonism to Chavalit in the Bangkok press. Villagers were bussed to Bangkok to provide an audience for Chavalit inveighing against his urban critics from the steps of Government House. In a speech in mid September, Chavalit (*TN*, 18 Sep 1997) pictured himself as the leader of rural Thais fighting the self-interest of the city and its (Chinese-origin) inhabitants:

> Thai people own this country and allow others to share the land. But when this second group of people loses benefits and doesn't get what it wants, they make noise. . . . They want to destroy this land. I want to see my people rise up to protect our country.

After his fall from the premiership in November 1997, Chavalit emphasized the NAP's rural and regional bias. He forged links with some of the farmers' groups in the northeast. He and other party leaders travelled constantly in the region on speaking tours. To aid the party's growing populist bent, Chavalit improved his public speaking abilities (he had become famous for incomprehensibility) and extended his skill in northeastern dialect. More significantly, he recruited into the NAP Thailand's most promising populist politician, Chalerm Yubamrung. Chalerm was an ex-policeman who had first excelled in precinct-boss politics in Bangkok, and subsequently developed a broader reputation as an orator through exposure on television. In 1998, he dissolved his small party and threw in his lot with Chavalit. His reputation, macho personality, and lively speeches added to the audience numbers and entertainment value of the NAP's speaking tours through the northeast.

Through the first half of 1998, the NAP took up the cause of "the poor." When the Democrats reversed the concessions to the Assembly of the Poor, an NAP leader warned, "the government is sparking a war against the poor" (Adisorn Piangket in *TN*, 23 Apr 1998). When Thirayuth Boonmee raised the issue of rich against poor over the financial decrees (see p. 74), the NAP

The perils of populism: Chavalit in Isan

slated the government strategy against the crisis as "helping the rich and ignoring the poor."

With the recession of rural protest during the rains, this rhetoric temporarily faded. But the NAP continued to broaden its popular support in the northeast. It produced newspapers which addressed regional issues. It convened seminars of monks to discuss "sustainable development in the northeast." Party MPs addressed the seminars, and monks pledged support. One provincial monastic head noted that the NAP was "the only political party" which paid attention to the region, and argued "we have to teach northeastern people to have pride and vote for one political party [as] the southern people do for the Democrats."[12] The NAP sponsored local and regional contests for northeastern *khaen* music, and included performances in its campaign tours. The use of monks and music took the NAP into an area of demotic politics which Thai parties had traditionally shunned.

In late 1998 and early 1999, the NAP resurrected the rich-poor rhetoric and blended it with the accusation that the Democrat government was too subservient to the IMF. Chavalit attacked the US for engineering the installation of the Democrats and for directing economic policy. The Democrats, he accused, were appeasing foreigners while neglecting the poor. Later in the month, the NAP issued a policy statement which argued Thailand should ignore the IMF, and should channel more resources to the poor through decentralization. On the stump through the northeast, Chavalit and Chalerm delivered this same populist message. The Democrats were too subservient to the IMF. They were bailing out the rich at the expense of the poor, the city at the expense of the countryside. The no-confidence motion filed in December 1999 blended the nationalism of devastated business with the populism of support for the poor (see p. 172).

But over late 1999, Chavalit and Chalerm appeared to step back from this attempt to define a new populist politics. They scaled back the rural tours and dropped the populist rhetoric. Instead, Chavalit made a half-hearted attempt to copy the Democrats' successful format of young technocratic leadership. He elevated Chaturon Chaisaeng to the post of party secretary-general, displacing Snoh Tienthong, one of the three barons whose competing ambitions had tested the political skills of Banharn. Chaturon was a member of the 1973–76 generation, and had made his parliamentary mark through a critique of Tarrin during the no-confidence debate. But rather than painting a new image for the New Aspiration Party, this move merely rekindled the baronial wars. Snoh prepared to quit, and other factions looked set to follow suit. Chaturon quit the general secretary's post after six months because of growing factional strife. New Aspiration began to look less like the cradle of a new rural-based populism, and more like a disintegrating memento of the era of *chao pho* politics.

THAIS LOVING THAIS

The transformation of the Democrat Party into the local representation of a neoliberal worldview generated a countervailing trend among groups which opposed this view, particularly domestic capital resentful at the mauling it suffered during the crisis, and at the government's neglect of the real economy. Through the crisis, this force attempted to raise support through nationalist appeals, but with little success (see pp. 165–73). In late 1998, a new political party was launched to capture exactly this growing trend of corporate disaffection with the Democrat-led government's policy. The party's leader, Thaksin Shinawatra, emphasized his difference from the Democrats' finance-led strategy with the remark, "I wouldn't solve this crisis just from a commercial banker's point of view" (*FEER*, 17 Jun 1999, 25).

Thaksin had been the single most successful new entrepreneur over the boom. On the eve of the crisis his net worth was estimated at 80 billion baht. Most of this wealth had been made from monopolistic concessions to supply telecommunications services. Thaksin dabbled in politics through the 1990s, joining Chamlong's declining Palang Tham Party, serving as a minister, and briefly taking the party leadership. In the late 1990s, he began to project himself as an alternative national leader.

Thaksin positioned his Thai Rak Thai (Thai Love Thai) Party as a party of small and medium business which could lead Thailand to an economic revival through a mixture of local entrepreneurship, local craft heritage, and high technology—an adaptation of the "Italian" or Tuscan model. This position made a direct appeal to the feelings of neglect, sublimated nationalism, and entrepreneurial pride of Thai business. Taksin claimed, "if I'm the government, I will open up choices for people who have the leaning and the ability to be entrepreneurs. People who earn salaries now will have the opportunity to quit and become entrepreneurs without facing excess risk" (*TN*, 25 Oct 1999). The party was successful in attracting a core of business and technocrat leaders, and scored well in opinion polls among potential urban voters. Barons fleeing from New Aspiration and other crumbling parties petitioned for entry to the party. Thaksin appointed a shadow cabinet to emphasize that he could match the technocratic cadre which had become the Democrat Party's claim to be the natural party of government (Thai Rak Thai 1999).

He spent lavishly on a national campaign to present himself as a more visionary alternative to the Democrats. The party's manifesto promised to "bring about reform in the fundamental structure of the country in all respects, so that Thailand is strong, modern, and ready to face the challenges of the world in the new era."[13] Taksin hoped to exploit the known tendency of the Bangkok electorate to veer between wild enthusiasm for the Democrats and total rejection of them. For success in the provinces, he resorted more to the old method of recruiting footloose factions. In early 2000, Snoh Tienthong led his faction from NAP to TRT. This was Snoh's fourth party shift in a decade. Each earlier shift had made him kingmaker of the subsequent cabinet. Thaksin also flirted with the possibility of recruiting rural support without the intermediation of the provincial barons. In early 2000, he promised a three-year moratorium for rural debt.

Thaksin offered a mix of the new politics and the old. On the one hand, TRT was launching towards the 2000 elections with a party programme— of support for small business and peasants—which offered a very different alternative to the globalized direction of the Democrats. On the other TRT appeared to be the new successor in a line of "Messiah parties"—like Chamlong's Palang Tham and Chavalit's NAP. Such parties have leaders who promise to save the country, but no depth of talent. They end up attracting a motley following, and decay from the inside.

OVERVIEW: TRANSFORMATIONS OF THE 1990s

The late 1990s have been a time of immense change in Thai politics—both in the institutional structure, and in the alignment of political forces. This should not be viewed simply as a response to the crisis but as part of a longer and deeper process of change in the political economy (Surin 1997; Hewison 1997; Pasuk and Baker 1997, 1998). In the early part of the decade, Kevin Hewison (1993, 181) flagged that "Thai social and political life has reached a watershed. . . . a new amalgam of social and political forces is emerging to reshape the Thai state." But the nature of those forces was subject to debate and the ultimate destination of this transformation was not clear. Hewison stressed the growing dominance of business capital. Anek (1992, 1995) and Thirayuth (1993) focused on the role of the urban middle class. The Chulalongkorn political economists foresaw a more complex contest involving businessman, peasant, and worker (Sungsidh and Pasuk 1993).

The starting point for the transformation of the 1990s was the compromise, negotiated over the 1980s, between the old forces of the bureaucratic polity and the new forces of metropolitan and (to a larger extent) provincial business. The essence of the compromise was simple. The provincial barons learned how to manipulate the new electoral politics and came to dominate parliament and cabinet. After some fractious negotiation, the heads of the bureaucracy learned to live with this new situation. They attached themselves to leading politicians and political parties. The framework of the bureaucracy remained in place with only minor qualifications of bureaucratic power. The barons gained political status, access to business opportunities, and the ability to trickle public goods back to their baronies. The scandals listed in the previous chapter had a significant new characteristic. In most of the plots to profit from the budget or from the control of natural resources, bureaucrat and political baron worked hand in hand.

In retrospect, it can be seen that this compromise depended on two strict conditions: first, the relative protection Thailand enjoyed from outside forces, both financial and political; second, the weakness of civil society. Over the 1990s, both these conditions were reversed. The outside world intruded. Civil society strengthened. The resulting changes occurred in two phases.

The first revolved around the attack on the bureaucrat-baron compromise mounted by urban-based pressure groups and eventually backed by broad urban support. This phase climaxed with the passing of the constitution and the felling of Chavalit in late 1997. Two groups with different backgrounds and agendas allied to mount this campaign. The first group included the heirs of 1970s radicalism. Their voice was most clearly articulated by Thirayuth Boonmee. This group operated largely at the level of discourse, and within a limited circle of the politically aware. But at times of political and social strain, it was able to recruit a wider base of support among the urban middling classes, and draw on a network of 1970s veterans now risen to positions of influence within the bureaucracy, political parties, media, NGOs, and pressure groups. Earlier, this lobby had campaigned for "democracy" to break down Thailand's centralization and bureaucratic paternalism. But when the party politicians chose to ally with the old centralized paternalist state, the 1970s activists lost faith in "democracy" and took up the cause of "civil society." They now aimed to shift power away from the state to the individual and community, by strengthening community and non-governmental organizations, and by demanding *rights* which limited, qualified, or transferred state power (Anek et al. 1995; Chuchai and Yuwadi 1997; Naruemon 1998; Phitthaya 1998a).

The second group consisted of "establishment radicals" or "conservative modernists" from the ranks of senior bureaucrats, professionals, modern businessmen, and executives. Again they operated largely at the level of discourse within a limited elite, but gained power from their collective status and influence, and their ability to raise wider support from the urban middling classes at critical points. Through the 1990s, this agenda was most clearly represented through the voice of Anand Panyarachun.[14] This group argued (as the army previously had) that the major threat to the Thai polity was Thailand's primitive capitalism uncontained. It held up a vision of national unity and social harmony secured by containing the power of Thailand's primitive capitalism through the paternalistic influence of good, ethical people. It looked outward to the West for models (constitution, separation of powers, good governance) and sometimes also for direct assistance to achieve this vision.

The alliance of these groups shaped the drafting of the new constitution which enshrined many of the rights and reforms on the liberal agenda, much of the political engineering on the conservative agenda, and a battery of new judicial and semi-judicial institutions required for implementation. However, the passage of such an ambitious new charter was doubtful until the onset of the economic crisis recruited wider support among big business and the urban middle class in 1996–97. These latter recruits had little idea of the charter's content, but adopted it as the symbol of an urban desire to exercise greater control over both politics and economy. After the constitution had passed, the reactionary forces regrouped. The reform alliance had to fight further battles to implement the constitution's provisions. At elections for the new senate in March–April 2000, the Bangkok electorate plumped for this alliance. Of the city's eighteen seats, eight were won by NGOs and activists, while five fell to conservative modernists.[15]

This alliance was also the vanguard of the urban revolt which drove Chavalit out of power at the onset of the crisis. But beyond this historical point, the alliance ran up against its own limitations. Neither of the two major groups in the alliance had the will or the electoral base to translate its agitational influence into parliamentary power. Moreover, in the aftermath of the constitution's passage, the huge ideological gap between the two groups drew them apart.

The second phase of the transformation took place within the realm of parliamentary politics. At the start of the decade, all the major parties were coalitions of provincial businessmen. In the mid 1990s, the Democrat Party went through an initial stage of transformation driven by the urban upsurge described above. In the late 1990s, this transformation broadened with the arrival of new and powerful forces in Thai politics against the background of economic crisis.

The first of these new forces were external influences, particularly those emanating from Washington. In part, the exposure of Thai politics to these forces was a simple consequence of the growth and liberalization of the Thai economy—Thai politics became subject to the judgement of "the markets." But in part, this was also a direct result of the neoliberal project to open up markets and impose on them new rules and practices. Quite explicitly, Washington seized the opportunity offered by the Asian crisis to advance this agenda. The initial focus was on reform of financial markets, but logically had to broaden into a reform of the legal and political systems which framed these markets.

Kanishka Jayasuriya has summed up this process around Asia as the replacement of "developmental states" by "regulatory states." In a developmental state, government seeks economic growth by promoting domestic capital. In a regulatory state, the administration of the economy is transferred to rule-based institutions (central banks, law courts), power is concentrated within a social and technocrat elite, parliaments become puppet shows, and civil society is "managed" (Bell et al. 1995; Jayasuriya 1996, 1999, 2000). Jayasuriya's analysis is based on East Asia with its political tradition of dictatorships and one-party states, and needs to be modified somewhat to suit Thailand. The space for political contestation is more open, hence this "regulatory" agenda is not the single state project, but one of several competing projects in the political arena. By aligning itself with the IMF and US ambition to seize on the crisis as an opportunity to restructure Thailand's financial system, regulatory framework, capital market, and much besides, the Democrat Party became the local representation of this agenda. As predicted by the Jayasuriya model, this led to increased aggression towards (and isolation from) civil society activism.

The second of these new forces in Thai politics was the growing assertion of rural interests. Driven largely by conflicts over resources, rural politics had become more organized, more sophisticated, and more assertive. Through the early 1990s, a series of marches, sieges of Government House, road blocks, and protest networks indicated an insistent demand for space within the formal political process. This trend continued through the crisis as economic hardship and social stress increased, the political allocation of hardship became a matter of public debate, and the pro-urban, pro-globalist Democrat Party attempted to suppress rural demands. The New Aspiration Party toyed with the opportunities offered by populist appeals reaching down to this rural surge. However, there were considerable barriers to any expansion of populism on a Latin American or even a Philippine scale. Many of the old mechanisms (military, political, cultural) for controlling rural politics, built up during the cold war, were still in place or capable of revival.[16] The New Aspiration Party itself was wary of unleashing a strident populism which the party would find difficult to control. Rural protest leaders were also aware of the dangers and limitations. But whether or not Chavalit chose to leap up on the tiger's back, the tiger was certainly there.

Thaksin's Thai Rak Thai Party was invented to capture the reaction to the Democrats' urban bias and commitment to globalism. It sought support from local businessmen and farmers who felt they had been neglected during the crisis in favour of Thailand's small cadre of globalized firms and urban middle class who profited on the coattails of globalization.

In the early 1990s, liberal optimists like Thirayuth and Anek imagined that an alliance between the urban middle class and a peasantry upgraded by wealth and education could reduce the chronic tendency to "instability" and carry through a liberal agenda of reforms. In their models, globalization was a benign force assisting the liberal agenda. At the end of the decade, the political shock of the crisis, the intrusions of neoliberalism, and the innovations of political reform had transformed the political environment. The prospect for an alliance of peasant and middle classes derived from European models of the nineteenth century had proved to be of little relevance to the globalized world at the outset of the twenty-first. Globalization was no longer perceived as a benign ally of liberal aspirations. Thai party politics had moved beyond the stage of competing business gangs, but hardly in ways which were predicted. The divisions in Thai politics increasingly ran along two main axes.

The first axis tracked attitudes to neoliberalism and globalization. At one end stood the Democrat Party with a base of support among business and white collar middle class who either saw their interests best served by globalization, or were attracted by the image of internationalism and modernity. At the other end stood businesses which had been mauled by the crises, social conservatives concerned about the consequences of greater foreign penetration, dissident activists, and the Thai Rak Thai Party manoeuvring to mould this material into a political force.

The second axis tracked the social distance from city to village. At one end stood the coalition of urban activism which had been so successful in changing the political structure and shrinking the space of the elected politicians. At the other stood rural Thailand petitioning ever more insistently for political space.

NOTES

1. Families returning more than one MP at the 1996 elections: Chidchob in Buriram; Iasakul in Nong Khai; Watcharapon in Sisaket; Moolasartsathorn in Surin; Srisurin in Surin; Chintavej in Ubon; Masdit in Nakhon Si Thammarat; Suwankhiri in Songkhla; Senniam in Songkhla; Sundaravej in Bangkok; Khunpleum in Chonburi; Sasomsap in Nakhon Pathom; Harnsawat in Pathumthani; Angkinand in Phetchaburi; Thienthong in Sa Kaew; Asavahame in Samut Prakarn; Kraiwatnusorn in Samut Sakhon; Adireksarn in Saraburi; Silpa-archa in Suphanburi; na Chiang Mai in Chiang Mai; Jongsuthanamani in Chiang Rai. Besides these, there were other constituencies where the seat passed from father to son or daughter at these elections: Krairiksh in Phitsanulok; Pattano in Songkhla; Uaphinyakul in Phrae; Khamprakorb in Nakhon Sawan; Piangket in Khon Kaen; Thongsawat in Lampang; Wongwan in Phrae; Chaisaeng in Chachoengsao.

2. Suwit Khunkitti and Korn Dabbarangsi.

3. Abhisit Vejjajiva and Chaturon Chaisaeng.

4. It is widely recognized that the south has a different political culture from the rest of Thailand. Vote buying is much less widespread. Political debate is more prevalent and more passionate, political oratory is more appreciated, and so on. What accounts for this difference is more controversial. Some attribute it to the rubber tree, some to the influence of Islam, some to the (cultural) distance from Bangkok, some to the longer and deeper urban tradition—the south's port towns are very old while most provincial towns in other regions are very young and raw.

5. With the exception of the economic team; see below.

6. Bangkok Democrat MPs who became ministers: Bhichai Rattakul, Savit Bhotiwihok, Abhisit Vejjajiva, Tarrin Nimmanhaeminda, Sukhumbhand Paribatra. Another Bangkok MP, Akkapol Sorasuchart, became government spokesman. Phisit Lee-ahtam, a Bangkokian and non-MP, also became a minister on the Democrat quota. Two other Democrat ministers, Pradit Pattaraprasit and Pornthep Techaphaibun, were returned by provincial constituencies but were essentially Bangkok people. Jurin Laksanavisit and Surin Pitsuwan, who qualify as both southerners and youngbloods, also received ministries.

7. After the death of Chatichai, Chuan brought Chat Patthana into the coalition to increase the majority and provide some extra insurance against coalition accidents.

8. By January 1999, the work-in-progress sheet of the World Bank/IMF consultants working inside the central bank listed twenty covering: restructuring and recapitalization of the core financial institutions, action plans for specialized financial institutions, a taskforce on a comprehensive supervision framework, drafting of new

banking legislation, changes in the legal framework, facilitating the sale of distressed assets, monitoring of debt restructuring, rationalizing accounting standards, improving financial data, and improving accountability and shareholder rights.

9. We are not saying such attention is "a bad thing." We are merely noting that something is changing, and this change will have consequences. Pasuk has been a significant and grateful recipient of the Asia Foundation's funding.

10. ITV evening news, 27 March 2000. As with Dong Larn, they gave government an ultimatum to provide them with land or else they would start cutting the trees.

11. The issue was raised at the *thammarat* meeting of NGOs and local groups convened by Thirayuth Boonmee, at Chulalongkorn University on 25–6 July 1998. Several speakers expressed a wish for some kind of central organization to provide better coordination of local movements, and to create a stronger bargaining position with official agencies. Local movements are all very well, the argument went, but they are too easily picked off one by one. Over two days, this sentiment became one of the major themes of the meeting. The second meeting was the third anniversary of the Assembly of the Poor in December 1998. The question posed by Piphob Thongchai was: will the Assembly remain vulnerable and ultimately powerless unless it develops some way to enter the formal political process. The answer at both meetings was negative. At the first, Banthon Ondam (a respected senior NGO leader, formerly an academic) argued that forming a central body would result in splits and discord. The strength of local movements lay in the locality. Loose networking remained the best organizational strategy. At the Assembly meeting, the proposal was not formally addressed.

12. Phra Ratchawanwethi of Sisaket (*TN*, 12 Oct 1998).

13. Some suspect that Taksin, whose business wealth was made through government monopoly concessions, merely represents "money politics" of a new and more sophisticated sort (see Ukrist 1998).

14. The choice of Thirayuth and Anand to personalize these two visions is a little vexed by the fact that these two made a concerted effort to collaborate. As noted above, however, they were pulled apart by their respective constituencies.

15. Outside the city, the results were different. A handful of activists succeeded in some major towns. But the majority of provincial seats were shared (roughly equally) between retired officials on the one hand, and wives, relatives, and associates of the dominant local political families on the other.

16. One major aspect of the increased politicization of the crisis was an increase in political violence. Murders of village headmen and other fixers who serve as vote brokers became an almost daily item in the news. Two MPs were victims of professional assassination attempts in 1999. Political parties invested in bulletproof vests for their more valuable members. The interior minister launched a campaign to disband the gangs of gunmen kept by politicians. Earlier a TV documentary had described these gangs in some detail, and had hinted that one was kept by this minister.

Out of place: walking the streets of Bangkok

SELLING THE COUNTRY, SAVING THE ELEPHANT

GREAT EXPECTATIONS

Shortly after the Chuan government was installed in November 1997, a group of Thai and foreign businessmen met at a prestigious Bangkok hotel for a regular session of updates on the political and business outlook hosted by an international network. The baht was already into its stomach-hollowing slide. Assessments of the likely scale of the crash were changing from bad to brutal. The speakers expected the crisis "to entirely disembowel Thailand's financial sector" and spill a lot of Thai corporate blood.

The session proceeded to open discussion. The head of an international bank took the floor. After a few preliminary remarks, he paused for effect and said with great emphasis:

"Thais must not become nationalistic."

After surveying the room, he repeated the message in a louder tone.

"THAIS MUST NOT BECOME NATIONALISTIC."

He talked on for some time, but the words were lost. These ringing phrases had increased the level of tension. The moderator took over and swung into his usual good-natured wrap-up with less confidence than usual. One of the Thais present intervened and asked for the floor.

He talked for around ten minutes. He gave the impression of being in a rather emotional state, but holding these emotions under control. His words were not very articulate but the meaning was clear. He was both baffled and bothered by the banker's forceful statement. He wanted to make it clear that Thailand would survive the crisis, however bad it might be.

The banker could have said Thais should not become defensive, negative, antagonistic, or a host of similar words. However, he chose the word "nationalistic." This choice might reflect several things. First, nationalism has been one of the most powerful movements of the past two centuries in the Europe from which the banker originated. It has shaped countries, and motivated the most destructive wars mankind has experienced. Second, nationalism has enjoyed a resurgence in Europe following the collapse of the cold war and the advance of globalization. The revival of Balkan nationalist wars and of neofascist political parties has raised fears that the post–cold war era is regressing to an earlier era of nationalism, rather than moving on to a more rational and optimistic era of globalization.

Third, these fears might have special importance for a senior executive in one of the banks most aggressive in exploiting the wider spaces of globalization. Possibly he had knowledge and experience of earlier crises of financial liberalization in Latin America, Scandinavia, and elsewhere, in which case, he would be aware that great financial opportunities would become available during the coming Thai crisis, and that political opposition would be the only barrier to economic logic. Although this particular banker left Thailand shortly afterwards, his bank became a player in the auctions of bankrupt Thai financial empires.

The immediate and emotional Thai response might at first sight seem to confirm these fears about the rise of nationalism. But on closer inspection, the picture is more complex. The individual who responded is one of the most successful Thais in the world of multinational business. He had made his entire business career in one of the world's largest and best-known companies. He had been posted outside Thailand as a department chief. He was now the first Thai to serve as country head of the company's operations in Thailand, and virtually unique in Thailand in holding such a position in a multinational company of this status.

Moreover he went on to take a very public role during the crisis, campaigning that Thailand must not resist change, but must reform its business practices exactly along the lines which the IMF and other Western bodies advocated. He campaigned by starting a regular television programme, by writing columns in the daily press, and by appearing regularly at business seminars.

In other words, he might be counted as an enthusiastic supporter of the banker's intended theme. What seems to have made the exchange in the business seminar so fragile and emotional was the vocabulary and the tone of voice. By choosing the word "nationalistic," the banker had essentially accused the Thais of being about to adopt an ideology which had been such a destructive force in European affairs. On top of that, the banker had lapsed, perhaps unthinkingly, into a colonial mode of repeating and shouting his message to make sure it was understood.

FOREIGNERISM

Between the baht float on 2 July 1997 and the conclusion of the IMF package in mid August, an article appeared in the *Bangkok Post*, the oldest and largest circulation English language newspaper. The article was positioned in the main slot on the editorial page, and was signed by one of the most experienced international correspondents working in the region.

The writer opened by recording how his Thai teacher had told him on arrival in 1982, "Of course, you know we Thais don't like *farangs*." His subsequent experience had proved this was indeed true. Thais hated foreigners. But this train of thought was not developed in the remainder of the article. It was merely a preface which excused what the writer wanted to say.

This was that Thailand was "a man-made disaster waiting to happen" as a result of "pure greed, corruption and a disregard for the law, alongside a callous attitude towards foreigners and their standards." In Thailand, "bleeding foreign investors" had become "almost a creed." Foreigners had lent "so generously" to local banks and companies, but now were worried about retrieving their money. The writer admitted that these investors may have been a little "carefree with their funds," but he failed to chide them for investing in such a foreigner-hating and lawless place, and insisted instead on their right to remove their money rather than living with the consequences of their "carefree" behaviour.

The article then moved on to the political context. Foreigners, the writer asserted, were now wondering how much Thailand's democracy "truly reflects the people's wishes." In fact, he claimed, "it is more the foreigners with their affection for Thailand and the people's charisma than the Thai people themselves who shake their heads" about all the terrible things done by the powerful. Things had now become so bad however that "the same concerned foreign community is wondering if it's still worth the effort to try to influence ingrained, venal mindsets by example."

There are several remarkable things about this article. The first is its overt racialism. The world is divided between Thais and "foreigners." The Thais are corrupt, callous, selfish, venal, incompetent, greedy, ignorant, and of course xenophobic. The foreigners are concerned, affectionate, generous, and exemplary. The second remarkable trait of the article is the resurgence of colonial attitudes. The Thais have clearly proven themselves unfit to rule a country. It is the foreigners who really care about the real people and who have the power to change things "by example." Third, there is the implication that the coming crisis (whose full magnitude is not yet known) is just retribution for the Thais' failings including their hatred and exploitation of foreigners. Finally it is remarkable that the article appeared in such a prominent place, that it was written by a relatively important journalist, and that nobody appeared to take a blind bit of notice.[1]

Although this article was an unusually articulate example, it was far from isolated. Particularly after the IMF arrival subtracted something from Thailand's sovereignty, there was a spate of similar opinions. Passionate letters to the local English-language press dismissed Thailand as a "small, corrupt and insignificant country," blustered about "no more Thai way," and demanded that US tax money should not be devoted to a bailout (the writers failed to recognize that the IMF money was an interest-bearing loan, and that the US, unlike several Asian countries, contributed nothing on top of its regular IMF contributions).[2] The popular end of the regional and international press was also susceptible to these attitudes. For a *Time* story on the Thai crisis in August 1997, the editor instructed his writers to bypass the usual stuff about an economic crisis and paint a picture of wholesale social collapse. The journalists concocted a slightly different theme, but the editor believed that his readership wanted to know about an Asian society coming apart.[3] Much later, a *Newsweek* cover article (12 Jul 1999) dismissed the possibility of a Thai recovery with a cheap jibe that the country's only comparative advantage lay in "sex and golf," and a cover headline sneering: If only the economy looked as good as its temples. Further up the editorial scale, *Far Eastern Economic Review* articles adopted an imperious lecturing tone (Thailand must do this, Indonesia must do that) quite unlike anything the magazine practiced before it was purchased by Dow Jones, the US-owned finance and publishing group.

SELLING THE COUNTRY

In the months following the baht float, there was little overtly nationalistic reaction. At this stage, the crisis was still expected to be mild (a decline to 3-percent annual growth), and Thai public opinion was confused. This phase ended during the transition from 1997 to 1998. The contagion to Indonesia and Korea made it obvious that Thailand's crisis would be much deeper than earlier expected, and that a "fire sale" of Thai-owned assets loomed. The second LoI (25 November 1997) clarified the IMF's intention to break down barriers to foreign entry, to privatize state enterprises, and to demand a programme of legislation to overhaul the financial industry. The contagion through Asia and beyond also clarified that the crisis was not solely a Thai problem. The dominant international discourse began to blame the crisis on the instabilities in the international finance market. The local discourse focused also on the failures of policy making (the Nukul Report). This was now a bad crisis which could be blamed on international financial instability and technocratic incompetence, which posed a severe threat to Thai capital, and which gave the IMF leverage to open up the economy to foreign penetration.

Some leading businessmen began to adopt the language of imperialism. At a USIS seminar, one commented: "This IMF thing is just like being colonized." Another said: "We avoided old-fashioned imperialism, why can't we avoid this?" Chumphon Pornprapha, the local partner of Suzuki motorcycles and other automotive ventures, argued that the crisis had created the opportunity for "neocolonialism."[4]

Through early 1998, there formed a loose and discordant coalition of dissidence against the IMF and against the Democrat government's acceptance of IMF strictures. This coalition had four main components. The first were medium-sized businessmen whose businesses were severely at risk. Some came from the terminally bloated real estate sector. Others were scattered through commerce, export industries, and other services. The second component were academics and activists, particularly many who had belonged to the 1970s generation of radicals. Many retained an instinctive antagonism to outside domination. A few belonged to a newer generation of unfashionable leftists. The third component included organized labour in the state enterprises. The fourth were farmers' organizations.

While these groups had very varying perspectives on the crisis, they found some common ground in opposition to foreign penetration, whether through fire sales or privatization. In January 1998, the former 1973 student leader Thirayuth Boonmee called the crisis a "political and economic war" between the US and Asia, and urged "we must not offer to sell everything to foreigners while inviting investments. While going international, we have to uphold the Thai spirit. . . . we have to preserve our important resources, state enterprises, occupations and businesses for national development" (*BP*, 10 Jan 1998).

In March 1998, the third LoI laid out more detailed plans for privatization and financial reforms, including a programme of legislative measures. In April–May, government proposed four decrees giving the executive extra powers to restructure the financial industry. Thirayuth took the opportunity to oppose the decrees unless the government agreed to countervailing measures which would ensure that the bailout of the financial industry was not loaded onto the poor. Some of the dissident businessmen cheered this opposition to the decrees. Farmers' groups demonstrated in parallel for a moratorium on agrarian debt. The parliamentary opposition took up Thirayuth's theme. This bandwagon effect generated a miniature political crisis. The finance minister protested that the decrees were "life and death" for the economy. The decrees passed parliament with some ease, but then the opposition prolonged the mini-crisis by challenging their validity in the newly formed Constitutional Court.

After this manoeuvre failed, this dissident coalition raised a demand for a two-year debt moratorium to stem the outward flow of capital. The government again reacted with the language of disaster. The deputy finance minister claimed a moratorium "would be like triggering an atomic bomb and the chain reaction will be enormous" (*TN*, 18 Jun 1998). The government also appealed to a wider urban audience by reminding them of the pre-liberalization past when foreign travel was restricted by currency controls, and many imported items were expensive or unavailable.

Following this mid year crisis, the dissident coalition quietly fell apart. Over the next eighteen months, opposition to the strategy of government and IMF was divided among three different groups which focused on different specific issues and which cooperated little with one another.

The core of the first group were debt-strapped entrepreneurs. In November 1998, the government launched a legislative programme of eleven bills. All had been set out in the fifth LoI in August and hence could be portrayed as an IMF-imposed programme. Two made adjustments to property laws to allow a slightly wider opportunity for foreign ownership. One enabled government to transform state enterprises into corporations for privatization through the stock market. One amended the law restricting businesses open to non-Thais. Two were designed to improve the law on bankruptcy and foreclosure in order to facilitate debt and corporate restructuring. This legislative programme touched on the sensitive issues of land ownership, corporate ownership, bankruptcy, and the foreign penetration of the economy.

Business opposition to these bills rallied in the senate. In 1995, Banharn had appointed several leading businessmen to the senate. Around thirty were known to be heavily indebted. Two were among the most indebted and the most notorious in encouraging businessmen not to pay their bankers. These were Prachai Liaophairat of Thai Petrochemical Industries (TPI) and Sawat Horrungruang, owner of a group of steel companies. These businessmen campaigned against the legislative programme as a whole, but particularly the bankruptcy bill. In a television interview, Prachai argued that the crisis had been engineered by the "great powers" (*maha amnat*),[5] and that "the foreigner businessmen and foreign banks have colluded to take us over at the world's cheapest price possible." He lamented that "the government has been fooled into helping the farangs to pressure us to pay back our debts," concluding that "it's like the government handing them a knife to stab us from behind." Sawat claimed that "90 percent of Thai people will become bankrupt" under the proposed law, and Prachai insisted "the 11 bills together . . . could blow up the whole country" (*TN*, 8 Jan 1999).

The indebted businessmen gained support from associated professionals and bureaucrats. Dej-udom Krairit, vice president of the Law Society, warned that the legislation "might wipe out this generation of local entrepreneurs" (*TN*, 3 Dec 1998). The retired political leader, Thanat Khoman, suggested the bills would "turn Thailand into something like a colonial state" (*BP*, 28 Nov 1998). Meechai Ruchupan, lawyer and president of the senate, argued that the legislation would give advantages to foreigners to buy Thai assets cheaply, particularly land. He asked, "Is it worth the efforts trying to revitalize the economy if everything ends up in foreign hands?" (*BP*, 21 Nov 1998). He objected to the state enterprise bill on grounds it would "hand over state power to foreigners" and could result in "anarchy" (*TN*, 6 Mar 1999). Another senior senator argued that "several tens of thousands of debtors will face bankruptcy suits from creditor banks which have been taken over by foreigners because the value of their pledged collateral has dropped. It is nobody's fault that the value of their assets has fallen" (*BP*, 11 Mar 1999). He proposed that the bills should be delayed for two years so that the "breathing space will enable debtors to bounce back" (*TN*, 16 Jan 1999). Another businessman urged, "It's not too late to protect the country from economic colonization by the superpowers if we stop these draft bills" (*BP*, 25 Nov 1998).

A deputation of these senators travelled to the US to lobby support. The government responded with a public relations offensive including ministerial visits to the major newspapers and appearances on television. Tarrin insisted that "we are not following IMF orders" and the bills were "our only way out" (*BP*, 24 Nov 1998). The final senate debate on the bankruptcy bill had to be suspended at one point because ministers were lobbying by passing notes into the chamber and waylaying senators in the corridor outside. The bill passed comfortably with only minor modification.[6] Other bills in the legislative programme also passed with little difficulty. Only the revised Alien Business Law underwent any serious delay and modification.

The second stream of protest was focused against privatization and spearheaded by the organizations of public sector workers. This protest reemerged in April 1999, immediately after the legislation to enable corporatization had been passed. The state enterprise workers had a long history of activism, and had contributed to delaying plans for privatization since the late 1980s. But the issue was now broadened by the fact that privatization was part of the IMF agenda. Government representatives added to the impression that privatization was an outside imposition by arguing that it had to take place because government needed the money, because government had made a commitment to the IMF, and because foreign confidence in the Thai economy would suffer if the plans were stalled.[7] The opposition campaign also attracted support from academics and activists. They argued that privatization undertaken during a financial crisis would result in national assets being sold to foreign capital at cheap prices without adequate safeguards for Thai consumers. The labour academic, Lae Dilokvidayarat, related the opposition against privatization to socialist and nationalist themes. He pointed out that state industries had been set up as part of the new democratic and nationalist politics that had emerged after 1932, and he argued that these state industries should be retained as social assets. Witayakon Chiangkun added that the government could not be trusted to manage privatization in a fair and clean manner, and hence privatization would amount to a social loss.

A third stream of protest emerged as a subset of the opposition to privatization. This protest focused on government's plans to sell off its stake in the Bangchak oil refinery. Bangchak was a small refinery of doubtful efficiency which was owned 80 percent by various government agencies and 20 percent by the public. Government wanted to sell the combined 32 percent stake held by the Krung Thai Bank and the Petroleum Authority (PTT). Kuwait Petroleum was interested, largely because Bangchak had developed the second largest network of petrol stations.

Bangchak became a focus of protest because of the company's involvement with NGOs and community organizations, developed by its managing director, Sophon Suphaphong. This involvement took three main forms. First, Bangchak encouraged local NGOs and community organizations to own and manage petrol stations as a form of ancillary income generation. Second, Bangchak had developed an accompanying retail store network which was organized on cooperative principles, and was used to distribute products made by community development projects. Third, Bangchak donated to NGOs and community associations, and sponsored radio and television programmes which advocated community-based development. Bangchak had hence become an example of efforts to develop a "social capitalism" which brought together business principles, social responsibility, and community development. The retired health official Dr Sem Pringpuangkaew argued that the movement to "save Bangchak" was "based on Buddha's principles of love, compassion, sympathy and neutrality." He insisted that "we are not against foreign investors and this has nothing to do with nationalism at all" (*BP*, 24 May 1998). Meechai Viravaidya added that "If we could do this with every major organization in the country we could create a social-capitalist regime and reduce the gap between the rich and poor" (*TN*, 1 Jun 1998).

This project drew sympathetic support from three groups. First, there were established senior social activists such as Prawase Wasi, who saw Bangchak as a marriage between capitalism and Thai-Buddhist values of mutual cooperation. Second, there were other business leaders, such as Khunying Niramol Suriyasat of Thai Toshiba and Narong Chokewattana of Sahapat (a leading Thai manufacturer of consumer goods), who also embraced this vision of social capitalism and sponsored such schemes. Third, there were sympathetic social activists and community workers including Khru Prateep, Chirmsak Pinthong, and Meechai Viravaidya; Meechai had promoted similar schemes through his Population and Community Development Association.

In the second LoI (November 1997), government proposed to complete the sale of Bangchak "by mid 1998." Sophon opposed this crash programme and the government backed away from this schedule. The issue reemerged after the privatization bill was passed in early 1999. Sophon argued that sale to foreigners "might harm the business of Bangchak which has good relations with Thai people" (*BP*, 28 May 1999). Narong Chokewattana formed a Bangchak Lovers Club which signed up 70,000 members, and claimed to receive questionnaire returns from over 300,000 people prepared to buy Bangchak shares.

In August 1999, Chamlong Srimuang, the former Bangkok mayor and leader of the Palang Tham Party, emerged from self-imposed political retirement to conduct a separate opposition to the Bangchak sale. He presented a petition of 30,000 signatures and argued that "Bangchak shows that it is possible to do business and benefit society at the same time." He added that this resistance was important because "the enemy's blade is at our throat" (*BP* and *TN*, 4 Aug 1999). The other group kept conspicuously separate from Chamlong, who soon after returned to his retirement.

Sophon successfully opposed a government plan to sell the full 32 percent stake to a single foreign strategic partner. However, when government continued with plans for an open sale, he resigned from the post of managing director of Bangchak and was elected to the new senate in March 2000, coming fourth among Bangkok's 264 candidates.[8]

In early 1999, the parliamentary opposition was swept into these dissident protests by the binary logic of parliamentary politics. In January 1999, the opposition called for a no-confidence debate, a parliamentary manoeuvre which had become a traditional annual event. In keeping with the usual form of such debates, the opposition started out with charges of corruption and maladministration. These attracted little public excitement. However, towards the end of the debate, Chaturon Chaisaeng entered a long and detailed critique of the government, and of finance minister Tarrin in particular, for being too obedient to the IMF, too accommodating to foreigners, and too negligent of Thailand's true economic interests. Chaturon's performance attracted considerable media interest. Recognizing the trend, the opposition leader, Chavalit Yongchaiyudh, elevated the relatively junior Chaturon to the powerful post of general secretary of the party. The opposition also launched two strategies to extend the impact of the no-confidence debate. First, it pursued the idea that the Democrat government had made "side letters" with the IMF beyond the LoIs, hinting that such secret agreements went further in opening up the economy to foreigners than the government dared admit in public. Ministers replied that the documents referred to by the opposition contained only some confidential technical data. Second, the opposition challenged that the LoIs were in effect treaties, and hence the prime minister and finance minister could be impeached for not following the constitution's provision that treaties must be approved by parliament. The Constitutional Court eventually ruled in the government's favour.

In March 1999, Chavalit embarked on an upcountry stump tour to spread the arguments which Chaturon had used in the no-confidence debate. He said that Tarrin "had allowed the United States to impose its will on the country," and that the privatization and bankruptcy bills would mean "the country would end up in foreign hands, with the people's dignity at stake." He accused the US of engineering his political downfall in November 1997 to make way for the pro-US Chuan government, and he vowed "never again to stand on the US side" (*BP*, 8 Mar 1999). At the end of March, Chavalit called for a "government of national salvation" (*TN*, 29 Mar 1999). Over the remainder of the year, opposition politicians occasionally made a fuss about the role of World Bank and IMF personnel in Thailand. In November 1999, the opposition launched another no-confidence motion. The formal motion not only switched focus from the usual corruption charges to the economic issue, but also went far beyond the usual rhetorical intensity of such motions:

The government is turning itself into a parliamentary dictatorship, acting in treason to the Royal aspiration of King Rama VII who had abdicated to benefit the populace. . . . This government has never cared for the poor. . . . It has allowed itself to become a puppet of foreign capital groups which aim to exploit the country, its people, and to drive local businesses to bankruptcy. It has also permitted foreign businesses to take advantage of local enterprises in an unjust way. . . . The country has fallen under foreign domination, like a victim of new colonialism. (*TN*, 13 Nov 1999)

NO DOGS STIRRING

These movements had produced some intense rhetoric, particularly over the six months (November 1998 to May 1999) which spanned the bankruptcy bill debate, the no-confidence debate, and the protests against privatization. But the popular response was very muted.

There was no truly major public demonstration on a nationalist theme. When the Assembly of the Poor staged a small protest against IMF policies outside the Bank of Thailand, staff came out to take photographs, claiming proudly that this was the first time the central bank had ever had a demo. At the height of the bankruptcy bill issue, a new organization was formed under the title of the Alliance for National Salvation (*phanthamit ku wikrit chat*).[9] When it held a rally in Sanam Luang, only 1,500 people turned up. At the height of the privatization issue, the state enterprise workers organized a march. Some forty other organizations joined in, including rural protesters acting in sympathy, and 1970s-era activists lodging a protest against the government's award of a decoration to one of the generals (Thanom) dislodged by the 1973 student revolt. Even with this broad support, the turnout was estimated around 1,500.

The Alliance for National Salvation erected some colourful billboards about the government "selling the country," but then quietly faded. Immediately after the campaign against the bankruptcy bill, one of the senators who had spearheaded the campaign was voted out of his executive post in the Chamber of Commerce for being too aggressive in public. The opposition New Aspiration Party, after espousing the nationalist theme, promptly began to fall apart. The party's renewed attack on the government's economic policy in the no-confidence debate of December

1999 was a total public failure. By early 2000, the economic-nationalist rhetoric had disappeared and the New Aspiration Party was struggling to hold the loyalty of competing factions.

The intensity of the proto-nationalist rhetoric in the political arena was not matched by an equivalent popular response. This impression is confirmed by a search for nationalist sentiments in popular culture. Very little shows up. The word "IMF" passed very quickly into popular usage. But its occasional appearances on demo posters and headbands were vastly outnumbered by its many adoptions as a synonym for "cheap" or "economical," especially on the signboards of roadside food stalls (*kwitieo IMF, khao kaeng IMF*). Promotions for everything from department stores to karaoke bars were "priced for the IMF era" (*rakha yuk IMF*) .

Popular songs traditionally comment on public affairs, and the crisis was quickly adopted in this medium. Again "IMF" appeared as an epithet for economy rather than threat. Songs such as "The Floating Baht" positioned the crisis as an affair of the rich city people, removed from the experience, control, and understanding of ordinary folk (Pasuk and Baker 1998, 325).

Television dramas also adjust quickly to popular attitudes in order to win share in a highly competitive market. Hence they can be read as a sensitive indicator of (urban) attitudes. At the outset of the crisis, one drama did play explicitly with nationalist themes. *Raya* imagined a fictitious episode from the Japanese occupation of Thailand during the Second World War. A small band of maquisards from the Seri Thai (Free Thai) movement confront a large contingent of the Japanese army on an island in the south. The maquisards speak about "saving the nation" (*ku chat*) in almost every scene. The drama ends with the defeat and wholesale slaughter of the Japanese by the small group of giant-killing heroes. However, this drama did not start a trend. Similar nationalist themes did not appear in later dramas, except perhaps in a rather subtle form. The crisis period saw increasing popularity of Thai-speaking foreigners (or foreign-looking *luk khrung*—Thai-farang mixes) as actors and actresses in television dramas. This was not new. But during the crisis, it became more common to cast them as buffoons and villains. A typical example was *Khu antarai dap khruang chon*, a caper story about a mysterious Arabian princess. The comedy was provided by one pair of "westerners" and another pair of "Japanese" playing secret agents of hopeless incompetence. The evil was provided by a Western-looking *luk khrung*, who displayed his villainy and

173

madness in the finale by systematically murdering the prettiest girls in the cast.

A much more noticeable theme of these dramas was the popularity of hospital scenes. Indeed, during the height of the crisis through 1998, it was hard to turn on the television during drama time without encountering a hospital scene on at least one channel. The saline drip had become the prop of choice. Typically in these scenes, relatives and girlfriends were seen gathered at the bedside of the young male hero whose wealth, lineage, talent, or charm was the focal point of the story. He had been lain low by a rare disease, car accident, or assassination attempt. The sentiment which these dramas were sharing with their audience was not resentment against some outside force, but the inward-looking experience of pain resulting from a mysterious and uncontrollable accident.

Similarly, movements of popular participation which emerged in response to the crisis tended to be focused inward rather than outward. In the early months of the crisis, there were calls for people to change dollars and other foreign currencies into baht, and for people to donate foreign currency or gold to help defray the national debt. In the "Thai Help Thai" campaign of this type, five thousand people joined a march through Bangkok in January 1998. This particular instance was orchestrated by the government and army. However, there were several others headed by popular monks. Luang Ta Maha Bua of Udon Thani, one of the country's most revered monks, started the *pha pa chuay chat* (donation to help the nation) which he described as "the final battle of my life." When the abbot travelled to Bangkok and delivered a fund-raising sermon in the largest city park, the event was organized by the city mayor, attended by royalty, and broadcast on TV. Mobile bank units were on hand to collect donations. The abbot presented the central bank with one billion baht in cash and 1.7 tonnes of gold. One of the more piquant images of this period featured the impeccably besuited governor of the central bank rather embarassedly accepting from this aged and berobed abbot a stacked pile of gold bars, in front of a barrage of press photographers and video crews.

Another abbot, Phra Phayom Kalayano, organized a smaller "National Emergency Fund" on similar lines. A Chumphon abbot arranged a "*pha pa IMF*" (IMF donation). Muslim leaders also took up the trend. A journalist, drawing a parallel with the defence of Ayutthaya in 1767, commented: "every time the country is in trouble, it is the ordinary people, not their so-

The central bank governor, the abbot, and the gold

called lords and masters, who have no hesitation in helping in what little way they can" (*TN*, 17 Jan 1998).

Others looked for help from beyond. Attendants at the Bangkok *lak muang* (city pillar) found that the numbers coming to pray for help or guidance increased ten times after the baht float.[10] Over the crisis, Princess Suphankalaya entered the pantheon of popular goddesses. According to the myth, she was the elder sister of the sixteenth- century King Naresuan who was taken hostage by the Burmese king and then killed by him while eight months pregnant with his child. This new cult was first promoted by a businesswoman who claimed the princess rescued her from bankruptcy. The businesswoman commissioned a historian to research the chronicles, and a popular romantic novelist to spin the tale. The historian tactfully wrote that the historical evidence was very sketchy and the violent death almost certainly imaginary. But an image of the princess appeared in the form of posters and votive objects which became very popular. The portrayal strikingly resembled the ideal entrant for beauty contests around the time of the businesswoman's youth. Suphankalaya's attraction seemed to arise from her connection to King Naresuan, who figures as a symbol of Thai nationalism, and from her violent death which traditionally invests a spirit with exceptional power.

NATION, NATIONALISM, NATIONALISM MILITANT

Why should nationalist sentiment have been so ineffective in politics, while so obviously powerful in other ways? This is a dangerous way to ask a question, since there is an infinity of possible answers to why something does not happen. But it is worth asking and speculating on—because, as the first section noted, non-Thais expected and feared a "nationalistic" reaction; because, as the third showed, some political actors aggressively propagated nationalist ideas; and because in other crisis-hit countries, some forms of nationalist sentiment were significantly more in evidence. Most obviously in Malaysia, Mahathir adopted an nationalistic stance, refused to accept IMF assistance, imposed capital controls in defiance of outside pressure, and postured aggressively on international public platforms. In Indonesia, even though the greater severity of the financial crisis increased the objective reasons for allowing foreign purchase of financial institutions, the government felt unable to take this step because of the fear of a political backlash. Meanwhile Korea is reckoned to have been the most nationalistic in reacting to the crisis. [11]

At a first level, Thailand's weak response to nationalistic ideas—at least in open, public politics—can perhaps be attributed to the lack of any mass nationalist movement in the country's history. By avoiding formal colonialism,[12] Thailand also avoided any experience of mass anti-colonial nationalism. A nationalist movement of sorts did arise between the 1920s and 1950s, and was heavily influenced by the international climate of anti-colonialism and claims to nationhood. But this movement in Thailand did not have to mobilize the mass of the people for a non-violent resistance movement or an anti-colonial war. The periods of serious threat to the existence of a modern Thai nation-state in the 1890s and 1940s were finessed by elite diplomacy not mass action. There was no popular struggle which left behind a history, mythology, heroes, heroic stories, or icons.

Partly as a corollary of this avoidance of anti-colonialism, Thailand also had little experience of *economic* nationalism. The period from the 1930s to the 1950s can be pictured as a time of economic nationalism when Thailand developed a limited form of state-led capitalism. But this picture needs to be qualified. This development was not underlain by any ideology of self-reliance, which was commonly a part of political nationalism in colonized states. There was a movement to regain fiscal autonomy by overriding the "unequal treaties" signed with the colonial powers in the 1850s. But there was no strong movement for tariff protection and state funding to build a national capitalism. Most of the state industries founded in this era were products of the wartime economy. In the 1950s and 1960s, Thailand adopted an idea of "development" but under US tutelage. There was no sign of the economic-nationalist ideologies which drove the ECLA phase in Latin America, or the socialist regimes in India and Indochina in this same era.

At a second level, perhaps there are severe limits on the idea of the nation as imagined in Thailand. The formation of the Thai nation-state was not the result of any popular movement. The boundaries of the Thai state were a residual of colonial expansion. The geography so enclosed included parts of at least three areas with distinctive histories and cultures (Ayutthaya-Siam; Lanna; Lao) and a periphery of transitional zones. The idea of Thailand as a nation was imposed over this jumbled geography by the rulers, often working explicitly in imitation of models they perceived in the West and in colonized states. The conception of national unity was built around one language, one history, one imagined ethnicity, one ritual centre—all imposed from above (Thongchai 1994).

Of course, many Western nation-states first originated in the imagination of a ruling elite. Yet in most cases such "lateral" or aristocratic nations (Smith 1995, 58–60) subsequently developed more of a mass character, particularly through the experience of the nationalist wars which characterized two centuries of European history.[13] These wars left behind a raft of stories, myths, memories, monuments, rituals, and other cultural products which are the fibre of popular nationalism in Europe through to the present. Thailand has not fought a nationalist war. Of course, the wars between Ayutthaya and Hongsawadi have been reimagined as a Thai-Burmese national conflict, but in reality these wars belong to a pre-national, dynastic era (Sunait 1994). Perhaps the closest modern Thailand has come to a nationalist military conflict is the short engagement with France in 1940–41. This is the event which is commemorated in Thailand's most important military memorial, the Victory Monument. But the incident was a short skirmish rather than an involving war. It is probably significant that the monument was designed by an Italian,[14] that it has no reference to Thai architectural style, that its association with a "victory" against the French is now almost wholly forgotten, and that it is being steadily buried by modern Bangkok.

This forgetting has been part of a broader forgetting of nationalist themes. Thailand's new rulers who set out to develop a Thai nationalism between the 1930s and the 1950s imagined a "Thai people" building a modern nation-state in order to participate in the modern, international world. This period saw the production of monuments, symbols, songs, and myths which dramatized a history in which the monarchy was a part rather than the whole, and a future in which the major themes were democracy and progress (Reynolds 1991). But over the past generation, there has been a strenuous effort to forget this period and its ideas, heroes, and cultural products.[15] This effort has been a joint venture between two very different political agendas. On the one hand, the revival of the monarchy since the 1950s has elevated the monarch as the central symbol of the nation to the exclusion of almost anything else. On the other hand, the democracy movement, reacting against the association of nationalism with military dictatorship, has tended to ignore this earlier phase of democratic development in the 1930s, and to erase any connections between this period and later (post-1973) history.[16]

The fate of the Democracy Monument, the most impressive and enduring memorial of the nationalist period, illustrates the result of these separate but strangely allied forces. In royalist history, the commemoration of Thailand's 1932 transition towards democracy has been transferred away from this monument to King Prajadhiphok's statue at the new parliament (Thongchai 1999). In royal pageantry, the Democracy Monument has become an unfortunate but manageable intrusion on an avenue regularly used for royal display. In radical history and pageantry, the monument has been repositioned as part of the movement against military dictatorship dating from 1973. Both royals and radicals suppress the association of the monument with the attempt to manufacture a mass, popular nationalism between the 1930s and 1950s.

There is of course a strong idea of a Thai nation, bound up in particular with the monarchy, the language, and the state boundaries. But there is little *militant history*—about war or popular movements—to act as a foundation for contemporary militancy on any popular scale.[17]

The early stages of the crisis provoked two historical comparisons. The first was to the defeat of Ayutthaya by the Burmese in 1767. The conventional shorthand for this event, *sia krung* (the fall of the city), lent itself easily to metaphors of an urban economic crisis. The second reference was to the period of colonial threats to Siam's existence in the 1890s. Both references tended to be interpreted as indicating a need for strong *leadership* to survive the crisis, rather than any broader popular action. In official history, Thailand lost to Burma in 1767 because of the weakness of king and aristocracy, and revived under the new leadership of Taksin and Rama I. The crisis of the 1890s was overcome by King Chulalongkorn and his entourage. In addition, the 1890s reference provided support for a modern, economic form of Thailand's traditional bamboo diplomacy. In popular history, Thailand survived the colonial threat by modernizing its administration to counter colonial claims to impose rule as part of a civilizing or modernizing mission. By analogy, Thailand would have to confront the economic crisis by self-reform, rather than resistance.[18]

SAVING THE ELEPHANT

In Thailand, the elephant is a sacred beast in a very special way. It figures in the religious culture—in the Buddha's birth story, in the image of the Hindu god Ganesh, and in many Jataka tales. It figures too in royal history as military equipment, parade transport, and as the magical protector of the realm, the white elephant. But the elephant today is much more than a religious and royal icon. It is a working animal and a popular symbol. Elephants are loved for their combination of power and vulnerability. In a curious way, the nation's experience of the crisis became transferred onto the popular symbol of the elephant.

After the crisis hit, elephants were in the news a lot. A glossy coffee-table book about elephants appeared. At least three art exhibitions were held on elephant themes. Another exhibition featured art *by* elephants—the inspiration of a Russian pop artist who called the style "dumbolism." The prime minister's wife in late 1997 went everywhere clutching an elephant doll rigged out in a wedding dress, diamond pendant, and ear-rings. The mascot chosen for the Bangkok Asian Games in 1998 was an elephant named Chaiyo, the Thai cheer word.

The elephant also conveyed important public messages. While nobody had much success in predicting the crisis, close observers of elephants in mid 1997 should have twigged that something was amiss. In the month before the baht float and the slide to disaster, an elephant ran amok and hurt a young boy in a Samut Prakan housing estate; another in Phayao

The prime minister's wife and mascot

killed his own mahout and fled into the forest; two were possibly poisoned by pineapple growers in Prachuab; one died after having a leg broken by a speeding car in Nakhon Pathom; and another was rammed by a car in Rangsit. Things were going wrong.

We know now that the worst impact of the crisis was through early 1998. The economy was shrinking at a rate of 12 or 13 percent a year. Some two million lost their jobs. The numbers in severe poverty shot up by a fifth. The public reaction to all of this was deceptively quiet. No major riots. No mass demonstrations. No disastrous violence. Of course, in the background there was a gradual disintegration. More drugs. More gunmen. More violence inside families. More petty crime. More summary killings. More suicides and mental distress. More children abandoned. But this huge social hurt was somehow disguised. Unless you paid attention to elephants.

Through this peak period of the crisis, there was an unusually large number of stories about elephants in trouble. In March 1998, two were shot and burned by pineapple planters in Kanchanaburi. Another fell off a cliff in the forest divided by the Yadana pipeline. In April, eight died mysteriously in Chiang Mai, probably as a result of rivalry among tourist operators. In May in Surin, a baby elephant died from eating pesticide-laced grass, and an adult died probably from starvation. In Prachuab, one elephant entertaining tourists died falling down a hill. Another was shot in the leg by a poacher. In October another was rammed by a car in Chonburi. In early 1999, fourteen were mistreated by tour operators in Phrae; one was shot and wounded by a hunter in Chachoengsao; and a pregnant female died in Kanchanaburi after being hit by a speeding train.[19]

The epicentre of the crisis was Bangkok, and through mid 1998 the media focused on the plight of elephants in the city. Like everyone else, the elephants suffered from unemployment. Like everyone else, they were forced to make a living in desperate and risky ways—in the elephants' case, by tramping the city streets to solicit alms. Tipped into this unnatural environment, they suffered. They were hit by cars and trucks, harassed by officials, fed amphetamines to keep awake at night. In July 1998, one fell into a city drain and died agonizingly on live TV after failed attempts to lift him out with a crane.

Towards year end, this theme was used as the plot line for a whisky ad. A young Adonis drinking in a bar for the rich and beautiful is suddenly drawn to the plight of an elephant mother and child in the crush of nighttime

Elephant in crisis

traffic. He rushes out and hands over not just all his money, but his Rolex-style watch which had been such a symbol of affluence in the boom. Two of the elephants killed in falls into Bangkok's subterranean infrastructure happened to be named Pang Thong Kham (gold) and Plai Setthi (millionaire). The elephant had come to represent not just the shock of unemployment, but the collapse of dreams of wealth, the dethronement of the god of money.

Elephants also predicted the timing of recovery from crisis. The Thai government and IMF had been forecasting recovery "within six months" since the crisis began. They had long since lost any credibility. But elephants were another matter. Again the message came in an ad, this time for a beer. The ad appeared first in March 1999. Though the statistics were unknown at the time, this was exactly the point when GDP, exports, and investment showed the first signs of an upturn. Unlike in the whisky ad, the elephant is not oppressed and threatened, but upbeat and resurgent. He is shown coming through the elephant gate of the ancient city of Ayutthaya, whose destruction in 1767 had been evoked many times as a metaphor of the current crisis. He is clad in finery, bathed in sunlight, surrounded by traditional dancers and fluttering pennants, trunk aloft, and preceded by songs-for-life star Ad Carabao singing a jubilant anthem and prancing in obvious triumph. Witnessing this display of national resurgence, groups of Japanese and westerners smile and raise their glasses in gestures of international confidence from East and West. Over the three months after this ad's appearance, the stock market index doubled.

In February 2000, the Board of Investment held a fair portrayed as a crisis-ending festival. Inevitably the mascot was an elephant, decked out in a Superman-style cloak, and a Japanese robot-style helmet—the modern magic from West and East required to achieve recovery.

But the crisis was not fully over, and elephant stories continued to punctuate the stumbling recovery. In August–September 1999, confidence slumped over reports of soaring bad loans, mismanagement, and possible cronyism in the government's Krung Thai Bank. Simultaneously, an elephant contracted on logging operations across the Burmese border stepped on a land mine which blew away her left foreleg. For several weeks, press and TV news reports were shared between ministers scrambling to manage the Krung Thai scandal, and veterinarians struggling to save the injured Motala. Crowds flocked to the elephant hospital. Donations poured in. The surgery was filmed live from a discreet distance. Medical progress reports were issued daily. Foreign help was sought for the prosthesis. A TV reporter broke down in mid transmission and begged viewers to pray for Motala's recovery. Reports came in of four other elephants injured by landmines at the Burmese border. The king suggested rehabilitated forests should be developed as elephant sanctuaries. As Motala slowly recovered, the Krung Thai story also faded from the headlines.

The Motala affair set off competition among NGOs and wildlife organizations to raise donations for elephants in distress. Over the following weeks the media were dominated by stories of the disputes between debtors and creditors to cooperate on debt restructuring, and stories of the squabbles between charitable organizations over elephants.

The issue of removing elephants from Bangkok's streets had been debated several times, without result. But in February 2000, an elephant which had only just arrived in the city and was probably upset by the traffic, went on a stampede along the city centre's main highways, pursued by squads of helpless policemen. The authorities decided that the forty or so elephants in the city must be forcibly removed. Headlines screamed, "National

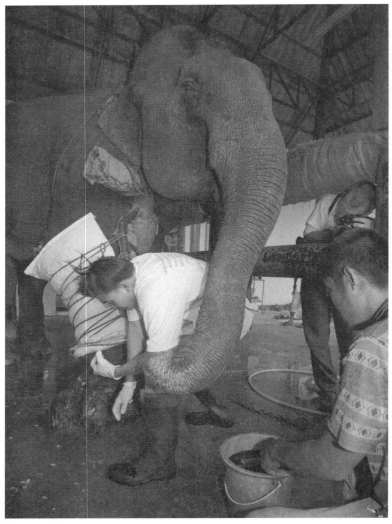

Motala undergoes pre-op

Symbol Sent Into Exile." TV talk shows discussed the issue with passion. Bangkok shivered at reports of elephants massing in Surin to invade the city in protest at the ban.[20] In the four days following the decision, the stock market index dropped by 20 percent.

ELEPHANTISM

Obviously much of the above account is fanciful and light-hearted. But there is also a serious suggestion. Perhaps the public media have an ability to express public sentiments which are not at all articulate.[21] The current problems of the elephant—exploitation by tourist operators, distress in the inappropriate environment of the city, clashes with farmers—are not new. They have existed since the 1988–89 logging ban put many out of work, and since the shrinkage of the forests deprived many of a natural habitat. The surge of elephant disaster stories during the crisis did not reflect a change among elephants but among those writing and reading the stories.

The elephant in Thailand has become a focus of popular emotions in an unusual way. It is not now part of official state iconography, although elephants (and especially the white elephant) are common in royal symbolism. It is not a specifically Thai national symbol, as other countries in the region treat the elephant in a similar way. It is much more intimate and accessible than most iconic material because of the real presence of actual beasts. Although the elephant has an aristocratic history as a ceremonial and military mount, its role in recent decades has been as a working animal. In the crisis the elephant became a focus for expressing emotions shared among people without invoking narratives about the nation or other imposed structures.

Three qualities appear to have qualified the elephant to play this role in the specific context of the crisis. First, the elephant is a reminder of the past and more specifically of a non-urban past and a natural environment—before the rise of the modern city where the crisis arose. Second, it is a working animal associated with the peripheral areas of the country, and with poor, peripheral communities (Kui, Suay) who specialize as mahouts. These migrant elephants and their keepers were in a similar position as the migrant rural workers who in the end bore the brunt of the urban crisis. Third, the elephant has become displaced and vulnerable in the modern world. Like the country itself, and like many individuals whose jobs or businesses

Elephant demo at Victory Monument

disappeared, elephants seemed powerless in the face of modernity, despite their great physical strength and their glorious history.

After the authorities resolved to ban elephants from city streets, the mahouts protested by marching thirteen elephants through the city centre. The procession recalled old royal and military parades. But in this case the procession was a protest about the right to livelihood. In one of many anguished editorials about the taxis, drains, mines, and pesticides inflicting damage on elephants, the writer advised:

How we respond to the responsibility of taking care of nature's gifts is an indication of our humanity. In the process of economic and social recovery, we must not lose sight of ourselves or what defines us—as human beings and as Thais. (*TN*, 8 Jan 1998)

In one incident, the nationalist undertones in the elephant stories came more clearly to the surface. In early 1998, reports trickled in about six Thai elephants which had gone to work in Indonesia. One had already died. The others were being mistreated and were increasingly at risk as Indonesia's crisis worsened. As months passed, the story became darker. The Thai mahouts had been tricked, short-changed, and sent home early. The deal had been set up by shady middlemen and "politicians." In returning the tusks of the dead beast, the Indonesians had tried to substitute a smaller pair. The story took on the shape of tales from the world of human trafficking—initial promises of wealth giving way to trickery, exploitation, and slavery.

A campaign was launched to bring these "Thai" elephants home. Groups got up petitions. The Prime Minister's Office, zoo organization, Foreign Ministry, and Commerce Ministry became involved. Negotiations took place at government-to-government level. The Indonesians refused to return the elephants. Emotions rose. Street demonstrations demanded that the Thai government do something. Popular outcry over this incident forced the government to kill a deal with China to exchange twelve Thai elephants for four pandas, two snow leopards, and a yak. Activists threatened to bring eighty tuskers into the city to "storm Government House" to enforce their demand (*TN*, 28 Nov 1998). This was perhaps the biggest threat of public disorder throughout the period of the crisis. The call to "bring the Thai elephants home" evoked more popular nationalist sentiment than all of the protests against the IMF, "selling the country," and the bankruptcy bills.

The five elephants were finally shipped back from Indonesia on the very last day of 1998, the year of economic disaster. They were welcomed at Phuket by the provincial governor, the local MP, and a flag-waving crowd. Journalists reported that the beasts were "thin and some with wounds, looking weary." One was perceived to have "tears in his eyes." As a group they trumpeted to show their "joy of being home" (*TN*, 31 Dec 1998; *BP*, 17 Jan 1999).

CONCLUSION

In the aftermath of the cold war, nationalism has become one of the fixations of Western political theorizing. Among the American right wing, this reflects a fear of resistance to US domination as is totally explicit in Samuel Huntington's *Clash of Civilizations* (1997). In Europe, the concern is more complex. The dissolution of the Eastern Bloc has led immediately to a range of nationalist wars which look horribly similar to conflicts which were smothered when the bloc was formed eighty years earlier. Some Western European states have seen the rise of nationalist parties whose slogans and policies echo those of fascism half a century earlier. European political thinkers have engaged in a passionate debate over the nature of this neonationalism—is it a reversion to permanent "primordial" sentiments, or is it a new construction provoked by globalization?

The outbreak of the Asian crisis provoked fears of a resurgence of Asian nationalism. The incident cited in the first section of this essay is only one example. The Hong Kong-based Political and Economic Research Consultancy began to provide regular reports on the levels of nationalism in the crisis-hit countries as part of its monitoring services for multinational firms. In part this sensitivity was a simple perception that political nationalism was the only potential barrier against economic penetration. But there was a more complex side. At the same time, there was a resurgence of frankly colonial attitudes, possibly triggered by relief at the collapse of the Asian boom with its vocabulary of magic (miracles) and animal aggression (tigers, dragons). Nationalism and colonialism are a yoked pair.

In the event, the fear of nationalism proved almost totally ungrounded in Thailand. Of course there was resistance to the transfers of power and ownership implied by the IMF's agenda of financial restructuring, market liberalization, and privatization. But that was business.[22] The attempts to organize this resistance publicly around a nationalist theme went nowhere. The loose coalition which formed in early 1998 broke up into three groups with separate agendas. Debtor entrepreneurs rallied round the defense of domestic capital. Conservative idealists imagined a new form of "social capitalism." Public sector workers argued for the retention of public capital. Opposition politicians toyed with the nationalist theme, but discovered that it drew little in terms of popular support and did nothing to hold the opposition together. Throughout the crisis, there was no single nationalist demonstration of any weight, no pebble tossed in anger at a foreign bank or fast food store.[23]

The gap between the foreign expectations of a nationalist resurgence and the subsequent reality is largely a reflection of the West's current concern about nationalism nearer home. But it also reveals something about the Thai concept of the nation. Since the late nineteenth century, the Thai elite had worked hard at building a Thai nation and nationalism by drawing on the best available examples from the outside world—flag, anthem, national rituals, national history, a traditional enemy (Burma), language, ethnicity, and especially the institution of monarchy and its own powerful array of symbols, rituals, and stories. But this nationalism proved difficult to mobilize to meet the country's toughest modern crisis. Perhaps this is because this nationalism was very much an elite creation. Perhaps the suppression (by both royalist and radical) of the nationalist interlude from the 1930s to the 1950s has damaged nationalism's political utility. Perhaps Thailand has simply not experienced anything like the unification movements, anti-colonial movements, or national wars which elsewhere have translated elite nationalism into a *nationalism militant* with a popular history, popular heroes, and wider popular appeal. Perhaps the elite has been careful to reserve nationalism as an elite property, and not to let it loose for mass use in fear of the dangerous consequences.

Perhaps in the absence of such a militant tradition, the reaction to the crisis turned inward rather than outward. Certainly this was true at the level of articulate elite expression. The king's famous speech of December 1997 emphasized *self*-sufficiency and *self*-reliance. Prawase Wasi called for a "war of national salvation" but then defined that war as campaigns of *self*-awareness, mental readjustment, and reform of school, *wat,* and local community. In radical debate, the two dominant themes were again a strengthening of *local* communities as a phalanx of resistance to globalism, and alternatively, involvement in *transnational* attempts to reform the one-dimensional, finance-based, neoliberal interpretation of globalization. In this radical debate, the nation hardly featured as a domain of struggle.[24]

Perhaps too this inward-looking trend was even stronger at the level of popular culture, as seen in the occasional press fads over such topics as suicide, in the television dramas' fascination with the hospital bedside, in the manufacture of new historical deities, in the emotions excited over an oil refinery, in the extraordinary passion for donating one's bangles to the central bank, and in the surge of *elephantism*.

NOTES

1. This last point is important. Consider the likely reaction to such an article appearing prominently in the equivalent newspaper in Malaysia, Singapore, or India.

2. This is a wonderful genre. A recent example (*TN*, 2 Apr 2000) talked about the Thais' "psychological and cultural problems rising from a misplaced ethnocentrism. To deal with them today, it would require a 20-year countrywide deprogramming by a full team of anthropologists and psychologists."

3. This editorial brief was sent to us to solicit our help with the story. The journalists rebelled against the brief and wrote a fairly conventional account of the financial bubble. The editorial side then displayed its less-than-adequate knowledge of Asia by misspelling the Thai currency in the front-cover headline: "From Bhat to Worse" (*Time*, 25 Aug 1997).

4. This was the general theme of businessmen attending the TDRI's year-end seminar in Pattaya in December 1997.

5. Interestingly the *Nation's* edited transcript of this TV interview omitted this bit.

6. The crucial vote fell 127-44 with twelve abstentions. The main amendment reduced the time a convicted bankrupt was debarred from business from ten years to five.

7. Piyasawasti Amaranand, head of the National Energy Planning Office, was especially fond of arguing that privatization was a financial necessity and a commitment to the IMF, without apparently realizing the political implications.

8. Meechai Viravaidya was also among the eighteen elected to the new senate from Bangkok.

9. For its logo, the Alliance chose an outline map of the country (cf. Thongchai 1994, ch. 7) surrounded by four linked hands.

10. Thanks to Paritta Chalermpow Koanantakool, who was researching on the city pillar, for this information.

11. The Hong Kong-based Political and Economic Risk Consultancy ranked the Asia-crisis countries in order of "scores for nationalism" as follows: Korea, India, Vietnam, China, Indonesia, Malaysia, Thailand, Taiwan, Japan, Hong Kong, Philippines, Singapore (*TN*, 22 Feb 1999).

12. Of course many like to describe Siam's unconventional accommodation with the colonial powers as "semi-colonialism." But by the same token, the response was "semi-nationalism," with mass militancy part of the missing half.

13. The European debate on nationalism tends to ignore the importance of war for developing the mass base and the mass mythology of nationalism. But an outsider visiting contemporary Europe is struck by how much popular culture and official nationalism draw on the great nationalist wars of the twentieth century.

14. Corrado Feroci, better known by his given Thai name of Silpa Bhirasri.

15. Terwiel (in Reynolds 1991, 145) comments how the nationalism of the 1930s now has to be rediscovered by historians.

16. "I believe that it is . . . because it is associated with the ideology of militarists, that nationalism is seen by most Thai academics as a concept of limited interpretative value in Thai language historiography" (Reynolds 1999, 263).

17. The national mythology has of course been filled with war stories, but these are almost exclusively about the exploits of kings, particularly their feats of single-handed combat against the Burmese. The exception is perhaps the story of the resistance of the Bang Rachan village against the Burmese in 1767. But this is also a construction in the royal chronicles and its main purpose is to emphasize loyalty to the throne. The Bang Rachan story was used by the electricity generating authority (EGAT) as the theme for an ad intended to rouse the Thai people to face the crisis.

18. This was the theme of the presidential address by Dr Vichit Suraphongchai at a seminar in December 1997 to commemorate the centenary of King Rama V's visit to Europe. Globalization, argued Vichit, is big, accelerating, irresistible. Just as King Chulalongkorn recognized the power of Europe and modernized Siam for survival, so Thailand today must recognize the powerful forces of globalization and reform internally to cope with them. "How capable and ready are our leaders," Vichit asked, "to implement the changes necessary to prepare Thailand for the future?" In 1999 Vichit became chairman of the Siam Commercial Bank.

19. The World Wildlife Fund estimates that Thailand has 2,705 domesticated elephants and 1,975 in the wild. These casualties represent a significant percentage of this population.

20. These reports seem to have been manufactured by city fears. The mahouts (by now equipped with a formal organization and well on their way to "civil society") denied any such plan.

21. Possibly another non-articulate response to the crisis was youth culture's tilt towards Japan. Of course, such fashions tend to go in cycles. Yet it is striking that in the mid 1990s, Bangkok's youth culture was largely fascinated with Western materials—alternative music, jeans, rap, MTV, and especially Hollywood movies. But the crisis period saw a big change. The fashionable clothes became the tubular sweaters, hooped designs, spaghetti straps, and platform soles already popular in Japan. Many new music groups were closely modelled on Japanese originals. Youth-oriented TV magazine programmes adopted a Japanese look and style. And dyed hair became de rigeur.

22. Prachai kept up his nationalist rhetoric to oppose bankruptcy proceedings. When he finally lost, he shrugged and called the fight "a boxing match" in which victory was the goal and any strategy permissible.

23. The US opposition against Supachai Panitchapakdi's bid to head the WTO evoked possibly the strongest public reaction, but this was focused solely against the US for being a "bad friend." On the eve of Finance Minister Tarrin's first visit to Washington to bargain with the IMF, Witayakon Chiangkun lamented on a TV talk show that a good placard-waving demo outside a foreign bank would significantly strengthen the minister's bargaining hand.

24. The magazine *Withithat* illustrates this division, with its two main writers, Yuk Si-ariya and Phitthaya Wongkun, espousing respectively the internationalist and community-retreat tendencies.

WALKING BACKWARDS INTO A *KHLONG:*[1] THINKING SOCIAL ALTERNATIVES

Being a tiger is not important. What is important is to have enough to eat and to live; and to have an economy which provides enough to eat and live. Having enough to eat and to live means supporting oneself to have enough for oneself . . .

I have said before that this sufficiency does not mean that each household has to produce its own food, weave its own cloth. That is too much. But within a village or district, there must be a certain amount of self-sufficiency. Anything which can be produced beyond local need can be sold, but maybe not sold too far away, to minimize transport costs . . .

If we can change back to a self-sufficient economy, not completely, even not as much as half, perhaps just a quarter, we can survive . . .

But people who like the modern economy may not agree. It's like walking backwards into a *khlong*. We have to live carefully and we have to go back to do things which are not complicated and which do not use elaborate, expensive equipment. We need to move backwards in order to move forwards. If we don't act like this, the solution to this crisis will be difficult.

H.M. King Bhumibol Adulyadej
4 December 1997

Since the early 1980s, ideas about the importance of locality and community have been proposed in opposition to the emphasis on growth and urbanization. This "localism discourse" has largely been ignored by mainstream economists and social scientists. If it is addressed at all, it is

193

seen in the context of Luddism, allotment movements, Amish communities, Ranters, and Shakers—futile attempts to obstruct history's march to modernism in the name of backward-looking rural utopianism.

Yet this discourse, and in particular some of its keywords—locality (*thongthin*), community (*chumchon*), self-reliance (*phung ton eng*), self-sufficiency (*pho yu pho kin*)—achieved considerable prominence in the context of the crisis. A number of intellectuals and social commentators associated with this discourse were very vocal. Moreover, the spread of the discourse was not limited to academics and public intellectuals.

The king's birthday speech in December 1997 gave the discourse new legitimacy. The speech was delivered (on television) at an especially bewildering stage of the crisis—the sort of time when the king has traditionally provided public guidance. The speech linked the crisis, the principle of self-sufficiency, and the idea of going back to a simpler economy. The importance of this message was immediately recognized. The press recounted the key sections of the speech at much greater length than normal. Extracts were constantly rerun as inter-programme fillers on television and radio. Quotations appeared on billboards outside government offices. The whole speech was quickly printed and distributed—the manual for the Great Leap Backwards. While the speech had ranged over many topics, these replays focused on the short passage in the speech about self-sufficiency (see above).

Even more striking was the reception, especially in rural Thailand. Anyone visiting villages in early 1998 could not avoid being struck by the frequency with which key words and phrases from the speech would appear in conversations with farmers—particularly *pho yu pho kin* (enough to eat and live—self-sufficiency) and *thritsadi mai* or "new theory," which became the shorthand reference to the king's ideas. Partly of course this reflects the great respect for the king and the success of the official effort at dissemination. But not every phrase uttered by the king is so readily adopted. Clearly these words had struck a chord. Or, to put it another way, the speech reflected the king's sensitivity to ideas and sentiments circulating in rural society. Moreover, this rural response cannot be simply attributed to the crisis. At this stage, farmers were relatively insulated as the 1997 harvest had been good, and the baht price of rice had soared to record levels (see pp. 91–2). The rural interest in self-sufficiency and self-reliance had emerged during the preceding boom which had increased social dislocation and social division.

Taking its lead from the king, the Ministry of the Interior adopted the principle of self-sufficiency and self-reliance (Ministry of the Interior 1998). In early 1998, the ministry launched into a major programme to educate its own personnel on the meaning of the principle and its application. A large slice of the ministry's budget was earmarked for programmes to promote self-sufficiency and self-reliance to counter the impact of the economic crisis. The team assembled to work on this project was intriguing. Alongside the ministry officials were some veterans of the coup-making Young Turk military group and some former student radicals who had spent time in the jungle with the Communist Party of Thailand.

The Royal Thai Army also adopted the policy, and allocated plots of land within military establishments for growing crops for military consumption. To publicize this project, the army commander appeared on television broadcasting rice seed into a flooded paddy field (he wore wellington boots).

Other organizations fell in with the trend. The Democrat Party, now at the head of the ruling cabinet coalition, officially committed itself to the policy—though not without assuring everyone that it would continue to pursue export-led growth in the "upper economy" while promoting self-sufficiency in the "lower economy" (*BP*, 19 Apr 1998). Other parties, including New Aspiration, began to promote rural projects based on the self-reliance ideal as part of their campaigns to build rural support. At least three television programmes appeared devoted to propagating the idea and showcasing successful local examples. Several leading monks publicly espoused the principle. The attempt to domesticate and propagate the idea of "good governance," promoted by the World Bank, was transformed by Thai NGOs into a restatement of the ideas of locality, community, and self-reliance (see pp. 124–6).

The "localism discourse" had emerged from the late 1970s, and by a decade later was running under the title of *watthanatham chumchon* or "community culture." The two words were significant. The discourse made the *community* central both as a source of value and as a political construct. The discourse made *culture* (rather than economics, politics, or whatever) the area of contestation between the community and outside forces (state, capitalism). Two quotations from Chatthip Nartsupha's (1991) review of the discourse give the main flavour. In the first, he is summarizing Bamrung Bunpanya, and in the second, Prawase Wasi.

> The village culture is independent of the middle class and upper class culture. It is related to a way of life which is in close touch with nature, and relies on the use of physical labour; a community of kinship and a village community. It is "the oldest form of society." No matter what outside circumstances have been and how they have changed, the essence of a village or a community, its economic, social and cultural independence has remained for hundreds of years. The village community thus has its own independent belief systems and way of development. However this line of economic development that Thailand follows is an imported idea, which is linked to internal state power. This is, namely, the capitalist way of development geared to supply the needs of Westerners. We are at a disadvantage in this kind of development. The more development there is, the poorer we are. Those who get rich, of whom there are few, apart from the Westerners, are those who serve the Westerners. . . . The direction of development should be changed so that the villagers rely on themselves as they had done in the past. They must begin by being independent minded and conscious of their own identity. (121)

> The rural communities must be strengthened [through] a subsistence mode of production of integrated agriculture; economic self-reliance and the eradication of external dependence; communal life, the institutions of family and *wat*, and a common culture of mutual aid. This rural community will develop its knowledge and expertise from original knowledge which is called "popular wisdom" . . . and combine it with international knowledge. . . . without a moral and ethical base, there can be no real development for the people, because human beings will promote themselves, be selfish, have *kilesa* (vices) and *tanha* (desires), which will overshadow wisdom and other virtues. (124–5)

The global-local theme has not been limited to Thailand but has become an international debate. This paper examines how some of the main propositions of this localism discourse developed in Thailand in the context of the economic crisis. The paper is divided into sections examining specific themes within the debate, namely: the role of Buddhist values relating to economic issues; the ethical values summarized in the concept of community; the importance of agriculture; and the political role of culture. At the end, we look briefly at the main objections raised against the discourse and consider some possible impact on Thailand beyond the crisis.

BUDDHIST ECONOMICS

> In truth, if we look from another angle, maybe it's lucky that this failure and this crisis make us take a good look at ourselves.
>
> P. A. Payutto, 19 December 1997

The idea that the Buddhist conception of moderation could serve as a counter to the principle of acquisitiveness at the heart of market economics has been around for a long time. However, the idea gained greater popularity and precision against the background of rapid growth and associated social change from the mid 1980s onwards.

In 1988, the leading Buddhist scholar, P. A. Payutto (Phrathammapidok) published a small book on *Buddhist Economics* and lectured several times on the topic over the next few years. Payutto made the whole concept of Buddhist economics more precise in three important ways. First, he related the major propositions (about moderation, wealth, work, acquisition, and the role of government) back to scriptural references. Second, he positioned his Buddhist economics as a direct criticism of market economics. He contended that "economics has become a narrow and rarefied discipline; an isolated, almost stunted, body of knowledge, having little to do with other disciplines or human activities" (Phrathammapidok 1992, 15–6). From a Buddhist view, economics could not be separated from an ethical stance, a view of nature, and a concept of society. By using the concept of "well-being," he adjusted what he saw as the central motor of market economics: "in contrast to the classical economic equation of maximum consumption leading to maximum satisfaction, we have moderate, or wise consumption, leading to well-being" (Phrathammapidok 1992, 69).

Payutto himself used this basis to criticize the rapid growth of materialism and a consumer society in the boom-and-bubble economy. However, others were more interested in the implications for environment and agriculture. Around this same period, several *achan* incorporated Buddhist economics as a part of courses on development, environment, and agricultural

197

economics—particularly Aphichai Phantasen at Thammasat. For a broader public, Prawase Wasi had already become an important popularizer of Buddhist concepts applied to everyday life. In the early 1990s, he brought together two ideas: first, the importance of reviving agriculture as it remained the economic base of the majority of people (on which more below); and second, the importance of Buddhism and especially the Buddhist concept of moderation for constraining materialism. Out of this juncture came *Phutthakasetakam* or Buddhist agriculture. As Aphichai (1996, 362) explained Prawase's idea, "Briefly and simply, it means agriculture for self-reliance, meeting the basic human needs through a way of production and a way of life which match together. Production is related to nature and religious principle."

This growing interest on the relationship between Buddhism and economics had two important consequences. First, it provided a base for criticism of the destructive impact of economic growth on the environment and on local communities. Second, it helped to popularize two concepts— self-sufficiency (*pho yu pho kin*) and self-reliance (*phung ton eng*). Self-sufficiency summarized the Buddhist concept of moderation as an antidote to acquisitiveness. Self-reliance conveyed both an idea of insurance against the dangers of market exposure, and also an idea of personal freedom. As Aphichai (1996, 364) stated, "Among the principles of Buddhist agriculture, self-reliance is the very heart, because it is an important principle which helps farmers to determine their own way of life."

Is this just academic debate? Talking to northeastern farmers in mid 1998, we were struck how often they themselves referred to the concepts of self-sufficiency and self-reliance without any prompting. Their thinking was very practical. Many were aware that in recent years their usage of cash had increased. During the boom, their cash income had grown with proceeds from migrant labour and ancillary industries. In parallel, cash outlays on both farming inputs and consumer goods had grown. With the crisis now squeezing their cash position—through the decline in migrant labour opportunities, and the rise of input prices—they were aware of the need to reduce cash outlays. Several mentioned the electricity bill, which had not existed before the coming of an electricity connection, but which was now a regular monthly event. Plans to increase local self-reliance, either at the household or community level, were appealing.

But in the crisis, the meaning of self-reliance was set for expansion beyond its application to the household or community. In a talk delivered just a week after the king's speech and hence in the same context of bewilderment, Payutto (Phrathammapitok 1998, 3–4) reflected on the crisis:

When we study the reasons which made us fail . . . did it arise from misguidedly developing the country in a way which relied too much on the outside? We did not try to stand on our own. We were rich because we borrowed money to use, happy because we borrowed others' property to enjoy.

This is the lesson. We should not lose our way again. Don't get lost playing around in the world on a stage set by others. . . . Don't get lost in free trade, the globalized financial system, and false freedom. In the end we get pulled into the whirlpool of freedom. But deep down it means becoming a slave. Because we mis-developed the country towards consumerism, we ended up slave of the countries which produce, slave of the countries which have more financial strength, because the principle is that big money sucks up little money.

The journal *Withithat* extracted the word "slave" as theme for a special issue on the crisis and its impact on the locality (Phitthaya 1998a). In various different ways, the contributors to this volume—and to many other forums—attributed the crisis to the *nation's* over-reliance on things from outside—capital, consumer goods, ideas, technology.

Through early 1998, Prawase Wasi expounded this theme in a series of speeches and seminar presentations which attracted the interest of a press sensitive to the popular need for guidance. One of Prawase's major themes was that the Buddhist search for moderation was threatened by mental subjection to the materialism learnt from the West. The pursuit of self-sufficiency and self-reliance were thus important at a personal level, community level, and national level.

COMMUNITY AS BASE

> We were like the Royal Plaza Hotel which was heavy at the top and shaky at the bottom [this Korat hotel collapsed because structural pillars had been removed].
>
> Prawase Wasi, March 1998

In many parts of the world, the idea of strengthening local communities as a counterweight to globalization arose in counterpoint to the enthusiasm for globalization from the early 1980s onwards. Just three points can be noted about the development of this idea in Thailand before the crisis. First, the discourse on the importance of community culture became a rallying point for NGOs and local activists in the late 1980s and early 1990s. Second, the main proposition was that to resist the destructive forces of globalization and outward-oriented development, communities needed to look inwards and strengthen their own foundations of resources and culture. Third, the discourse was criticized from many angles but particularly for imagining and idealizing a community which had possibly never existed, or had been much less benign, or had been superceded by the modernizations of the last half-century.

In the context of the crisis, the idea of the community was developed most subtly and most effectively by Saneh Chamarik. His authority to speak on the issue was enhanced by the fact that he had retired from academe to a northeastern village where he founded a school and project to put the discourse into practice.

Saneh expanded the community discourse in several important ways. First, he broadened the importance of looking inwards for a basis to resist the destructive forces of globalization. The real crisis, he argued, was not the short-term financial bust but the longer-term commitment to a Western-oriented, export-oriented growth which placed the Thai economy ever more at the mercy of the world's great economic powers. The financial crisis was just a stage, a result of this longer-term misdirection. The costs of this national strategy were evident in the destruction of the environment, neglect of agriculture, increasing social division, and growing human problems. Moreover, he went on, "the problem today of world society, not just of Thai society, is the problem that mankind, human values and social values are falling under the destructive dominance of economics" (Saneh

1999, 28). Up until Keynes, economics had still been concerned with social values, but more recently economics had become focused wholly on concepts of efficiency and business profit to the exclusion of any social dimension.

Second, the idea of community thus became the basis for restating ideas of human and social need in opposition to the dehumanization of economics. In this sense, community was much more a *moral* idea than a physical idea. It was not, he made clear, the same concept as the government's definition of a community or village—as a geographic and administrative unit. Saneh (1999, 35) argued that "to escape from the world economic order which destructively threatens mankind, human values, and society, we must look to the community in this light—as a target or answer for building a new order of society." In other words, it did not matter whether the community had never existed or never been as good as imagined. It was still necessary to *invent* or reinvent the community *as a principle*. The ultimate aim would be to "create a new social order in which the economy serves society, rather than society serves the economy" (Saneh 1999, 37).

Third, this reinvented community was not seen as a means of escape from globalization and modernity—a rat-hole down which people could hide away from destructive forces. Rather the community strategy would offer a long-term way to integrate everyone into the national and international economy from the bottom up, in opposition to the processes of peripheralization and exclusion within globalization. Communities had to build from their own wisdom and resources, but not statically and not in isolation. Local wisdom should be developed by adoption from modern ideas and technology. While the primary aim of the community economy should be self-reliance and security, the next step should be the development of a surplus, the evolution of ever more sophisticated local economic institutions including banks and industries, the gradual broadening of external economic networks, with the ultimate goal of full integration with the national and international economy on a basis of strength (Saneh 1998; Phitthaya 1998b, 78–81). This of course would be a long process: "I don't want to call it a 10-year plan or a 20-year plan. But I think we must look at the development strategy, not just plans of this sort" (Saneh 1999, 37).

Saneh's thinking around this time amounted to a mobilization of the idea of community which had been a rather passive element in the earlier construction of *watthanatham chumchon*. This more assertive attitude to the role of community also shaped the adaptation of "good governance" into the Thai context. In early 1998, the 1973 student leader turned "social critic," Thirayuth Boonmee, proposed that the idea of "good governance" could serve as the focus for a wholesale social reform to move beyond the crisis. He offered a (later controversial) Thai translation for the phrase "good governance" (*thammarat*, see p. 125) and an interpretation intended to be relevant to Thailand. He began from the international interpretation of the phrase—transparency, honesty, accountability, efficiency—but reinterpreted with "a Thai soul and international heart," and elaborated as a "national project" involving government, private sector, and local communities (Thirayuth 1998). But Saneh called this definition elitist. He argued that good governance in the Thai context should be reinterpreted to mean grassroots participation. Prawase Wasi redefined *thammarat* as a self-sufficient, community-based economy and society. In July 1998, Thirayuth called up meetings of NGOs, activists, and local community groups to discuss the issue.

Thirayuth opened by proposing that *thammarat* meant that each person is the owner of the nation, that in the past government had been too powerful and too centralized, and that the task was to shift the balance between individual and state. He offered several models for this change including a liberal model, a citizenship model, and a community-based model. The meeting ignored all except the latter. The debate concentrated wholly on shifting the power balance between local community and state. The ideal was defined as *chumchon aphiwat*, community rule. Thirayuth (1998, 16, 31) later summarized the concept along these drastically modified lines:

National good governance is a movement based on the power of local organizations, community civil society, to understand the problems, be self-reliant, self-help, self-reform; and at the same time to build the strength to truly examine what is bad and ugly. . . .

Mainstream thinking on development has created problems over the environment, society, disease, and the problems from this crisis. As a result, the development strategy based on self-sufficiency is growing ever stronger day by day, side by side with mainstream development.

Bamrung Bunpanya, one of the early conceptualizers of *watthanatham chumchon*, proposed that all legislation should be limited to four or five clauses, so that local communities could interpret and adapt according to local needs and circumstances.[2]

THE REVIVAL OF AGRICULTURE

> Since our economy now completely depends upon foreign capital, it is time for the government to go beyond and select a way of relying on the country's original potential to become independent.
>
> Saneh Chamarik, November 1998

The crisis revived interest in agriculture and rural society. The contrasting impact of the crisis on Thailand and Indonesia emphasized the importance of national self-sufficiency in food. As currency values dived, the cost of imported food in Indonesia soared, resulting in food riots and widespread distress. In Thailand, the price of food—virtually all locally produced—stayed steady. Moreover, the fall in currency value initially boosted the baht earnings from crop exports and helped to cushion the rural economy against the impact of the crisis. Further, as some two million were disemployed in the urban economy, the village was expected to serve as the social safety net (see pp. 92–4).

The rural sector had been neglected in the previous two decades. As long as the urban economy was growing rapidly, it was fashionable to assume that the rural sector would decline into insignificance, as in other industrialized nations. Growth could be achieved more easily by transferring people out of agriculture to the urban sector, rather than by improving the productivity or efficiency of farming. The crisis restated the economic importance of the rural sector, but even more, its *social* and *political* importance.

While localist advocates like Saneh Chamarik welcomed this revived interest, they argued strongly against viewing the rural sector simply as a shock absorber for the urban economy's volatility. Rather Saneh (1999, 35–6) pointed out that the rural economy had significance for itself, and that this significance would increase on a global scale in the near future:

Why do I attribute such importance to the countryside? Because the Thai countryside is not like that of England, Europe, and cold countries. The Thai countryside is part of the hot zone of the world which is rich in resources and biodiversity. . . . The hot zone covers just 7 percent of the surface area of the world but has 60–70 percent of the biodiversity, and is important to major industries of significance for mankind, namely the food industry and many others . . . Seventy to eighty percent of the pharmaceuticals made from bio-resources from the hot zone have been taken by foreign scientists from the local wisdom of villagers. This statistic is very revealing. It indicates the potential. And this potential can develop the Thai economy, society, and politics in the future.

In parallel, Chatthip Nartsupha, who had earlier helped define community culture, recognized that one major failure of the theory had been its lack of any economics. He began to redress this problem by restating that the strength of the approach was its peasant's-eye view of the world:

The community culture approach starts from the concept of survival. The peasants' rights in production stem from their moral right to survival. The organization of economy and society is designed to ensure survival. . . . The approach attempts to explain peasant society as one form of society which exists on a basis of equality with other societies outside the peasant's world. It focuses study on four main aspects of the peasantry: community culture; the peasants' world view; mixed farming; and self-reliance. (Chatthip et al. 1998)[3]

However, the community approach, Chatthip continued, had concentrated too much on culture, and too little on economics. This had effectively allowed agricultural economics to be conducted with the tools and perspectives of urban economics:

Agricultural economics has tended to analyze the farm as a capitalist enterprise. It has concentrated on the market and the pricing of different agricultural products, rather than studying the organization of family production which is at the heart of the Thai peasant economy. Also there has been almost no study of peasant economic networks, and of the relations between the peasant community economy and other economic sectors in the national economy. (Chatthip et al, 1998)

Chatthip's group proposed that what was needed was "a theory of production organization of the peasant family"—perhaps using the perspective and methodology of the Chayanovian school, perhaps adopting from the Gandhian tradition, perhaps drawing on Latin American experience—but adjusted to the political and economic realities of contemporary Thailand. That would have to begin with village-level research.

Moreover, as with Saneh's approach, the aim was not to portray or promote a view of the village economy as autarchic and isolated. Rather, "study should also be made of the relations between the local economies and the national economy, with the ultimate objective of a national prosperity founded on the flourishing of local community economies." As with Saneh, the objective would be to increase the productive capacity of the rural economy, and find appropriate institutional ways to integrate it with the national and international economy on more equitable terms.

The journal *Withithat*, which appeared on the eve of the crisis, became a focus for debate on the origins, meaning, and implications of the economic crisis. The issues through 1998 concentrated on the structure of globalization and Thailand's vulnerability. In searching for solutions and responses to the crisis, the journal's editors and regular contributors were drawn bit by bit to concentrate on the importance of the community as the basis of the society, and agriculture as the basis of the social economy. In late 1998, the journal published the works by Saneh and the Chatthip group cited above. In February 1999, it issued a volume on the *Sustainable Economy* which gave space to some long-standing advocates of village self-reliance (Banthon Ondam, Seri Phongphit), expounded Gandhi's ideas on community economics, and advocated a transnational peasant response to the crisis. In the editor's introduction, Phitthaya Wongkun (1999, 10) argued that Thailand could survive this and previous economic crises such as the 1930s depression because of the self-reliance and sustainability of the peasant economy which still supported the majority of the population.

> For this reason [the loss of sovereignty to the IMF], the national spirit of developing the community and Thai society should be the main direction in the future. The national economic and social development plans and the government's economic strategies should focus on developing the structure and the diversity of the community economy, and on building communities

205

as centres of diversity across the country. Then development will harmonize with the social foundations, natural foundations, cultural foundations, and the thinking of present day community leaders. And Thailand will have a civil society which is civilized, secure, and sustainable.

CULTURE AND GLOBALIZATION

Today Thailand faces a catastrophe in the economy, in politics, and in culture. Each day more people realize that this crisis is more violent than any instance in all our previous history.

Yuk Si-ariya, 1997

In the early 1990s, the political scientist Chai-Anan Samudavanija had been one of the most enthusiastic exponents of globalization. On the eve of the crisis (1997), he published a book, *Watthanatham ku thun* (Culture as Capital), which marked a significant rethink.

Chai-Anan began by taking issue with Samuel Huntington's "clash of civilizations" argument which not only posited cultural warfare replacing politico-economic warfare in the post–cold war world, but appeared to give little room for non-major cultures such as those of Thailand. Chai-Anan proposed instead a "splash of civilizations," an efflorescence of local cultures rather than homogenization within a major model.

Chai-Anan went on to endorse the idea, first put forward in the Thai context by Rangsan Thanapornphan (1996), that culture represents a form of capital. He noted that the crisis emphasized that Thailand has little of its own stock of other forms of capital, particularly financial capital and technology; that Thailand had tried to develop by borrowing this other capital from the advanced world; and that the crisis had arisen because these loans could be easily withdrawn. By contrast, Thailand has a large stock of cultural capital. This was evident from surveys which showed tourists choose Thailand as a destination because of monuments, cultural performances, food, and service attitude—all products which embody a high element of cultural capital. Similarly they rate Thailand low for products which embody technology (hotels, communications) and public capital (infrastructure, traffic).

Chai-Anan pointed out that the inheritance of cultural capital also extends to social values—such as mutual sympathy, respect for elders, compassion—which would not only help Thailand to survive the crisis, but would provide a basis for the construction of a superior social model over the long term.

This stock of cultural capital, Chai-Anan noted, had been built up through past investments, and needed to be maintained by constant reinvestment. He summed up (1997, 85–6):

> . . . when we appreciate culture as a form of capital, we can have a culture strategy which can serve as a tool for the Thai state in the context of globalization. . . . Even though Thai society has little economic capital, low economic production capacity, low savings, low labour skills, yet we still have people who smile easily, a long-standing heritage of cultural capital, values that remain strong and do not need to be rebuilt. This is different from many western societies which need to rebuild a foundation of values and principles (such as gratitude to parents, family warmth, respect for elders).

Over the 1990s, Suvinai Pornvalai put out a prodigious volume of writing combining economics, aspects of Eastern cultures, and sophisticated versions of "how to" literature—the manuals for success in anything, but especially business, which became the largest segment of Thai publishing. In early 1998 he published *Sethakit fong sabu: bot-rian lae thang rot* (The Bubble Economy: Lessons and Ways to Survive), introduced as a book to help non-economists understand the crisis.

Suvinai explained the economic crisis through two processes at work in parallel within international capitalism. First is the gradual increase of financial capital in comparison to industrial capital. Speculative financial investment now far exceeds productive investment, resulting in the series of over-investment bubbles which have afflicted Europe, the US, Japan, and now Southeast Asia in the past two decades. Second is the advance of consumerism, through which Thailand has become ensnared in this trail of bursting bubbles.

According to Suvinai (1998, 31–2), capitalism grows by continually expanding the limits of consumption. From the fourteenth to the nineteenth century, this was achieved by overcoming boundaries of space through exploration and colonialism. In the early twentieth century, this phase reached a dead end with the advent of world wars, socialist revolutions, and anti-colonial struggles. In a second phase from around 1930 to around 1980, expansion was sustained by increasing the levels of consumption within the heartland countries of international capital, by reshaping and redirecting "wants" to focus on "products." Since 1980, this same process has been extended across the world:

> Globalization is the last manifestation of capitalism which uses communications technology and builds a high image for the modern lifestyle to stimulate people's wants and expand the borders of people's wants with a success that the socialist countries could not match. (Suvinai 1998, 33)

In the advanced stages of this phase, consumption becomes an end in itself. For countries—like Thailand—absorbed into the fringes of the spread of consumerism, patterns of consumption become separated from the local heritage of culture and ways of life. Borne up by the illusions of the over-investment bubble, consumption focuses on goods whose whole purpose is to display the fact of consumption itself.

Until ten years ago, Suvinai continued, Thais' consumption patterns reflected the restraint and limitation of wants common to a peasant-based society. But in the bubble and under the influence of consumerism, the middle class has pioneered an expansion of consumption culture which has affected the whole society. Suvinai (1998, 84–5) concluded:

> The first thing everyone must do to pull the country out of this economic disaster is to change from the consumption habits which come with the bubble and the ideology of consumerism. . . . the real route to survival will begin, not from any political change which is far from certain, but from change by the Thai middle class itself.

In a similar vein, Phitthaya Wongkun (1998d) argued that a society which blindly follows an outside model, fails to see its own value, and fails to understand its own cultural roots, will suffer a gradual change in its own culture and way of life, such that "in the end that society will gradually change to a slave society, modern-style." The spread of a Western model across the world has created an "imperialism of the mind" which is reproduced across economics, politics, and culture. The free market ideology provides cover for speculative capital to invade weaker countries, collapse their economies, and buy up the wreckage cheap. The command of weaponry and international organizations enables the USA and Europe to dominate world politics. The spread of Western images through advertising and film, Phitthaya continued (1998d),[4] have led to a gradual adoption of a Western lifestyle:

> Cultural slavery has already spread through Thai society. . . . Now that the knowledge, mentality, way of thinking, and way of life of most people is westernized, in what way will we still be a Thai society? . . . This kind of society is a modern-style slave society, under a mental imperialism which is spreading throughout the world.

In 1994–95, Prawase Wasi had spoken and written extensively on the issue of culture in connection with the effort to make the Eighth Plan a very different document from its predecessors. He used a concept of culture to criticize the imbalance in Thailand's previous development. He defined culture as a society's accumulated knowledge and practice. Implicitly, culture is a more powerful concept than people, nation, or state. Past development has been marked by "compartmentalized thinking," which focuses on a few parts rather than the whole. In particular, it focuses on developing wealth rather than humanity, business profits rather than society.

In 1997–98, Prawase extended this line of thinking against the background of the crisis. The result of this compartmentalized approach to development is not only lopsided and unsustainable, but represents a deep form of threat to Thailand *as a culture*:

> If Thailand focuses only on developing business, Thai culture will disappear from this country called Thailand. When you lose culture, it's equal to losing nation. (Prawase 1998, 13)

The old path of development was at odds with the cultural base, and particularly with the economy of local communities. This badness of fit had resulted in the neglect of agriculture, widening gap between rich and poor, destruction of the environment, and loss of ethics. The solution lay in redefining development on a community base.

209

Prawase's thinking went beyond a simply economistic interpretation of self-reliance. Speaking at the height of the crisis, he depicted self-sufficiency as a "moral economy" in contrast to "the economy that presses for money and that destroys everything including the culture" (*BP*, 2 Feb 1998). Later Prawase (1999) came to prefer the terms "cultural economy" or "basic economy" to stress the need for an economic ethic which placed social values above profit:

> The foundation of a society is culture. . . . Cultural economics is not about money alone, but also about family, community, culture, and the environment. All these must be considered together in order to integrate life, spirit, society and environment in a balanced way.

The route to recovery, according to Prawase, lay not in the finance industry and the macroeconomy, but in the school, *wat*, family, and local community. At the peak of the crisis in mid 1998, he called for a "war of national salvation" in which the National Culture Commission would be wheeled out as one of the battalions (*BP*, 21 Jul 1998).

In sum, from a variety of perspectives, intellectuals looked to a concept of culture as defence against globalization. They defined culture very broadly—as way of life, the society's accumulated learning from the past, or simply as knowledge. While there is an implicit us/them theme present, this is not the driving force of these arguments. The call is not so much to defend Thai culture, but to draw on Thai culture and local community cultures to rescue the society from disaster. The strategy is to look inward, have less faith in globalization, and leverage benefits from the society's inheritance rather than relying on borrowed money and technology.

RUNNING AWAY FROM THE *KHLONG*

One measure of the importance of this discourse of locality against globalization lies in the fierceness of the opposition it provoked.

In the period before the crisis, the idea of community culture was challenged from the angle of liberal modernism, most notably by Anek Laothamatas (1995; Anek et al. 1995). In the context of the crisis and the heightened profile of the self-reliance idea, this challenge was restated in fiercer and more emotional terms by Kamchai Laisamit (1998). Besides attacking assumptions and logical inconsistencies in the localism discourse, these challenges make four main points.

First, the idea of the local community as a source of moral values is a hopeless idealization. The local community in this form probably never existed. It has certainly been transformed by the ever closer relations with urban capitalism over the last century. And it could never be invented or reinvented in real physical form within the contemporary context.

Second, the dominant reality of rural society is not egalitarian and cooperative communities but the patronage system (*rabop uppatham*) characterized by inequality, economic exploitation, and political domination. This patronage system constrains the development of the rural economy and undermines Thailand's progress towards democracy. Provincial bosses with an electoral base in rural society dominate parliament and other representative bodies and pervert their operation. As elsewhere in the world, democracy cannot flourish in the context of a backward peasant society.

Third, for Thailand to progress both economically and politically, the village should not be conserved but transformed. Farmers should not try to revive local wisdom but should try to become better capitalists so they can compete more efficiently. Farmers should not try to preserve local communities, but should escape from them into free individualism so that they can recombine in the free associations which are the basis of civil society and democracy (Anek 1995, 82–92).

Fourth, the localism discourse is a conservative force, promoted by utopians and conservative nationalists, which threatens the march of progress and may even damage what urban modernism has achieved. Kamchai (1998, 79) railed:

> Why should we think of going back to recall the community culture as a direction to fight the economic crisis at the national level, when this community culture is weaker than capitalism and has already collapsed once in the past? This time it will not only be the community which will be in a mess. It will lead the city, which is the most progressive element in the country, to total collapse along with it.

DIVERTING THE *KHLONG*

At the outset of the crisis, many mainstream thinkers and public leaders made similar statements reaffirming their faith in urban-led progress. Anand Panyarachun, for instance, argued that the crisis should not be blamed on globalization but on Thailand's failure to manage it. He insisted Thailand should not react by turning away from the world. However, the length and depth of the crisis eventually sparked a broader interest in the localism discourse. The aggression shown by foreign interests, the extent of the damage to the Thai urban economy, and the prospects for social distress and disorder, persuaded even some ardent globalizers to think again. Even Anand's faith seemed to waver. In December 1999, the Thailand Development Research Institute—the leading technocratic think-tank and spiritual home of mainstream economics—devoted its flagship year-end conference to the theme of the "Sufficiency Economy" laid out in the king's 1997 speech.[5] Anand was chairman of the institute. Aphichai Puntasen opened the event with a discourse on Buddhist economics.

The conference statement of definition presented the concept of a sufficiency economy as "moderation and due consideration in all modes of conduct, as well as the need for sufficient protection from internal and external shocks." This moderation was needed in order "to cope appropriately with critical challenges arising from extensive and rapid socio-economic, environmental, and cultural changes occurring as a result of globalization." In the hands of TDRI, the principle of sufficiency had been transformed into a technique for negotiating a more conditional accommodation with globalization: "The philosophy points the way for recovery that will lead to a more resilient and sustainable economy better able to meet the challenges from globalisation and other changes." Anand closed the conference by describing the sufficiency economy as a tool for adjusting mainstream development economics to be become more self-reliant, balanced, and sustainable, and for containing globalization's tendency towards social division:

> We can summarise that the approach of the sufficiency economy does not conflict with mainstream economics which emphasises optimality. It's an approach which offers an "optimum" strategy for all aspects of development. For the sake of the Thai way-of-life, it is necessary to lay a new theoretical

foundation in the future which does not rely on others, stands on its own feet, is self-critical, takes the middle path, and adopts a development process which is continually adjusted. . . . Besides, the sufficiency economy accords with the unique character of Thai society with its mutual consideration, mutual assistance, goodwill and good intention towards others, resulting in pursuit of the common benefit more than personal benefit. (TDRI 1999b)

Not everyone welcomed this broader interest in the localism discourse which snowballed over the crisis. Those who see the discourse as an attempt to shift the balance of power between state and locality resented the Ministry of the Interior's official adoption and promotion of self-reliance which they felt was opportunistic and damaging to the power of the discourse in the long run. Similarly some opposed the business sponsorship of community projects, such as Suphon Suphaphong's Bangchak schemes and Meechai Viravaidya's TBird, as distorting the concept of self-reliance for political and business gain. Some felt that the attempts by Anand and others to yoke the sufficiency principle with mainstream economics was an attempt to preempt and neutralize a powerful radical message (Kasian 2000).

CONCLUSION: BEYOND COMMUNITY CULTURE

The discourse on *watthanatham chumchon* which jelled in the late 1980s and early 1990s has been substantially changed against the background of the economic crisis. The earlier version focused on community *as a culture*, encompassing knowledge, local practices, and social relations. It asserted the importance of this culture as a counter to centralized political domination, top-down development planning, and urban-triumphalist cultural segregation. It amounted to an assertion of the importance of the rural locality. However, as a concept it remained rather passive. It attracted a rather confused debate over whether the "community" was supposed to be a description of historical fact, or an idealized image guiding the way to the future.

The king's speech on self-sufficiency broadened interest in the discourse. Many of the official actions which stemmed from this initiative—particularly those of the Democrat Party and the Ministry of the

Interior—were conceived as forms of short-term disaster management. However, at the same time, the discourse also advanced in ways that may be important over the longer term.

Saneh clarified that "community" is important as an ethical construct needed to reassert human and moral values in the face of the dehumanizing narratives of modern economics and in face of the propensity to social catastrophe built into the international economic system. As such, "community" has much the same status in the discourse as the idea of a "state of nature" had in the evolution of modern Western liberal theories. It is a philosophic statement about the human condition and human needs, which serves as the starting point for building social and political theories.

Religious scholars such as P. A. Payutto and academics such as Aphichai Puntasen gave the ideas of self-reliance and self-sufficiency a grounding in Buddhist philosophy, and sparked interest in "Buddhist economics" as a counter-discourse to modern economics.

A very broad range of intellectuals including Rangsan, Chai-Anan, Suvinai, Prawase, and Phitthaya drew attention to *culture* as a social, economic, and political asset. As with other assets, culture needs to be protected from losing its value, and constantly renewed by reinvestment. Also as with other assets, culture can deliver profits in the form of social strengths and economic revenues whose value becomes evident when a crisis leads to the rapid destruction of other forms of asset.

These clarifications and extensions of some key concepts within the discourse of community culture served as the basis for a more activist and assertive version of community or locality-based theorization. In the thinking of Saneh and of Chatthip's group, the restatement of the community as a moral necessity became the basis for a rescripting of rural economics based on the existing natural and human resource endowment, rather than as an adjunct of theories of urban economic expansion. NGO and community groups adopting and adapting *thammarat* called for a more aggressive approach to decentralization and "community rule." In the thinking of Buddhist scholars such as Payutto and lay popularizers such as Prawase Wasi, self-reliance became a national project, not only a personal or community strategy. Similarly the idea of "culture" was adopted much more widely than the idea of "community culture" to provoke debate on visions of a Thai future which need not follow the pattern or the urging of the West. The severity of the crisis induced some ardent globalizers to look at the community discourse as a framework for adding some conditions to global integration and rampant development.

Critics of the localism discourse reflect a different vision of the Thai future—a vision of urbanism, capitalism, and democracy triumphant. While delivered in the name of liberalism and progress, this critique is sometimes surprisingly alarmist and frankly intolerant. These critics interpret "self-reliance" as meaning a complete withdrawal from the market economy, which seems a deliberately exaggerated view of what the localists propose. Some critics see the call for a rural focus as a denial of the right of the city to exist and prosper. This alarmism seems to reflect a lack of self-confidence in the urban liberal camp.

The rise of the localism discourse has been a function of the social division and environmental damage which are features of the development of urban capitalism all through history and all round the world. The localists argue that the liberal-modernists have no arguments, no social philosophy to manage these destructive consequences. The liberal modernists reply that this is simply a stage that has to be traversed, and costs which have to be borne—resisting the flow of history will ultimately be more costly. The localists reply that the modernists' vision of capitalism and democracy is losing adherents even in its Western heartland. Besides, the trend of the world economy is to freeze more and more areas, more and more segments of the population, as peripheral and excluded, rather than fully integrated into the benefits of capitalism. Localism is a form of guerrilla resistance to this peripheralization.

In nineteenth-century Europe, against the background of the rise of industrial society, arguments in favour of free trade were locked in combat with arguments that the excesses of the free market were a threat to human values, social values, and the growth of democracy. Critics pointed out that the free market not only generated massive economic inequality but also cultivated utilitarian ways of thinking which threatened the European inheritance of humanist values. These critical arguments often looked backwards to a "golden age" or "state of nature" to build philosophical foundations for their critique; and simultaneously looked forward to visions of utopia or improvement. There were many strands in this critique which variously led towards romanticism, nationalism, and socialism. As a whole, they were eventually successful in bringing about state-led and society-led initiatives to moderate free market liberalism.

215

This comparison is not meant to suggest that Thailand will follow the same path. The era is different, and Thailand's intellectual inheritance is different. The comparison is merely meant to indicate that the mobilization of ideas about community, locality, and Buddhist values to oppose the neoliberal agenda follows a known historical pattern. Societies under pressure discover that social and cultural values which do not figure in market economics are important to the society's survival and well-being. The increased salience of these localist ideas, and their intellectual development during the crisis, offer some hope.

NOTES

1. To walk backwards into a *khlong* (*thoi lang khao khlong*) is a Thai saying meaning to regress or to become more conservative.

2. Proposed at an NGO think-tank in Mae Rim, Chiang Mai, 9–11 October 1999.

3. See especially the final chapter of Chatthip et al. (1998). All the quotes used here are taken from the English-language summary of this book, prepared for the Thailand Research Fund.

4. This preface does not have page numbers. The quote comes from the penultimate page.

5. This mainstream reinterpretation liked to take the "self" away from the "sufficiency" in order to downplay the element of withdrawal from the wider economy. This linguistic nicety, of course, only meant anything to those sophisticated enough to know English.

BEYOND CRISIS: CHANGES, FEARS, FUTURES

The crisis brought a large number of changes in a very short time. Some of these followed the clear-cut agendas laid out at the onset of the crisis (see chapter 1). But the crisis was deeper, longer, and more complex than most had predicted at that early stage. The Washington Consensus crumpled in the face of international economic turmoil and sustained academic attack. It had to be rewritten with greater attention to the dangers of over rapid and poorly planned liberalization, and the need for more sensitive social policies. The visions of Thailand's modernizers had to be scaled back in the face of economic damage and social stress. The calls for a retreat to self-reliance and community roots had to be tempered in the face of global realities.

This chapter looks at the possible directions of the Thai political economy in the aftermath of the crisis. It begins with a summary review of four major economic changes—higher foreign investment, corporate acquisitions, trends in exporting, and the rise of public debt. Then it briefly reviews three major political shifts—the shrinkage of formal political space, the restoration of Bangkok dominance, and the rise of political activism. Finally, it examines how all these changes are likely to interact, and sketches two main visions for the future.

ECONOMIC IMPACT

Foreign investment

After the float, foreign investment flowed into Thailand in much greater volume than ever before. Very little of this was new investment. Almost all was buying up cheap assets.

Over the eleven-and-a-half years (1986–mid 1997) of the prior boom—a boom which many attribute to foreign investment—the total inflow of private FDI was 487 billion baht. In the thirty months following the July 1997 float, the total inflow was 589 billion baht—about a fifth higher in roughly one fifth of the time. Over the boom, the annual inflow averaged 42 billion baht, over the bust, 235 billion baht—six times higher in baht terms, four times higher in dollar terms, and over three times higher in relation to GDP (5.0 versus 1.6 percent).

These FDI inflows increased immediately after the baht float, peaked in the first half of 1998, and remained high through to the end of 1999. Some of the inflows came from joint venture partners obliged to inject capital to keep a company functioning. Some came from bottom fishers. Most came from international companies taking advantage of very good pricing. Almost none went into new ventures. Of this post-crash inflow, around 185 billion baht went into the buyouts and recapitalization of the banks. Another 164 billion baht went into industry, especially into automotive, electrical, and metal industries (table 9.1). Other major destinations were trade (103 billion baht), the financial sector (33 billion), and services (35 billion). The major source was Japan (107 billion baht, 2.7 billion US dollars). In addition, 90 billion baht came from the EU, and 66 billion from the US. Other large amounts came from Hong Kong and Singapore, some of which possibly represents investments through subsidiaries of Western firms. In addition, over the two-and-a-half post-float years, there was a net inflow of portfolio investment of 139 billion baht or 3.8 billion US dollars, with the major sources being Hong Kong, Singapore, and the UK.[1]

Who was buying what? Brimble and Sherman (1999) tracked 130 acquisition deals by foreign capital between October 1997 and May 1999 representing a total value of US$4.5 billion (table 9.2), nearly a third of the total recorded in the FDI statistics.[2] Roughly a third of this amount represented deals in the financial sector, and the largest source of capital was Europe. In addition, Brimble and Sherman tracked 135 deals worth

Table 9.1: Foreign Investment

	Billion baht		Billion US$	
	1986– mid 97	Mid 97– end 99	1986– mid 97	Mid 97– end 99
Total FDI - including banks	486.9	588.7	19.1	14.9
Total FDI - excluding banks	480.9	403.4	18.9	10.3
Industry	184.3	163.5	7.2	4.2
Financial institutions	29.0	33.2	1.1	0.8
Trade	89.0	102.8	3.5	2.7
Construction	39.9	4.1	1.6	0.1
Mining & quarrying	14.6	-0.4	0.6	0.0
Agriculture	3.1	0.1	0.1	0.0
Services	21.7	34.6	0.8	0.9
Real estate	101.9	27.1	4.0	0.7
Others	-2.6	38.3	-0.1	1.0
Japan	144.2	107.0	5.6	2.7
Hong Kong	72.8	38.3	2.9	1.0
Taiwan	31.3	11.4	1.2	0.3
USA	71.4	66.0	2.8	1.7
EU	45.8	90.3	1.8	2.3
Singapore	41.6	59.8	1.6	1.5
Other	73.8	30.5	2.9	0.8
Total portfolio investment	259.5	138.7	10.2	3.8
Japan	2.8	1.2	0.1	0.0
Hong Kong	78.6	100.6	3.1	2.7
Taiwan	2.7	-0.2	0.1	0.0
USA	24.9	-60.8	1.0	-1.5
EU	23.5	28.5	0.9	0.7
Singapore	142.5	87.4	5.6	2.3
Other	-15.5	-18.0	-0.6	-0.4

Source: Bank of Thailand

US$1.5 billion made under a special provision for foreign investors to acquire a majority stake in firms promoted by the Board of Investment (BoI) on condition of the local partners' consent. Almost half of these deals were in the automotive sector, with others spread across chemicals, electronics, and light industry.

Table 9.2: Foreign acquisitions, Oct 1997–May 1998

	Number	Value US$ mil	Percent of number	Percent of value
Total	130	4526.5	100	100
Finance	36	1772.7	28	39
Electronic	19	586.5	15	13
Automotive	19	199.4	15	4
Japan	39	586.9	30	13
Europe	31	1772.4	24	39
USA	25	789.3	19	17
East Asia	17	628.6	13	14
Majority (51–90%)	38	2685.0	29	59
Outright (91–100%)	32	451.6	25	10

Source: Brimble and Sherman (1999)

These inflows resulted in a significant increase of foreign ownership, especially in three main areas—finance, export industries, and retail.

Finance industry

Perhaps the major impact of the crisis on the Thai political economy has been the devastation in the financial sector. As several commentators have shown, Asia's debt-based credit systems, once exposed by financial liberalization, are highly vulnerable to collapse in the event of capital flight (Wade and Veneroso 1998; UNCTAD 1998; Bhanupong 1999). The sudden withdrawal of capital undermines the asset base of financial institutions. It also causes the currency to depreciate and hence increases their foreign-exchange-based liabilities. The result is a double blow which affects all corporations which have borrowed overseas, and especially those which have acted as financial intermediaries.

On the eve of the crisis, Thailand had fifteen commercial banks and ninety-two finance companies. In the early years of the boom, the finance companies played an important role in financing the rapid expansion of domestic manufacturing firms which helped to create the export boom. After 1987 when government began to promote the stock market, they became more involved in developing brokerages and lending money for stock speculation. By the time of the crash, most finance companies were hopelessly exposed to foreign short-term borrowing on the one hand, and to real estate loans, consumer credit, and advances to stock speculators on the other. Fifty-six finance companies were closed down by government in December 1997. Others subsequently closed, merged, or were absorbed into a parent. By the start of 2000, only twenty-three were still in operation. Ultimately only one or two merged groups were expected to survive in the form of limited banks.[3]

The banks fall into four groups (table 9.3). First, six small and medium banks were taken over by the Bank of Thailand in early 1998. One were closed down, and the remaining five slated for sale to foreign interests. One was sold to United Overseas Bank of Singapore, and another to HSBC.

Second, three small banks sold a majority interest to foreign banks during 1998–99.[4] The buyers were ABN Amro, Standard Chartered, and the Development Bank of Singapore. In total the eight banks sold or up for sale represent over half the number of banks, but only a sixth of total deposit volume.

Third, Krung Thai (owned by government) and Thai Military Bank (owned by the army) enjoyed special status. In mid 1998, government had hopes of using Krung Thai (and other smaller state-owned financial institutions) as a mechanism for absorbing some of the damage to the financial sector, and for stimulating recovery in the real economy. But the bank was too weighted down by bad debts and poor management. It became not a tool for stimulating recovery, but a lightning rod for criticism of the government's strategy. However government committed to maintain its existence, pumped in 185 billion baht of new capital, and installed another batch of management. The Thai Military Bank was also badly damaged, but enjoyed a charmed life.[5]

Fourth, the four remaining large commercial banks struggled to survive and maintain the existing management control. All except the establishment Siam Commercial Bank viewed the government's financial rescue package (14 August 1998) as a poison pill, and refused to accept inputs of government capital. The smallest of the four, Bank of Ayudhya, survived by selling off other assets of the group (principally its cement plant). The other three floated international share issues which raised the foreign-owned proportion of their capital to 49 percent. All four converted some of their domestic deposits into share capital (at high cost). However, their situation remained highly uncertain. Government stated that it did not wish to see the whole

Table 9.3: Thai commercial banks, 1997–99

Bank	Controlling interest pre-crisis	Employees 1997	Deposits 1997(bt bn)	Status, end 1999	Foreign share (%) 1999
Bangkok Bank	Sophonpanich family	25,958	947		49
Thai Farmers Bank	Lamsam family	19,158	588		49
Siam Commercial Bank	Crown Property Bureau	12,908	559		49
Bank of Ayudhya	Rattanarak family	11,530	389		40
Krung Thai Bank	Thai government	16,286	580		
Thai Military Bank	Thai army	8,165	258		13
Thai Danu Bank	Tuchinda family	2,993	90	Acquired by DBS (Singapore)	51
Bank of Asia	Phatrapraisit family	2,519	80	Acquired by ABN Amro	75
Nakhon Thon Bank	Wang Lee family	2,162	47	Acquired by Standard Chartered	75
Bangkok Bank of Commerce	Jalichandra family	5,391	110*	Closed down. Good assets to Krung Thai.	
Siam City Bank	Mahadamrongkun family	6,260	158	Taken over by BoT. Being sold.	
Bangkok Metropolitan Bank	Techaphaibun family	5,916	80	Taken over by BoT. Sold to HSBC.	75
First Bangkok City Bangkok	Charoen Siriwattanaphakdi	3,765	132	Taken over by BoT. Merged to Krung Thai.	
Laemthong Bank	Chansrichawla family	1,162	27	Taken over by BoT. Sold to UOB (Singapore).	75
Union Bank of Bangkok	Chonwichan family	2,805	48	Taken over by BoT. Merged with 13 finance companies as BankThai. To be sold.	

* 1996 figure   Sources: Bank of Thailand; press reports

financial system converted to foreign ownership (as happened in some Latin American crises), but at the same time was highly nervous of being seen to give any direct support to the major banks.

Virtually the whole brokerage industry was taken over, largely by European firms, with some US and Asian (Singapore, Taiwan) participation.[6] The ownership mix in the insurance industry also tilted. Some local firms were bought out by their foreign partner (Prudential). Almost every other local firm sold a 25 percent stake to a foreign partner. Some foreign firms established before the crisis (AIA, John Hancock) took the opportunity to expand, with AIA becoming a dominant market leader in life insurance.

At the onset of the crisis, the financial sector was overwhelmingly Thai. At the exit, a handful of large banks, a couple of finance companies, and a smattering of brokerages and insurance firms were hanging on. But overall the sector had been internationalized in a very short time.

Export industries

In October 1997, government effectively relaxed remaining restrictions on foreign ownership of corporations with the exception of a small reserved list.[7] Over the next year, many of the manufacturing enterprises originally set up as joint ventures were converted into full or majority foreign ownership, particularly in the key sectors of export manufacturing—automotive, electrical, and electronics.

In the automotive sector, Mitsubishi bought out its local partner. Honda injected new capital, resulting in a halving of the already small local shareholding. Toyota injected 4 billion baht of new capital, further diluting the local partner's minority stake. Toyota also bought over three auto parts companies sold off by Siam Cement in its downsizing. Yamaha bought a majority stake from its joint venture partner in motorcycle manufacture. One of the largest auto part producers, the Somboon group, reduced its stake in nine of its companies from 51 to 5 percent.

The same pattern prevailed in electronics and electrical goods. Matsushita bought out the local National joint venture. Samsung and NEC bought out their local partners completely. The Sahaviriya computing business sold 51 percent to Acer and 10 percent to Epson.

Retail

The largest Thai player in the retail sector, the Central group, sold off the supermarkets, discount warehouses, and megastores which represented most of its corporate expansion of the past decade or more, in order to hang on to its original core business of department stores. The two main purchasers were the Dutch Ahold group and French Groupe Casino. The CP group sold majority stakes in its main retail holdings to Tesco of the UK and Delhaize of Belgium. In addition, Carrefour and Makro took the opportunity of cheaper property prices to expand into the space created by the collapse of other retail businesses. On a smaller scale, 7-Eleven stores continued a rapid expansion into space vacated by the collapse of corner stores.[8]

Other sectors

The other area of major interest to foreign investors were heavy industries, telecommunications, and infrastructure projects. Many investors focused their attention on the possibilities which might be opened up by privatization. Others targeted firms which had taken on spectacularly high levels of foreign debt, or firms in sectors which had been heavily over-invested during the early 1990s.

The Siam Cement Group (SCG) had the reputation as one of the most established, secure, and best managed of any Thai corporations. Yet SCG was caught with US$4.2 billion of foreign loans (mostly unhedged) at the time of the depreciation. In 1997 it recorded a loss of 53 billion baht, largely on foreign exchange. The group reacted by putting a third of its total assets up for sale. These assets included many joint ventures in electronics and auto parts which the group had acquired when incoming foreign investors sought a politically powerful ally as local partner. However over the following two years, SCG was able to increase its exports, convert some of its dollar loans to local debentures, and struggled back to profitability. The downsizing was cut back. SCG would shed around 13 percent of assets, mostly in ancillary businesses such as automotive and glass. Other cement firms were less resilient. Jalaprathan cement sold 80 percent to Cemente Francais. Siam City Cement sold 25 percent to Holderbank.

Thai Petrochemical Industries (TPI), the largest petrochemical company and one of the fastest growing companies during the boom, became the largest defaulting debtor (US$3.5 billion) and the first victim of the new bankruptcy law. The largest steel producer, Sahaviriya, was forced to sell majority control in two of its three core companies to Japanese partners. The Nakhonthai steel group was preparing to sell an 80 percent stake to foreign creditors. Singtel of Singapore bought a 20 percent stake in the cellular operator, AIS, and Somers of UK bought 36 percent in the Ucom telecommunications group.

In sum, the crisis saw levels of capital inflow several times higher than ever before. Very little of this funding went into new ventures. Most was directed to acquisition of Thai assets. These asset transfers had a definite geoeconomic pattern. Many manufacturing enterprises were transferred to Asian owners—mainly Japanese. Many service businesses (financial and retail) were taken over by Western firms—principally American and continental European.

Thai firms

Besides delivering a significant increase in the role of foreign capital in some key areas of the economy, the crisis also severely damaged the status and the prospects of some of the major Thai firms.

The handful of the largest conglomerates were able to survive, largely by selling off some of the outer regions of their sprawling empires. This group includes the top few banks, SCG, and Charoen Pokphand (CP), which reacted mainly by selling off businesses in China.

Among the next rank of conglomerates—and particularly among those associated with the smaller, collapsed banks—the damage was greater. Most of the groups survived, but their significance was considerably diminished. Many were weighted down with heavy investments in property. Most faced difficulties in adjusting to a very different financial industry. Some circumvented the credit seizure by floating bonds.[9] But most did not have the size or sophistication to take this option. Some (as described above) were obliged to sell out to foreign partners and incoming investors. By early 1999, half of the 1,200 local auto parts makers had reportedly closed down (Brimble and Sherman 1999, 21). Other firms had a core business in industries such as textiles which had failed to modernize, and the financial disruption of the crisis simply delivered the death blow. The Sukree textile group, for instance, seemed fated to disappear.

Among small firms the damage was greater, but more difficult to estimate. Large numbers of small firms simply stopped operating because of the fall of custom and lack of access to credit. Many had their asset base wiped out. Some four thousand firms had their assets auctioned off by the FRA. Many were small and medium family businesses which had made a disastrous foray into property speculation in the early 1990s.

In some areas of the economy, local firms did reasonably well through the crisis because their foreign debts were limited and the currency depreciation boosted demand. Examples are food processing, hotels, and other businesses related to tourism.

In sum, the apex of the pyramid of Thai capital seemed battered but fairly well intact. The middle slopes had been badly knocked around. The lower foothills were a terrible mess.

Exports

Export value in dollar terms stagnated from 1996 onwards. But the exchange rate shifts disguise some underlying dynamism. From 1996 to 1999 exports grew 57 percent in baht terms and 47 percent in volume.

Moreover, the crisis accentuated a sectoral pattern evident since the early 1990s. Traditional export sectors such as agriculture, resource-based industries (wood, food processing), and labour-intensive industries (textiles, shoes, toys) all suffered declines. The export growth was all concentrated in technology-based industries, particularly the duo of automotive and electronic goods. The Japanese auto makers not only bought full or overwhelming majority stakes in their Thailand ventures, they also directed them more towards export to offset the collapse in the Thai market. Automotive exports grew 166 percent in dollar terms over 1996–99. Some electronics sub-sectors followed suit. There were big increases in export of computer parts (21 percent), telecoms equipment (33 percent), and integrated circuits (28 percent).

Overall the technology-based exports grew by 22 percent in dollar terms over 1996–99. This was much below the 20+ percent per year rates of the early 1990s, but still increased this sector's share of total Thai exports from 40 to 46 percent. The other major export increase came in process industries

Table 9.4: Export breakdown, 1996–99

| | — Value, US$ billion — | | | | — Annual growth (%) — | | | | —Shares (%)— | |
	1996	1997	1998	1999	1996	1997	1998	1999	1996	1999
Agriculture	6.58	5.84	5.08	4.87	2.5	-11.2	-13.1	-4.0	11.8	8.4
Resource-based	7.05	6.92	6.37	6.66	-2.5	-1.8	-7.9	4.5	12.7	11.4
Labour-intensive	11.00	10.25	9.06	9.45	-14.9	-6.8	-11.6	4.4	19.8	16.2
Process	4.56	5.24	4.65	5.43	15.4	14.8	-11.2	16.7	8.2	9.3
Technology-based	22.10	23.92	24.00	26.89	3.0	8.3	0.3	12.1	39.7	46.1
Other	4.32	5.22	4.88	5.01	-0.6	20.7	-6.4	2.7	7.8	8.6
Japan	9.35	8.60	7.42	8.22	-1.1	-8.0	-13.8	10.8	16.8	14.1
Greater China	6.52	6.75	6.24	6.86	10.4	3.5	-7.5	10.0	11.7	11.8
Other Asia	13.04	13.38	10.43	11.72	0.0	2.6	-22.0	12.3	23.5	20.1
USA	9.99	11.26	12.04	12.63	-0.5	12.7	6.9	4.9	18.0	21.7
Europe	9.63	10.03	10.46	10.57	-1.2	4.2	4.3	1.1	17.3	18.1
Middle East	2.15	1.94	1.88	2.08	-15.8	-9.9	-2.8	10.4	3.9	3.6
Other	4.92	5.43	5.57	6.24	-12.0	10.4	2.6	12.1	8.8	10.7
Total	55.61	57.39	54.04	58.33	-1.3	3.2	-5.8	7.9	100.0	100.0

Source: Bank of Thailand

(cement, plastics, chemicals, paper), largely through the attempts by indebted firms like SCG and TPI to seek salvation through export revenues. From 1996 to 1998, Thailand's export markets in Asia declined, while Europe and especially the US took up some of the slack. But in 1999—and especially in the second half—this picture was reversed. The growth markets were again in Asia, while the Western markets slowed.

Government debt

Prior to the crisis, the public sector's foreign debt (including monetary authorities) had stood at 17 billion US dollars, equivalent to around 10 percent of GDP (Table 9.5). By late 1999, the foreign debt had doubled to 36 billion US dollars, and was predicted to increase further.

Table 9.5: Government debt

	92	93	94	95	96	97	98	99
Domestic debt (baht bn)	278.9	296.0	293.6	311.0	322.6	325.5	727.5	1,075.0
Central government	202.7	161.1	103.2	72.7	44.3	31.8	426.9	642.4
State enterprises	76.2	134.9	190.4	238.3	278.4	293.8	300.6	432.6
Foreign debt (US$ bn)								
Public sector	13.1	14.2	15.7	16.4	16.8	17.2	20.3	23.7
Monetary authorities	-	-	-	-	-	7.2	11.2	12.8
Total (baht bn)	611.5	655.5	689.6	720.5	749.4	1091.3	2037.2	2461.5
As % of GDP	21.6	20.6	19.0	17.2	16.3	23.1	43.9	52.5

Source: Bank of Thailand

The increase in public sector foreign debt resulted only partially from obligations to the IMF. The two other major sources were loans contracted through the World Bank, ADB, and Miyazawa Plan to fund the fiscal stimulus launched from mid 1998; and bonds launched to finance the debts of the financial firms taken under government control in late 1997 and early 1998.

In addition, the public sector's domestic debt (including debts of state enterprises) tripled from 323 billion baht before the crisis to 1,075 billion at the end of 1999 as a result of budget deficits and financial bailouts.

With the continuing deficit and full fiscalization of the money pumped into the financial industry, the total government debt was predicted to rise further. In early 2000, opposition politicians claimed the true figure was already around 75 percent of GDP, largely because of debts still hidden in FIDF. The government claimed this estimate included some double-counting.

Consequences

In sum these economic changes suggest that Thailand will return to the old pattern of export-oriented growth but with four important differences.

First, there is increased participation by foreign capital, especially in the two strategic sectors of finance and export manufacturing.

Second, export growth is more focused on a limited range of sectors which in turn are heavily dependent on foreign capital and technology. While Thailand's exports are spread across a wide range of sectors, many of these are stagnant or in decline, especially those in which Thai capital remains important or where local resources are significant. Over the crisis, international firms in the automotive and electronic industries committed more capital to Thailand. Automotive plants represent heavy investments both in plant and human capital, and thus have some degree of inertia. Electronics plants by contrast are much more footloose. Thailand's attraction as a location arises from its readiness to be an amenable host (welcoming, politically stable) rather than from any advantages in infrastructure or linkages. Foreign firms can easily be tempted away by countries, such as China, which offer equally amenable hosting plus extra advantages in the form of cheaper labour or better infrastructure. Future export-led growth is likely to depend heavily on the performance of those sectors in which Thailand contributes little more than labour and location and where international competition is strong.

Third, the setback to domestic capital during the crisis is likely to mark the beginning of a trend rather than a one-time shift. The two key supports of the pre-crisis phase—the central role of the banks, and the loosely protective role of government—have been knocked away. The domestic banks will take a long time to recover and overcome the antagonisms that developed between creditor and debtor during the crisis. The international banks are likely to favour international firms because the systems and relationships are already in place. They will concentrate on consumer banking and risk management, where they have clear advantages through technology and experience. They are much less likely to take over the Thai banks' old role of funding ambitious entrepreneurship on the basis of personal relationships and personal market knowledge.

Indeed, financial liberalization destroys the form of entrepreneurial banking pursued by many Asian banking sectors. In the old world of Bretton Woods, fixed exchange rates, and closed capital accounts, all the regulation of the international financial system took place at the international level. This created a relatively stable environment in which banks inside national economies could be very entrepreneurial. Now, all the international regulation has been removed. The international financial system is a barely restrained anarchy. All the regulation now has to take place at the national level or, more exactly, at the level of each bank. Hence governments clamp stringent rules onto the way banks operate—rules which extend to the procedures banks have to follow before making each and every loan. In this new world, old Asian-style entrepreneurial banking becomes impossible.[10]

Fourth, government faces the future with a high level of debt. At present around 64 percent of the budget is devoted to current expenditure (salaries and overheads), while 36 percent or around 300 billion baht per year goes on capital expenditure. If the public debt does rise over 3 trillion baht as expected, a 10-year repayment programme would require *all* of the current capital expenditure budget for that decade.

Government proposes to lessen the problem by paying off some of the FIDF debt using excess central bank reserves, and covering some with another bond issue. But the excess from the reserves will only marginally dent the problem, and bond issues will only delay it. The budget for fiscal 2001 shows the problem. Despite ambitious revenue targets, fixed spending will take up 64 percent of the total, and debt servicing another 12 percent, leaving only 24 percent for capital expenditures. The government's capacity will be severely limited by its sheer lack of cash.

The World Bank claims the Thai government will be able to reduce this debt rapidly, in the same way that it did in the 1980s when the upturn in the economy resulted in a high budget surplus. But this time it may not be so easy. First, the surplus accumulated quickly in the 1980s because the economy (and tax receipts) accelerated very fast. Few expect such a sharp upturn this time. Second, revenue depends heavily on trade taxes which are being reduced under regional (AFTA) agreements.[11] Third, government expenditure was low in the 1980s because government failed to invest in infrastructure, but this may no longer be an option.

Government will undoubtedly attempt to increase tax demands, reduce budget leakage, and raise funds by privatization, but will face considerable resistance in all these endeavours.

POLITICS AND SOCIETY

These shifts in the economy have run in parallel with changes in politics. These can be summarized under three headings: the contraction of the space available for formal politics; the restoration of Bangkok dominance; and the growth in dissidence and civil society activism.

Formal political space

Globalization, as Susan Strange (1996) so clearly said, is nothing more or less than a transfer of power. Some of the powers once exercised by national governments (and by other national power holders) are transferred to international institutions or dominant countries. Other powers just seem to disappear.

The crisis has merely completed changes in the ambit of state power that were a consequence of the growing exposure of the Thai economy over the previous fifteen years. From the mid 1980s, the growing wealth and sophistication of the Thai economy attracted the interest of international manufacturers, vendors, and financiers. Thailand's rulers came under pressure to make changes to accommodate these new entrants. Since the financial liberalization of 1991–93, these pressures have become more insistent. The crisis presented an opportunity for international organizations, banks, firms, and lobby groups to press for a wide range of reforms in finance, law, government institutions, and social policy. Many of these reforms are designed to restrict the discretion of government, particularly in the area of economic policy making.

As the crisis eases, the direct pressure of these forces will diminish. But because of the highly exposed economy, government will remain vulnerable to the "judgement of the markets" on a daily basis. Throughout the crisis, the government faced down opposition to unpopular measures by arguing that "the markets" would desert Thailand with results compared to atomic bombs and other forms of devastation. In addition, because the government budget is crippled by public debt, government will be dependent on loans (especially from the ADB) for any significant policy initiatives. Such loans will come with advice and conditions. This advice and these conditions will be difficult to resist. These budget-strapped circumstances will persist long enough for habits and practices to change.

In the 1960s, the US assisted Thailand to found institutions and policies for developing a national capitalism as part of the US strategy to commit countries *economically* to the non-communist camp. In the crisis, much of this structure has been dismantled. Of course, this change was inevitable with the ending of the cold war and the rapid development of Western interest in expanding its access to world markets. However, the speed with which policies have been reversed and institutions reoriented will mean there will be a period of uneasy adjustment.

The return of Bangkok

With the expansion of electoral politics from the mid 1980s, Bangkok lost its grip on government. The provinces reigned. In the crisis, this trend was abruptly reversed. The new constitution, developed over the period since 1994, was designed to break the provincial barons' tightening grip over the cabinet. The prospects of passing the constitution were unsure until the advent of the crisis built support for an urban agitation both to pass the constitution and drive the incumbent provincial barons out of the cabinet.

As part of the same process, the Democrat Party was transformed from one among many provincially weighted parties, into the party best able to reflect an urban demand for cleaner government and better management of the economy. The post-1997 Democrats represent a new pattern for Thai parties, with a core of economic technocrats, an inner ring of businessmen and middle class, and a periphery of provincial barons, many of them in allied coalition parties. The success of the Democrats meant that the opposition New Aspiration Party, after a flirtation with populism, began approximating itself to this model. The newly formed Thai Rak Thai Party also based itself on the same pattern.

Civil society

Outside formal political institutions, levels of protest and activism had already been growing through the 1990s. The crisis exposed the failings of both politicians and officials, and stimulated popular moves for greater participation, for closer monitoring of the rulers, and for more self-help organizations outside the formal political domain. In these activities, four groups were especially prominent and are likely to shape the broader political world after the crisis: urban civil society activists, disgruntled businessmen, rural protesters, and a cadre of "establishment radicals."

The success in passing the constitution and felling the Chavalit government in late 1997 raised the hopes of urban civil society activists. Several groups and networks were formed to monitor the implementation of the constitution and to take advantage of its provisions. Conservative attempts to blunt some of the charter's more ambitious provisions stimulated these efforts. Against the background of the crisis, pitched battles were fought over the implementation of the charter's provisions on freedom of information, liberalization of the media, the setting up of an election commission, and community control on resources. Activist groups also quickly mobilized provisions of the constitution to submit the first "people's bill" (on community forestry), and to demand investigation over a public health scandal.

In other ways, there was an increase in the level of civil society activism. Groups launched campaigns on biodiversity, on the issue of genetically modified foods, and on the implications of the ADB's plans for Thai agriculture. Activists also expanded their international horizons. The Assembly of the Poor linked up with rural networks across Asia. The staging of the Unctad X conference in Bangkok in February 2000 provided an opportunity for international networking by Thai NGOs. In recognition of its increasingly prominent role in public debate, the press began moves towards self-policing.

Attempts to activate new counter-corruption provisions, coupled with greater daring on the part of both print and broadcast media, made the years 1998–99 a vintage period for political scandals. For the first time ever, three ministers were forced to resign by sheer public disgust over their alleged involvement in schemes to profit from the public budget. In March 2000, the National Counter Corruption Commission set up under the new constitution found that the interior minister, Sanan Kachornprasart, had falsified documents in his declaration of assets. He was forced to resign. This was the first time any senior Thai political figure had been brought down by legal process.

Battered business

In the eye of the crisis, domestic business proved unable to defend the forms of state protection and assistance it had earlier enjoyed. The instincts of big business are to work behind the scenes of parliamentary politics, but this proved ineffective in the circumstances of crisis. Some sections of business attempted to raise a standard of economic nationalism, but were unable to generate any widespread movement either within the business community or within a wider population because Thailand has no tradition of mass nationalism stemming from anti-colonial struggles. The aftermath of the crisis is likely to find businessmen showing renewed interest in party politics, but also increased activism by business lobby groups.

Rural protest

The crisis increased the economic pressure on rural society. Income transfers from the urban economy were severely reduced. Many disemployed migrants were forced to fall back on the village family as their social welfare system. Falling international commodity prices undercut farm incomes. In 1998 and again in 1999, farmers' groups demanded debt relief. In early 1999, some landless groups, swollen by unemployed migrants, launched "land invasions" into state-claimed forest areas. From early 1999 onwards, government faced a wave of demands for subsidies to offset low crop prices. These movements were contained by a mixture of repression and compromise.

The crisis changed the context of rural politics in several ways. It demystified the supposed superiority of the urban economy, and emboldened groups which promote rural self-reliance and groups which demand greater government attention to agricultural development. It halted—at least temporarily—the gradual transfer of population from village to city, undermined faith in the reliability of urban employment, and increased the importance of the village as a social cushion.

At the height of the crisis, government implemented its Keynesian stimulus of the economy by pushing funds (from the Miyazawa scheme and budget deficit) into the rural localities to cushion distress and deliver the fastest multiplier. On the exit from the crisis, rural demands are likely to increase. As past governments have tried to minimize rural pressure by denying space for rural politics, there are no good mechanisms for handling such demands. Government will find it hard to scale down palliative schemes such as the Miyazawa funding.

Two trends in rural politics established before the crisis are likely to continue and strengthen. First, conflicts over resources of land, water, and forest will lead to more radical demands for the relaxation of central control, and for the devolution of power from centre to locality. Every attempt to locate a large, disruptive, polluting project in a rural locality—dam, power plant, waste disposal—now faces strong opposition. Second, the rearguard action against the declining profitability of agriculture will throw up demands for more government attention to debt relief and crop pricing and for more diversion of national resources to the rural sector.

The crisis also began a fierce debate about the need for representation of rural groups in national politics. The new rural activism of the 1990s had been organized through local groups and umbrella networks. This strategy avoided faction-fighting over leadership, and avoided the risk that leaders would be neutralized by patronage or bullets. But during the crisis, several rural activists began to argue that the rural lobby would always be defeated unless it achieved some foothold in national parliamentary politics. Most rural activists opposed the idea by arguing that such a change in strategy would risk sacrificing what had been gained by the networking approach. But by early 2000 advocates had begun to suggest that rural activism should develop a political party which did not supplant the local networks, but worked in parallel with them.

Establishment radicalism

In the past, in periods of heightened political conflict or worsening distribution, conservative forces often rooted in the established bureaucracy have come out to promote ideologies of national unity and programmes of economic redistribution. In the early stages of the crisis, such forces were enthusiastic about the notion of "good governance." However, as the crisis deepened, they became more concerned over growing social division and the increased foreign penetration of the Thai economy. This is not because they are anti-foreign in any cultural or political sense. Most of the individuals involved are very westernized. But they became concerned that the step change in foreign penetration might be too big and too sudden for the society to absorb. They feared some chemical reaction between increasing social division and economic nationalism. They became interested in the king's idea of a "sufficiency economy" as a strategy to moderate the speed of globalization, and to cushion society against globalization's divisive force.

Open politics

How these different forces of business nationalism, rural radicalism, urban civil society activism, and establishment radicalism will react together is impossible to predict. What is clear, however, is that Thailand's relatively open public politics will provide space for these forces. Government's ability to respond to these demands will be limited by the fiscal crisis, and by neoliberal pressure to constrict the scope of government. Initially, this is likely to lead to a fractious period of competing demands, confused alliances, and petulant reactions by government and bureaucracy under attack.

Elections for the senate in March 2000 offered a glimpse of the public's political mood. These were the first polls under the new constitution, the first supervised by an independent election commission, and the first ever for an elected senate in Thailand. The charter officially banned candidates belonging to political parties and limited public campaigning in the hope that the electorate would choose "good people." The level of interest was unprecedented. Initial estimates projected up to 10,000 candidates. The actual number fell to around 2,000, but this was still ten for every seat. Election day turnout was 72 percent, well above the usual 50 percent for assembly polls.[12]

The results offered a mix of old and new. Outside the major urban areas, the ban on campaigning effectively delivered the election into the hands of the old vote brokers. Most of those elected were retired officials or the wives, children, and associates of established political figures. In Bangkok the results were more interesting. The largest vote went to a retired irrigation official, Pramote Maiklad, whose main prominence came from his long association with the king. He had also been eased out of his job a year earlier under political pressure. Three others (Suphon Suphaphong, Chirmsak

Pinthong, and Meechai Viravaidya) were closely associated with NGO work and the campaign to save Bangchak from privatization. Three others (Khru Yui, Khru Pratheep, and Jon Ungphakorn) were long-standing NGO activists on children rights, slum communities, and AIDS. Another academic (Kaewsan Atipho) was an activist on urban renewal and scourge of suspect politicians, including the ruling interior minister. The only businessmen elected (Wichian Techaphaibun) had lost his bank in the crash and, along with two lawyers elected (Sak Kosaengrueng and Seri Suwanpanond), had been active in the campaign to defend Thai capital from the fire sale. The only successful Bangkok candidate with a political association was Chumphon Silpa-archa who had (quite uniquely) resigned a ministership and split from his brother Banharn.

The returns from some provincial areas (Chiang Rai, Korat, Songkhla, Bangkok outskirts) showed some of the same trends. Urban Thailand had voted for public activism, for the self-reliant response to the crisis associated with the king, for the campaigns to save Bangchak and prevent a fire sale, and against the intrigues and arrogance of the incumbent politicians.[13]

THE WAY AHEAD

Dividing society

Throughout Thailand's period of strong growth from the 1960s, the number of people below the poverty line fell, but the gap between rich and poor gaped wider. During the export-oriented boom from the mid-1980s, these trends were accentuated. By some estimates half of all the income gains of the boom went to just 10 percent of the population.

This economic division (as measured by the gini coefficient) appeared to reach its worst point in 1992. After that, labour markets tightened, real wages rose, and more of the benefits were spread more widely. The share of all incomes going to the top 10 percent of households stopped growing and contracted (chart 9.1). The shares going to the other deciles increased. But this redistribution was very slight.[14] Some hope this change in trend shows the Kuznets effect—that during growth, income distribution first gets worse and then gets better. But the slight improvement from 1992 to 1998 may result merely from the special labour market conditions at the end of a boom. The main factors behind Thailand's sharply skewed income

Chart 9.1: Incomes shares by decile, 1981–98

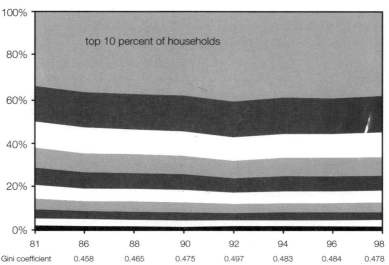

Gini coefficient	0.458	0.465	0.475	0.497	0.483	0.484	0.478

distribution are structural—the concentration of growth in certain sectors of the urban economy; the continued weakness of agriculture; and the poor distribution of economic assets (land ownership), social assets (education), and political assets (organizational strength and access).

On exit from the crisis, the tendency for this pattern of growth to divide society will remain. Indeed, the increased dependence on foreign investment may make matters worse. That is the conclusion of cross-country studies of FDI and export-led growth (Tsai 1995). It is also a lesson from Latin America after its financial crises, market liberalization, and increased foreign investment in the 1980s (Green 1995; Alvarez et al. 1998). There, one of the fastest-growing businesses became protection—selling everything from fortified condominiums to private armies to protect the rich from the angry.

Even more than before, growth is likely to be concentrated in a limited portion of the economy, namely a few leading sectors of export manu-facture. The linkage effects to other sectors will be weak. Because these industries are capital intensive and technology based, they will not have a large pull on the labour market. Because of fierce international competi-tion and the possibilities that firms will relocate away from Thailand,

237

government will be easily blackmailed into channelling resources towards these sectors. Other areas of the economy will be less dynamic and less favoured. The rural economy in particular will continue to languish. The urban bias built into the reformed parliament will obstruct pressures to reverse the trend of worsening distribution through any refocus on agriculture or any serious restructuring of the allocation of economic, social, and political assets. During the bubble and bust, rural land passed from small farmer-operators to urban speculators, investors, and banks. Accurate statistics are not available but it is most likely that the ownership of land became more skewed, and the numbers of landless and insecure farmers increased.

Competing agendas

At present two competing visions of the near future are available, though neither is yet sharply defined in public debate. The first accepts and welcomes the fact that Thailand is moving from an era in which the main aim of economic policy was to develop a local capitalism, to an era in which Thailand will prosper as a host for multinational capital. This is the vision implied by the neoliberal agenda, and also favoured by many Thai technocrats who have become more antagonistic to the old business conglomerates. It is also supported by many members of the Bangkok middle class who prospered during the boom, who hope the good times will return, and who like to imagine Thailand as a properly "modern" society. It is also implicitly the vision of the Democrat Party. For supporters of this agenda, the main priorities are reforms in education and infrastructure to create the manpower and environment which attract investors; and the "good governance" reforms in law and administration which the neoliberals demand.

The model of this future is Singapore. The major problem lies in managing the social consequences of worsening distribution. Singapore confronted this problem by building one of the world's most extensive systems of social welfare, concentrating public investment on education and infrastructure, and disposing of its rural sector (to Malaysia). Not all of these options are available to Bangkok.[15] However, educational reform has risen to the top of the national agenda, while the World Bank and ADB are supporting schemes to extend social safety nets at low cost by mobilizing and strengthening existing non-state provisions by family, community, and self-help associations. However the international agencies' thinking about social safety nets is very focused on the market failures of the urban sector. It makes no attack on the structural factors—poor land rights, low investment in agriculture, poor access to education, limited political rights—which lie behind the growing divide in Thai society. Besides, the fiscal constraint imposed by high levels of public debt, the possibility of competing political demands for public expenditure, and the increasing discontent in rural society, mean that this "Singapore solution" will require a significant retreat from democracy.

A second vision sees a resurgence of local capitalism among small and medium firms. This vision starts from the proposition that Thailand's entrepreneurial culture is still alive, and that the collapse of the conglomerates and the destruction of government-protected monopolies will create a more open space for the growth of a new wave of small and medium firms. These firms should concentrate on activities in which Thailand has some competitive advantage arising from its natural resources, cultural capital, or social capital. The model is Taiwan.[16] Advocates suggest that this model is more appropriate to Thailand than the earlier concentration of growth in big domestic conglomerates, and that the benefits will be more widely distributed.

This view finds support among formal business lobbies and some political parties. Thaksin Shinawatra has pitched his new Thai Rak Thai party as supportive of entrepreneurship, small and medium enterprise, and a more proactive government role in industrial planning and promotion. The Chat Phatthana party remains involved with some of the stronger of the surviving Thai conglomerates, and has argued (unsuccessfully so far) for a more active industrial policy. In early 1999, it proposed government should directly support the resurrection of a wafer fabrication project, which collapsed at the onset of the crisis, as a means to stimulate the electronics sector.

This view is also roughly congruent with the Japanese vision to develop Thailand's foundation of service and subcontract businesses to support another wave of region-wide growth based on an outflow of Japanese manufacturing. From before the crisis, Japan warned Thailand over the neglect of direct industrial policy. Through the crisis, it occasionally signalled dissent from the neoliberal, finance-accented trend of the IMF's anti-crisis strategy. However, the Japanese voice was undermined by the weakness of Japan's own economy, and by the sheer noise level of the neoliberal advocacy. The Japanese effort is also vulnerable to the criticism that it focuses aid in areas which are directly supportive of Japanese export firms in Thailand. Only after the Miyazawa initiative in late 1998 did the Japanese voice in policy making became stronger.

However, the prospects for this vision depend on the construction of a political coalition able to defeat the neoliberal-inclined Democrat-led regime and its background of support from Western business lobbies and international organizations. This model also faces the problem of budget constraints and competing political demands. If the Japanese economy revives and delivers a new phase of regional growth, Thailand's economy and its economic policy may be pulled into line with Japanese strategy. But if the Western economies remain significantly stronger, the Singapore model may come to the fore.

While the crisis has thus seen Thailand move along the neoliberal path, the future trend is not at all clear and uncontested. International institutions, led by the World Bank, have placed greater emphasis on an agenda of democratization, governance, social safety nets, and support for civil society. This new agenda—dubbed the New or Post Washington Consensus—recognizes that the earlier neoliberal agenda lacked social and political aspects, and that social and political reactions can threaten the economic programme. This new agenda enshrines a belief that more open politics will strengthen the prospects for the success of the neoliberal economic agenda of open markets. In Thailand, where politics are already more open than in most Asian countries and where the crisis has stimulated participation and competition, this belief is likely to be put to the test. The groups which we expect to assert themselves after the crisis—small and medium businessmen who do not understand why their businesses were wrecked; farmers who have borne much of the social strain; civil society activists who are emboldened to build on recent success; and establishment radicals who are concerned whether the society can absorb such a sudden step change in foreign economic penetration—these groups have many good reasons not to support open markets without reservation.

Localism

There is a third vision of the future, that of the localists. They do not necessarily oppose globalization. Rather they believe that the way for a relatively small and globally unimportant society to survive in the age of globalization is to pay close attention to its local foundations. Similarly they do not necessarily oppose the outward orientation of the Thai economy. Realists among them recognize that this trend has a long history, is firmly embedded in the structure of the economy, and has a large base of support in Thai urban society. But they argue for positive action to counter the social consequences of this outward orientation. The keywords of this agenda are *self*-reliance, *self*-help, *self*-sufficiency.

Support for this agenda grew through the duration of the crisis. This was partly due to the lead given by the king in his speech of December 1997, and partly due to the advocacy of Prawase Wasi, Saneh Chamarik, and many others. But this agenda also gained supporters because of the length and severity of the crisis itself. Many committed globalizers and ardent modernists, who argued at the outset of the crisis that Thailand must respond by espousing the reforms and further liberalizations advocated by the neoliberals, became more qualified and conditional over the next thirty months. The crisis revealed the vulnerability of Thailand, the rapacity of some whom Thais had considered friends, and the imperative to be more self-reliant. Reflecting on the huge public debt which Thailand had contracted in just two years, the central bank governor, Chatumongol Sonakul said, "Outside your country it's a dog-eat-dog world and little dogs that don't behave get their heads bitten off" (*TN*, 21 Oct 1999).

Many adopted the view that Thailand had to undertake the neoliberal-nominated reforms in order to survive in the global economy, but also needed to strengthen its social foundations for the same reason. The language of self-sufficiency and self-reliance spread surprisingly widely. At the end of 1999, the Thailand Development Research Institute, the leading centre of technocratic research and the spiritual home of the country's leading mainstream economists, devoted its flagship annual public conference to the king's ideas on the sufficient economy. The economist and financier, Narongchai Akrasanee, who had been a prominent enthusiast for market economics and export-led growth, started to imagine that he had all along been a believer in self-reliance. Bangkok Bank executives began to spout the language of sufficiency and self-reliance. Chatumongol even presented the legislation to reform the central bank as an example of the king's ideas on the self-sufficient economy.

In his famous 1997 speech, the king had talked about the importance of sufficiency and self-reliance for surviving the crisis. Over the first two years of the crisis, this was the point that was remembered from the speech. It was interpreted as strengthening the villages to withstand the social impact of unemployment and income loss. But in the same speech the king had also talked about Thailand's capacity as a self-reliant and competitive producer. He sat through the speech with a bongo drum in front of him. He explained that the maker had formerly imported the drums, but could not sell them at a profit after the crash. So he had worked out how to make the drums out of wood from Thai rubber trees and other local materials, and was now exporting to the USA and Europe. At first, this aspect of the king's speech was ignored. But as the crisis lengthened, more people, particularly in the business and administrative elite, began to find a broader interpretation of the king's ideas about sufficiency and self-reliance useful both as an insurance against social damage and as a strategy for the survival of Thai capitalism. The keynote statement from the TDRI conference argued that the king's strategy "points the way for recovery that will lead to a more resilient and sustainable economy better able to meet the challenges arising from globalization and other changes" (TDRI 1999b). In this new version, greater self-reliance meant a more conditional accommodation with the forces of globalization, rather than blind faith in globalization's benefits.

The impact of the crisis has been more complex than most expected. It has shifted Thailand decisively along the road towards a more open and globally integrated economy. At the same time it has opened up politics to a wider range of ideas and agendas, stirred up civil society, and directed attention back to the society's foundations and local roots. More than ever, Thailand's political economy is hostage to the fortunes of the major forces in the global economy. But also more than ever, Thailand's civil society is an arena for competing interests, visions, and agendas—including the view that success in the age of globalization depends (ironically) on greater self-reliance.

NOTES

1. Between July 1997 and mid 1999, forty-five large companies listed on the Stock Exchange of Thailand had offered their shares to foreign buyers. These included seven commercial banks, eight securities companies, three insurance

companies, and twenty-seven others. Report of the Stock Exchange Commission, cited in Kamon (1999).

2. Brimble and Sherman's sample included deals in which the foreign participant put in at least US$1 million *either* to buy an initial stake of at least 10 percent *or* to convert a minority stake into a majority or outright ownership.

3. Kiatnakin and Thanachart/Ekachart planned to apply for limited bank licences.

4. In the case of Nakhon Thon Bank, the private negotiation stalled and government stepped in, took over the bank, and completed the sale to Standard Chartered.

5. Thai Military Bank failed to raise new capital through an international roadshow in late 1999. The bank's advisers knew the project was doomed when at meetings with prospective foreign buyers some of the directors turned up dressed in full uniform.

6. Firms buying majority stakes included: Merrill Lynch, Vickers Ballas, Societé General Crosby, AIG group, ING Barings, Indosuez W.I. Carr, Lehman Brothers, BNP, Bankers Trust, and two Singaporean (DBS, Kim-Eng) and one Taiwanese (KG) firm (*BP*, 25 Aug 1998).

7. In October 1997, 100-percent foreign ownership was allowed in financial institutions (previously restricted to 25 percent), but with a ten-year limitation which is seen as only a cosmetic touch. The 40-percent limitation on businesses other than those US-owned or covered by specific export-promotion concessions was effectively lifted by a Board of Investment (BoI) provision. The Alien Business Law, which reserves certain sectors for Thai-only investment, has been revised. Full foreign ownership of land is still restricted, but leasehold has been significantly liberalized.

8. In 1999, the number of chain convenience stores increased 15 percent, and the market leader, 7-Eleven, increased its turnover from 11 to 13 billion baht (*BP*, 10 Nov 1999).

9. Total corporate bond issues were 125.8 billion baht in 1999, and 45.3 billion in the first quarter of 2000.

10. Several leading Thai bankers (e.g. Chartsiri Sophonpanich of Bangkok Bank in *TN*, 4 May 1999) have stated that they too will focus on consumer banking and compete with the international banks. Less convincingly, they claim they will develop more lending to small and medium enterprises—a claim which is rather more politically correct than realistic. Chartsiri stated: "Relationship banking used to generate 70 percent of business, now it's probably 30 per cent" (*TN*, 30 Jun 1999).

11. Import tariffs on 85 percent of goods traded within ASEAN are cut to a range of 0–5 percent from 1 January 2000.

12. Voting was (for the first time) officially compulsory but this was not well understood, and the penalties for not voting were minor (loss of certain political rights). Some of the high turnout was contributed by last-minute rumours that non-voters would lose access to public services such as schools and hospitals.

13. The Election Commission disqualified 78 of the 200 successful candidates for electoral malpractice. The second poll in Bangkok confirmed the overall pattern by removing the only businessman (Wichian) from the list of successful Bangkok candidates, and substituting another activist—Chodchoy Sophonpanich.

14. Thanks to Yukio Ikemoto of Tokyo University for these income calculations based on data from the *Socioeconomic Surveys*.

15. Many supporters of this vision often seem to imagine that they already live in a country very different from Thailand. They seem blind to anything beyond the city.

16. Thaksin claims inspiration from the Tuscan-Italian model. But Taiwan is probably closer in geographical, cultural and other ways.

LESSONS

Thailand's crisis was surprising because nobody expected the downturn could be so steep and so deep. The country's past record (forty years with GDP growth never dropping below 4 percent) was no guide to how bad things could quickly become.

Crises are created by ideology and politics. Many analysts locate the origins of the Thai crisis in the bad sequencing of financial liberalization—going for capital account convertibility without reforms in banking practice and macroeconomic stance. Few ask why these decisions were taken. The World Bank and Thai technocrats backed liberalization because they believed it would improve the Thai economy's prospects for growth. But they could not control the politics. Financial liberalization carried out in parallel with increased democratization delivered control of economic policy making into the hands of politicians with little understanding of economic management. The inflows of hot money helped create a political constituency to oppose reforms in macro management. The politics of liberalization are much trickier than enthusiasts expect.

Since the collapse of the cold war, the US has adopted a mission to reform economic and political systems around the world. The manifesto of this project—open markets and good governance—is the modern version of the civilizing mission of the colonial era. The manifesto also has some important subsidiary propositions. The fulfilment of this mission is opposed by "elites," "vested interests," or "crony capitalists." Periods of crisis and dislocation, when these opposing forces are in disarray, provide opportunities to fulfil the mission. The oppressed mass of "the poor" will benefit, and

245

their silent support legitimates interventions which undercut elected (or otherwise established) governments. Hence crises packages are divided between overcoming a crisis and taking advantage of it. These two aims conflict.

Modern crises happen in the capital account because of devastatingly large inward and outward flows. A stronger banking system and more appropriate macro stance will lessen vulnerability to such crises. But they will not prevent them altogether. Small and weak economies are constantly vulnerable to the large capital movements which are now everyday events. International financial institutions are constantly improving their ability to manage and profit from the risks inherent in this fluid capital market. They make money out of the volatility of markets.

Creditors and debtors make financial crises together. Every loan has both a borrower and a lender. Holders of short-term debt were quite rational in wanting to get out of Thailand after mid-1997. But they would also have been even more rational if they had decided *not* to come in over the previous two to three years. Some have excused themselves by arguing that the market was not transparent. True, the management of the reserves was covert, but that became critical only during the endgame. Any lender during 1994–96, could see data showing the unprecedented levels of loan inflows, the declining returns from SET-listed firms, the faltering of exports, and the widening current account gap. The problem was not the availability of information, but the will to learn from it—on behalf of both debtors and creditors.

The West and the international organizations are not going to reform the international financial system. The enthusiasm for reform which peaked in late 1998 has evaporated as the prospects for a crash of international proportions have receded. Only a major disaster in the US or European economies will prompt any significant reform.

When a crisis happens, the first priority for a country such as Thailand should be to stay clear of the IMF (in its present form). The IMF's first priority is to maintain the stability of the international financial system, and that means ensuring that the big players are not damaged. Its second is to enforce neoliberal policy reforms. Achieving recovery comes in third place. Thailand will have to establish early warning systems in order to redress problems before they get out of hand. A small country like Thailand should seek a more regional approach (over matters such as currency management) to create some form of immunity against the negative effects of global disorder.

Because modern crises are capital account crises, the recovery programmes need to work directly on the capital account. The IMF applied a solution designed for the current account crises of Latin America in the 1980s. The cure was not only irrelevant to the real disease, but the fiscal and monetary medicine was also very slow acting, while this new disease strikes fast. The headlong flight of capital out of Thailand from mid 1997 converted a crisis predicted to be relatively mild into a major disaster with international implications. The only way to prevent this happening in modern-style crises is to block the capital outflow. By different measures, Malaysia and Korea did this, and suffered less. These countries have had similar crises before. They had the learning. Thailand and Indonesia were more naïve. They paid the price. Some sort of capital controls, standstill agreement, or debt rollover arrangement is the only way to prevent the stomach-hollowing slide suffered by Thailand and Indonesia.

Once an economy has suffered this slide, the damage is large and probably permanent, and the way out from the crisis is a very steep climb. Any economy which has had its currency value cut by 50 percent, and suffered a steady outflow of capital equivalent to a sixth of GDP over two to three years, would find most of its companies technically bankrupt, its financial system in seizure, and its real economy stopped dead. Most would also face total social and political chaos.

Some Thai firms obviously contributed to the crisis. Many did not. But once the economy is stopped dead and virtually all firms rendered technically bankrupt, then this distinction disappears. All have a problem. And all can be blamed.

Once a crisis happens, it can be cited as evidence to prove every possible kind of theory.

The IMF will never admit fault. It has resisted virtually all criticism of its Asian packages, and has rushed to claim credit for the recovery. But consider this. The IMF's package was supposed to work by restoring international confidence, reversing capital outflows, and raising exports. But exports remained sluggish, while the capital outflows still have not stopped since the implementation of the package. Any recovery is happening despite these outflows, despite the IMF.

Crises will be handled better if those in charge have more involvement, more knowledge, more sympathy, and more at stake. Thailand started the Asian crisis but was essentially a sideshow. The Thai economy is not so significant to the world economy that its fate demands attention. This helps to explain why the initial programme was so carelessly done. Larry Summers remarked, "Thailand is not on our border." The IMF (according to Jo Stiglitz) shrugged off criticism of its original plans on grounds that it could always try something else if they did not work. But in modern crises, you only get one chance.

In countries such as Thailand, the unemployment rate does not measure the social impact of economic stress as well as in more developed economies. The labour market is less formal and more fluid. People have multiple and serial patterns of employment. With no formal social welfare, not working/earning is often not an option. Many react to crisis by taking low-paid work, launching a petty business, or working as unpaid family labour in order to have a claim on family support. People are likely to redefine themselves as unpaid labour or out of the labour force, rather then appearing as "unemployed." The unemployment rate only captured around half of the disruption in the labour market.

Crises end up hitting the most vulnerable—particularly the rural poor and landless who depend on income from migratory labour. The recent crisis shows that countries with unemployment insurance schemes (such as Korea) can cope with the social impact better. Thai workers have agitated for the introduction of the unemployment insurance scheme for some time. The Thai government has resisted introducing such schemes for fear of increasing the government's burden. But the ultimate cost—the public debts incurred from social bailout schemes—should change that assessment.

In the absence of significant social provisioning, self help is the best way to survive. However good their intentions on social policy, the international organizations were engaged in an entirely experimental project to provide a new kind of social provision in a social and bureaucratic context that they did not understand. These efforts were not quick or effective enough to cushion the impact of such a sharp downturn. But local society responded with techniques for sharing the strain and mobilizing community supports. Thailand is lucky that family and community have not yet been destroyed by the strains of industrialization and globalization.

The international organizations now highlight social policy. They have discovered that mass protests or mass distress which lead to movements of nationalism or populism are the only serious potential threats to programmes of economic and political reform carried out against the background of economic crisis. The social safety net is an attempt to preempt such reactions. But social safety nets, however necessary, are only strategies for cushioning crises. They do not address the issues which lie behind poverty and social division—the skewed distribution of economic, social, and political assets. Rural society is expected to remain a dependent department of the urban economy, gradually releasing labour supplies, and gradually falling apart.

The poverty business is becoming rather crowded. In May 1999 the president of the ADB declared that poverty reduction is the "overarching objective" of the ADB. In April 2000, the ADB announced it would banish poverty from Asia by a specific date—2025. In the weeks before his retirement, Michel Camdessus claimed that the IMF was the "best friend of the poor" and that "poverty reduction is at the heart of our programmes." James Wolfensohn constantly repeats that the World Bank is dedicated to the removal of poverty. At the tail of the crisis the Bank announced its commitment to the "quality of growth." Is all of this a change of heart or a crisis of legitimacy?

The crisis has made clear that the West no longer wants to promote local capitalisms. In the period of the cold war, local capitalisms were seen as bulwarks against communism. Now that the cold war has passed and the communist threat has become history, the poorer countries of the world have become peripheral again. Their role—explicitly stated by people like Larry Summers—is to be a good and secure place for investments of multinational companies.

Political elites get coopted into the neoliberal project. In an open and externally exposed economy, political leaders are vulnerable to the blackmail of the financial markets on a day-to-day basis. Once the public sector runs up a large debt, the political leaders must be responsive to the creditors. Acquiescence becomes a lot easier than resistance. Although the ruling Democrats opposed several parts of the IMF programme, in public they presented themselves as "good pupils" of the IMF. Whenever they faced opposition, they claimed "the markets" would punish Thailand, deepening the disaster. Balancing these outside pressures against the need to maintain local constituencies of support becomes a tricky business. Ultimately political leaders find it easier to sell the neoliberal programme to the locals than to sell local needs and demands to the outside patrons and creditors. The Thai government ceased to be responsible to its people. Instead it became responsive to its creditors and to its international patrons.

During the boom, Thailand's rural sector was ignored. The crisis restated its social and political importance. In the absence of any formal social welfare, the villages still take the strain of urban economic disaster. But they no longer do this without complaint. Through the crisis, the government was under siege by farmers demanding debt relief, crop price support, and control over natural resources. Politicians toyed with the idea of converting these protests into a more potent populism. Ultimately, the politicians backed away from such a dangerous project. But the pressure remains, because the problem remains.

Nationalism provides no platform for active resistance in the absence of any history of nationalist militancy. Attempts to build a network of resistance to the crisis programmes of the government and IMF on the basis of nationalism came to nothing. Although the elite has invested in building a Thai nationalism from top down over the past century, this nationalism was never turned into a popular, mass force through a nationalist war or an anti-colonial movement.

Rather than punching outwards, many people turned inwards. The king offered self-sufficiency and self-reliance as ways to manage the dangers of globalization. At first this message was interpreted as a strategy to strengthen villages to bear the strain of urban collapse. But as the crisis deepened and lengthened, the proposition that Thailand needed to understand the real foundations of its society, economy, and culture, gained a much broader interpretation. Sufficiency was reinterpreted as a strategy to place conditions on global integration, and to protect society against division and dissolution. Self-reliance started to be seen as a strategy to survive and succeed in the era of globalization.

The debate about the local community as a counterweight to globalization gained greater power and definition. The idea of the community was relaunched not as a cultural ideal but as a philosophical construct, underwritten by Buddhism, that elevated social values of humanity and human well-being above the profit motive and market clearing of pure economics.

The crisis reorganized Thai politics. The space for formal politics narrowed. The city reasserted its political domination. The ruling

Democrats were pulled into alignment with neoliberal policies. Civil society was stirred up by stress and frustration. The resulting political forces harbour a host of contradictions. Social demands have increased, but the capacity of the state to deliver against these demands may have shrunk.

Society should rely less on the state. As Robert Cox (2000) has argued, in a globalized world, governments of open economies become increasingly involved with an international world of business and finance, and increasingly detached from the needs and demands of their people. This detachment becomes even more marked when a large element of the people live within a political economy which is only loosely linked to this international world. Also as Cox notes, this new structure increases the importance of civil society and social movements. Here Thailand is relatively fortunate. Over the last two decades—and especially through the 1990s—many different types of NGOs, foundations, and popular movements have appeared to work for improvement in the quality of life of people at the grassroots. The groups working on issues of health, protection of children, human rights, environmental care, corruption, community building, and minority rights have become particularly strong. Popular movements have grown up from the roots among small-scale fishermen, landless peasants, victims of dam and power projects, AIDS patients, female workers, sex workers, hill peoples, and urban enthusiasts for political reform and environmental protection. In many ways, government failures have proved to be strong incentives. It is these social groups and grassroots movements which will be the conscience of the society and which will act as forces for change towards a better future.

ABBREVIATIONS

ADB	Asian Development Bank
BBC	Bangkok Bank of Commerce
BIBF	Bangkok International Banking Facility
BoI	Board of Investment
BoT	Bank of Thailand
CDA	Constitution Drafting Assembly
CERN	Carnegie Economic Reform Network
CP	Charoen Pokphand company/group
FCCT	Foreign Correspondents Club of Thailand
FDA	Food and Drug Authority
FDI	foreign direct investment
FIDF	Financial Institutions Development Fund
FRA	Financial Sector Restructuring Authority
GDP	gross domestic product
GSB	Government Savings Bank
IFC	International Finance Corporation (of the World Bank)
ILO	International Labour Organization
ITV	Independent Television
IMF	International Monetary Fund
ISI	import substitution industrialization
JETRO	Japan External Trade Organization
JICA	Japan International Cooperation Agency

LDP	Liberal Democratic Party (of Japan)
LFS	Labour Force Survey
LoI	Letter of Intent
MIT	Massachusetts Institute of Technology
MITI	Ministry of International Trade and Industry (of Japan)
NAP	New Aspiration Party
NESDB	National Economic and Social Development Board
NGO	non-government organization
NSO	National Statistical Office
OECD	Organization for Economic Cooperation and Development
OECF	Overseas Economic Cooperation Fund
PLMO	Property Loan Management Office
R&D	research and development
SAP	Social Action Party
SES	Socioeconomic Survey
SIF	Social Investment Fund
SIP	Social Investment Programme
SLIPS/CAPS	Stapled Limited Interest Preferred Shares/Capital Augmented Preferred Shares
TAO	Tambon Administration Organization
TDRI	Thailand Development Research Institute
TRT	Thai Rak Thai (Thai love Thai) Party
UNDP	United Nations Development Programme
UNESCO	United Nations Educational, Scientific and Cultural Organization
UNICEF	United Nations International Children's Emergency Fund
VAT	value added tax
WTO	World Trade Organization

GLOSSARY

achan	professor, teacher
chaebol	Korean business conglomerate
chao pho	godfather
chumchon	community
chumchon aphiwat	community rule
dao krachai	lit., scattered stars; protests scattered around in peripheral localities
farang	foreigner, westerner
Isan	northeastern region
khaen	traditional northeastern woodwind instrument
khao kaeng	curry and rice
kilesa	vice
khlong	canal
ku chat	saving the nation
kwitieo	noodles
lak muang	city pillar
luk chin ping	grilled meatballs
luk khrung	Eurasian, Thai-*farang*
maha amnat	lit., great powers; powerful countries
ngoen phan	lit., money transfer; local development funds, especially the 1975 tambon scheme
O Bo To	Tambon Administration Organization (*ongkon borihan tambon*)

pha pa	ritual of donating robes or money to monks
pha pa chuay chat	donation to help the nation
phanthamit ku wikrit chat	Alliance for National Salvation
pho yu pho kin	lit., enough to live and eat; self-sufficiency
phung ton eng	self-reliance
Phutthakasetakam	Buddhist agriculture
rabop uppatham	patronage system
rai	unit of land equivalent to 0.16 hectare
rakha yuk IMF	IMF-era prices
samakkhi	unity
sia krung	the fall of the city, especially Ayutthaya in 1767
So Po Ko	Land Reform Office (*samnak ngan kan patirup thidin phua kasetakam*)
songkran	Thai New Year's celebration in which water is sprinkled or poured on others as a blessing
tambon	sub-district
tanha	desire
thammarat	lit., righteous state; proposed translation of "good governance"
thongthin	locality
thritsadi mai	new theory
wat	temple
watthanatham chumchon	community culture

BIBLIOGRAPHY

AWSJ   *Asian Wall Street Journal*
BP   *Bangkok Post*
FEER   *Far Eastern Economic Review*
TN   *The Nation*
TR   *Thai Rath*

The Letters of Intent (LoI) between the Thai government and the IMF can be found on the Bank of Thailand's website: www.bot.or.th.

Akyüz, Yilmaz and Andrew Cornford. 1999. Capital Flows to Developing Countries and the Reform of the International Financial System. Unctad discussion papers no. 143, November.

Alvarez, Sonia E., Evelina Dagnino, and Arturo Escobar, eds. 1998. *Cultures of Politics. Politics of Cultures: Re-visioning Latin American Social Movements*. Boulder: Westview Press.

Ammar Siamwalla. 1997. Why are we in this Mess? *The Nation*, 12, 13, and 14 November 1997; *Bangkok Post*, 12 November 1997

Ammar Siamwalla and Orapin Sopchokchai. 1998. *Responding to the Thai Economic Crisis*. Bangkok: TDRI, August.

Amon Chantharasombun. 1994. *Khonsatitiwchannalisum (Constitutionalism): thang ok khong prathet thai* (Constitutionalism: Way out for Thailand). Bangkok: Institute of Public Policy Studies.

Anand Panyarachun. 1999. Democracy and Free Markets. *TDRI Quarterly Review* 14 (4), December.

Anek Laothamatas. 1992. *Business Associations and the New Political Economy of Thailand: From Bureaucratic Polity to Liberal Corporatism*. Boulder: Westview Press.

Anek Laothamatas. 1995. *Song nakhara prachathippatai: naew thang patirup kan muang setthakit phu prachathippatai* (A Tale of Two Cities of Democracy: Directions for Reform in Politics and Economy for Democracy). Bangkok: Matichon.

Anek Laothamatas, Seksan Prasertkun, Anan Kanchanaphan, and Direk Pathamasiriwat. 1995. *Wiphak sangkhom thai* (Critique of Thai Society). Bangkok: Amarin.

Aphichai Phantasen. 1996. *Khwam wang thang ok lae thang luak mai* (Hopes, Ways out, and New Options). Bangkok: Munnithi Phumipanya.

Aroonsri Tivakul. 1995. Globalization of Financial Markets in Thailand and their Implications for Monetary Stability. *Bank of Thailand Quarterly Bulletin* 35 (2).

Asian Development Bank. 1999. Assessing the Social Impact of the Financial Crisis in Thailand, by Amara Ponsapich and Peter Brimble. July 30.

Baker, Chris. 2000. Thailand's Assembly of the Poor: Background, Drama, Reaction. *South East Asia Research* 8 (1).

Banthit Thanachaisetwuni, ed. 1997. *Wikrit loek chang wang ngan lae thang ok* (The Lay-off Crisis, Unemployment, and the Way out). Bangkok: Arom Phonphangan Foundation.

Beams, Nick. 1998. The Asian Meltdown: A Crisis of Global Capitalism. At www.wsws.org.

Bell, Daniel A., David Brown, Kanishka Jayasuriya, and David Martin Jones. 1995. *Towards Illiberal Democracy in Pacific Asia*. New York: St. Martins.

Bello, Walden, Shea Cunningham, and Li Kheng Po. 1998. *A Siamese Tragedy: Development and Disintegration in Modern Thailand*. London and New York: Zed Books.

Bernard, Mitchell. 1999. East Asia's Tumbling Dominoes: Financial Crises and the Myth of the Regional Model. *Socialist Register* 1999.

Bhanupong Nidhiprabha. 1998. Economic Crises and the Debt-Deflation Episode in Thailand. *ASEAN Economic Bulletin* 15 (3), December.

Brimble, Peter and James Sherman. 1999. Mergers and Acquisitions in Thailand: The Changing Face of Foreign Direct Investment. Report prepared for the United Nations Conference on Trade and Development, 20 May.

CERN. 1999. *The Politics of the Economic Crisis in Asia: Consensus and Controversies.* Washington D.C.: Carnegie Economic Reform Network.

Chai-Anan Samudavanija. 1995. *Kan patirup thang kan muang* (Political Reform), Bangkok: Institute of Public Policy Studies.

Chai-Anan Saumudavanija. 1997. *Watthanatham ku thun* (Culture as Capital). Bangkok: P. Press.

Chaiyawat Wibulswasdi. 1996. How should central banks respond to the challenges posed by the global integration of capital markets? Bank of Thailand. *Quarterly Bulletin* 36 (1).

Chalongphob Sussangkarn, Frank Flatters, and Sauwalak Kittiprapas. 1999. Comparative Social Impacts of the Asian Economic Crisis in Thailand, Indonesia, Malaysia and the Philippines: a Preliminary Report. *TDRI Quarterly Review* 14 (2), March.

Chandrasekhar, C. P. and Jayati Ghosh. 1998. Hubris, Hysteria, Hope: The Political Economy of Crisis and Response in Southeast Asia. In *Tigers in Trouble: Financial Governance, Liberalisation and Crises in East Asia*, edited by K. S. Jomo. London: Zed Books.

Chang, Ha-Joon. 1998. South Korea: the Misunderstood Crisis. In *Tigers in Trouble: Financial Governance, Liberalisation and Crises in East Asia*, edited by K. S. Jomo. London: Zed Books.

Chatthip Nartsupha. 1991. The 'Community Culture' School of Thought. In *Thai Constructions of Knowledge*, edited by Manas Chitkasem and Andrew Turton. London: SOAS.

Chatthip Nartsupha, Chinasak Suwan-Achariya, Aphichat Thongyou, Voravidh Charoenloet, and Maniemai Thongyou. 1998. *Thritsadi lae naewkhit setthakit chumchon chaona* (Theories and Approaches to the Economics of the Peasant Community). Bangkok: Withithat local wisdom series 7.

Chittima Duriyaprapan and Mathee Supapongse. 1996. Financial Liberalisation: Case Study of Thailand. *Bank of Thailand Quarterly Bulletin* 36 (4).

Chuchai Suphawong and Yuwadi Katganglai, eds. 1997. *Pracha sangkhom: thatsana nak khit nai sangkhom thai* (Civil Society: Views of Thinkers in Thai Society). Bangkok: Matichon.

Committee on Democratic Development (CDD). 1995. *Patirup kan muang thai* (Reform of Thai Politics). Bangkok: Thailand Research Fund.

Connors, Michael K. 1999. Political Reform and the State in Thailand. *Journal of Contemporary Asia* 29.

Cox, Robert W. 2000. Political Economy and World Order: Problems of Power and Knowledge at the Turn of the Millennium. In *Political Economy and the Changing Global Order*, edited by Richard Stubbs and Geoffrey R. D. Underhill. Don Mills, Ontario: Oxford University Press Canada.

Deacon. Bob. 1997. *Global Social Policy: International Organizations and the Future of Welfare*. London: Sage Publications.

Finance and Banking. 1992. *Thai: sunklang kan ngoen nai phumiphak* (Thailand: Financial Centre for the Region). In *Kan Ngoen Thanakan* (Finance and Banking). March.

Graham, Carol. 1994. *Safety Nets. Politics and the Poor*. Washington: Brookings Institute.

Green, Duncan. 1995. *The Silent Revolution: Rise of Market Economies in Latin America*. New York: Monthly Review Press.

Greenspan, Alan. 1997. Speech at the New York Club. Reported in *The Nation*, 4 and 5 December 1997.

Handley, Paul. 1997. More of the Same? Politics and Business, 1987–96. In *Political Change in Thailand: Democracy and Participation*, edited by Kevin Hewison. London and New York: Routledge.

Heller, Peter S. 1999. Social Concerns for the New Architecture in Asia. Paper for the IMF's Manila Social Forum, 9 November.

Hewison, Kevin. 1989. *Power and Politics in Thailand*. Manila: Journal of Contemporary Asia Press.

Hewison, Kevin. 1993. Of Regimes. State and Pluralities: Thai Politics Enters the 1990s. In *Southeast Asia in the 1990s: Authoritarianism, Democracy and Capitalism*, edited by K. Hewison, R. Robison, and G. Rodan. Sydney: Allen & Unwin.

Hewison, Kevin, ed. 1997. *Political Change in Thailand: Democracy and Participation*. London and New York: Routledge.

Hewison, Kevin. 2000. Thailand's Capitalism before and after the Economic Crisis. In *Politics and Markets in the Wake of the Asian Crisis*, edited by Richard Robison, Mark Beeson, Kanishka Jayasuriya, and Hyuk-Rae Kim. London: Routledge.

Huntington, Samuel P. 1997. *The Clash of Civilizations and the Remaking of World Order*. London: Simon & Schuster.

IMF. 1992. Statement by IMF on the Realization of Economic, Social and Cultural Rights. UN Doc. E/CN.4/Sub.2/1992/57 of 14 September.

IMF. 1994. *Annual Report 1994*. Washington: IMF.

IMF. 1995a. Social Dimensions of Change: The IMF's Policy Dialogue. Contribution to the World Summit on Development. Washington: IMF.

IMF. 1995b. Social Safety Nets for Economic Transition: Options and Recent Experiences. Papers on Policy Analysis and Assessment by Expenditure Policy Division Staff. PPAA/95/3. February. Washington: IMF.

Jayasuriya, Kanishka. 1996. Rule of Law and Capitalism in East Asia. *Pacific Review* 9 (3).

Jayasuriya, Kanishka. 1999. The New Touchy-Feely Washington. *AQ* November–December.

Jayasuriya, Kanishka. 2000. Authoritarian Liberalism, Governance and the Emergence of the Regulatory State in Post-Crisis East Asia. In *Politics and Markets in the Wake of the Asian Crisis*, edited by Richard Robison, Mark Beeson, Kanishka Jayasuriya, and Hyuk-Rae Kim. London: Routledge.

Jomo, K. S.. 1998. Malaysia: From Miracle to Debacle. In *Tigers in Trouble: Financial Governance, Liberalisation and Crises in East Asia*, edited by K. S. Jomo. London: Zed Books.

Kakwani, N. 1998. *Impact of Economic Crisis on Employment, Unemployment and Real Income*. Bangkok: NESDB.

Kamchai Laisamit. 1998. *Wichan neung nak setthasat* (One Economist's Vision). Bangkok: Rujaeng.

Kamon Kamontrakun. 1999. *Ongkon lok aphi maha thun kam chat lae amnat setthakit thi ying yai nai kan khrop khrong lok* (Global Organizations, Large Global Enterprises and their Power of Global Control). In *Wikrit lok phan world bank yut chat thai* (World Crisis and the World Bank's Plan to Seize Thailand), edited by Phitthaya Wongkun. Bangkok: Withithat globalization series 12.

Kasian Tejapira. 2000. *Setthakit pho phiang thuan krasae a-rai?* (What Approach does the Sufficiency Economy Oppose?). *Nation Sutsapda*, 8 (403), 21–7 February 2000.

Khan, Mushtaq H. 1998. Patron-client Networks and the Economic Effects of Corruption in Asia. *European Journal of Development Research* 10 (1), June.

Klein, James R.. 1998. The Constitution of the Kingdom of Thailand. 1997: A Blueprint for Participatory Democracy. Working Paper No.8. Bangkok: The Asia Foundation. March.

Krugman, Paul. 1998. What Happened to Asia? January. web.mit.edu/Krugman/www/disinter.html

Lauridsen, L. S. 1998. Thailand: Causes, Conduct, Consequences. In *Tigers in Trouble: Financial Governance, Liberalisation and Crises in East Asia*, edited by K. S. Jomo. London: Zed Books.

McCargo, Duncan. 1997. *Chamlong Srimuang and the New Thai Politics*. London: Hurst.

McCargo, Duncan. 1998. Alternative Meanings of Political Reform in Contemporary Thailand. *Copenhagen Journal of Asian Studies* 13.

Ministry of the Interior. 1998. *Setthakit chumchon phung ton eng: naew khwam khit lae yutthasat* (Self-Reliant Community Economy: Thinking and Strategy). Bangkok: Ministry of the Interior.

Moore, Barrington Jr. 1967. *The Social Origins of Dictatorship and Democracy*. London: Penguin.

Morell, David and Chai-Anan Samudavanija. 1981. *Political Conflict in Thailand: Reform, Reaction, Revolution*. Cambridge, Mass.: Oelgeschlager, Gunn and Hain.

Naris Chaiyasoot. 1995. Industrialisation, Financial Reform and Monetary Policy. In *Thailand's Industrialisation and Its Consequences*, edited by Medhi Krongkaew. London: St. Martin's Press.

Narong Petprasoet. ed. 1999. *1999: chut plian haeng yuk samai* (1999: Turning Point of the Era). Bangkok: Setthasat kan muang (pua chumchon) 8.

Narongchai Akrasanee and Paitoon Wiboonchutikula. 1990. *Trade Policy and Industrialization in Thailand: Development Outlook and Future Issues*. Ottawa: WIDER.

Narongchai Akrasanee, Karel Jansen, and Jeerasak Ponpisanupichit. 1993. *International Capital Flows and Economic Adjustment in Thailand*. Bangkok: TDRI.

Naruemon Thabchumpon. 1998. Grassroots NGOs and Political Reform in Thailand: Democracy behind Civil Society. *Copenhagen Journal of Asian Studies* 13.

Nathan, Dev, Govind Kelkar, and Nongluck Suphanchaimat. 1998. *Carrying the Burden of the Crisis: Women and the Rural Poor in Thailand*. Unpublished paper. August.

NESDB. *Indicators of Well-Being and Policy Analysis*. Quarterly newsletter [abbreviated as *Indicators*].

Nipon Poapongsakorn. 1999. Agriculture as a Source of Recovery? Paper for Thailand Update, ANU, Canberra, 21 April.

Noranit Setthabut. 1987. *Phak prachathipat* (The Democrat Party). Bangkok: Thammasat University Press.

Nualnoi Treerat, Noppanun Wannathepsakul, and Daniel Ray Lewis. 2000. Global Study on Illegal Drugs: The Case of Bangkok, Thailand. Report for the United Nations Drug Control Programme.

Nukul Prachuabmoh. 1998. *Kho thet ching kiew kap sathanakan wikrit thang setthakit* (Facts about the Economic Crisis]. Bangkok: Ministry of Finance (the "Nukul Report").

Pasuk Phongpaichit. 1992. Technocrats, Businessmen and Generals: Democracy and Economic Policy-Making in Thailand. In *The Dynamic of Economic Policy Reform in South-East Asia and the South-West Pacific*, edited by A. J. MacIntyre and K. Jayasuriya. Singapore: Oxford University Press.

Pasuk Phongpaichit and Chris Baker. 1995. *Thailand: Economy and Politics*. Kuala Lumpur: Oxford University Press.

Pasuk Phongpaichit and Chris Baker. 1997. Power in Transition: Thailand in the 1990s. In *Political Change in Thailand*, edited by Kevin Hewison. London and New York: Routledge.

Pasuk Phongpaichit and Chris Baker. 1998. *Thailand's Boom and Bust*. Chiang Mai: Silkworm Books.

Pasuk Phongpaichit and Sungsidh Piriyarangsan. 1996. *Corruption and Democracy in Thailand*. Chiang Mai: Silkworm Books.

Phatra Research Institute. 1997. The Way out of the Economic Crisis. Unpublished. 30 September.

Phitthaya Wongkun. ed. 1998a. *Thammarat: jut plian prathet thai?* (Thammarat: Turning Point for Thailand?). Bangkok: Withithat globalization series 6.

Phitthaya Wongkun. 1998b. *Than chumchon prachasangkhom thammarat lae chumchon athippatai: thang rot nai yuk wikrit setthakit sangkhom thai* (Community Base, Civil Society, Good Governance, and Community Rule: Survival Routes in the Crisis of Thai Economy and Society). In Phitthaya 1998a.

Phitthaya Wongkun. ed. 1998c. *Thai yuk watthanatham that* (Thai in the Age of Slavery). Bangkok: Withithat globalization series 4.

Phitthaya Wongkun. 1998d. *Kamnam: phumpanya that sang watthanatham that* (Preface: Slave Wisdom Creates Slave Culture). In Phithaya 1998c.

Phitthaya Wongkun. ed. 1998e. *Pracha-aphiwat: bot-rian 25 phi 14 tula* (People's Revolution: Lessons from 25 Years of 14 October). Bangkok: Withithat globalization series 7.

Phitthaya Wongkun. ed. 1999. *Rap wikrit setthakit lok pi 2000: setthakit yang yun* (Withstanding the World Economic Crisis of Year 2000: The Sustainable Economy). Bangkok: Withithat globalization series 10.

Phrathammapitok (P. A. Payutto). 1992. *Buddhist Economics: A Middle Way for the Market Place*, translated by Dhammavijaya and Bruce Evans. Bangkok: Buddhadhamma Foundation.

Phrathammapitok (P. A. Payutto). 1998. *Khwam romyen nai wikrit thai: phutthawithi nai kan kae panha wikrit khong chat* (Shelter in the Thai Crisis: A Buddhist Way to Solve the Problem of the National Crisis). In Phithaya 1998a.

Praphat Pintobtaeng. 1998. *Kan muang bon thong thanon: 99 wan samatcha khon chon* [Politics on the Street: Ninety-nine Days of the Assembly of the Poor]. Bangkok: Krirk University.

Prasan Marutphitak et al. 1998. *Anant Panyarachun: chiwit khwam khit lae kan ngan khong adit nayok ratthamontri song samai* (Anand Panyarachun: Life, Thought, and Works of the Former Two-time Prime Minister). Bangkok: Amarin.

Prawase Wasi. 1998. *Watthanatham kan phatthana* (The Culture of Development). In Phitthaya 1998c.

Prawase Wasi. 1999. *Sethakit pho phiang lae prachasangkom naew thang phlik fun sethakit sangkhom* (The Self-sufficient Economy and Civil Society as a Way to Revive Economy and Society). Bangkok: Mo Chao Ban.

Prudhisan Jumbala. 1998. Thailand: Constitutional Reform amidst Economic Crisis. In *Southeast Asian Affairs 1998*. Singapore: ISEAS.

Rangsan Thanapornphan. 1996. *Thun watthanatham* (Cultural Capital). Unpublished paper.

Reynolds, Craig, ed. 1991. *National Identity and its Defenders: Thailand 1939–1989*. Clayton: Monash Papers on Southeast Asia No. 25.

Reynolds, Craig. 1999. On the Gendering of Nationalist and Post-Nationalist Selves in Twentieth-Century Thailand. In *Genders and Sexualities in Modern Thailand*, edited by Peter Jackson and Nerida Cook. Chiang Mai: Silkworm Books.

Rubin, Robert E. 1988. Remarks to Chulalongkorn University. June 30. www.treas.gov/press/releases/pr2568.htm

Saneh Chamarik. 1998. *Than khit su thang luk mai khong sangkhom thai* (Foundations of Thought for New Options for Thai Society). Bangkok: Withithat local wisdom series 3.

Saneh Chamarik. 1999. *1999 Chut plian haeng yuk samai: chak lokaphiwat su chumchon* (1999: Turning Point of the Era: From Globalization to Community). In Narong 1999.

Sauwalak Kittiprapas and Chettha Intharawithak. 1999. *Kan prap tua khong talat raeng ngan thai phai tai phawa wikrit setthakit* (Adjustment of the Thai Labour Market in the Crisis). Bangkok: TDRI.

Sauwalak Kittiprapas and Chettha Intharawithak. 2000. *Social Impacts of Thai Economic Crisis: What Have We Learned?* Bangkok: TDRI

Smith, Anthony D. 1995. *Nations and Nationalism in a Global Era*. Cambridge: Policy Press.

Snoh Unakul. 1987. *Yutthasat kan phatthana chat adit patchuban anakhot* (Strategy for Developing the Nation, Past, Present, and Future). Bangkok: United Production.

Srisuwan Kuankachorn. 1998. The Roots of the Thai Crisis: A Failure of Development. *Watershed* 3 (3).

Strange, Susan. 1996. *The Retreat of the State: The Diffusion of Power in the World Economy*. Cambridge: Cambridge University Press.

Suehiro, Akira. 1989. *Capital Accumulation in Thailand 1855–1985*. Tokyo: Centre for East Asian Cultural Studies.

Suehiro, Akira. 1999. East Asia's Currency and Economic Crisis: Liberalizing and Stabilizing Economies and Restoring Competitiveness. Speech at the Oriental Hotel, Bangkok. 26 March.

Suehiro, Akira. 2000. The Asian Crisis and Economic and Social Restructuring: Americanization and Social Governance. Unpublished paper.

Summers, Larry. 1998a. Remarks before the IMF. 9 March 1998. US Treasury RR-2286.

Summers, Larry 1998b. Opportunities Out of Crises: Lessons From Asia. 19 March 1998. US Treasury RR-2309.

Summers, Larry. 1998c. The New Economy and the Global Economy. Remarks at the Chemical Manufacturers' Association, 9 November 1998. US Treasury RR-2808.

Summers, Larry. 1999a. Reflections on Managing Global Integration. Speech at Annual Meeting of the Association of Government Economists New York City, 4 January 1999. US Treasury RR-2877.

Summers, Larry. 1999b. Remarks to Senate Foreign Relations Subcommittee on International Economic Policy and Export/Trade Promotion, 27 January 1999. US Treasury RR-2916.

Summers, Larry. 1999c. Roots of the Asian Crises and the Road to a Stronger Global Financial System. 25 April 1999. US Treasury RR-3102.

Sunait Chutintaranond. 1994. *Phama rop thai* (The Burmese Wars with the Thai). Bangkok: Matichon.

Sungsidh Piriyarangsan and Pasuk Phongpaichit, eds. 1993. *Chon chan klang bon krasae prachathippatai thai* (The Middle Class on the Tide of Thai Democracy). Bangkok: Political Economy Centre, Chulalongkorn University.

Surin Maisrikrod. 1997. The Making of Thai Democracy: A Study of Political Alliances Among the State, the Capitalists, and the Middle Class. In *Democratization in Southeast and East Asia*, edited by Anek Laothamatas. Singapore: ISEAS.

Suthep Kittikulsingh. 1999. Non-performing Loans (NPLs): The Borrower's Viewpoint. *TDRI Quarterly Review*. 14 (4), December.

Suthy Prasatset. 1997. *Kho sangket bang prakan kieo kap wikritkan setthakit thai pi 2540* (Some Observations about the Thai Economic Crisis of 1997). In *Kaliyuk kap hayana setthakit thai* (Kaliyuga and the Thai Economic Disaster), edited by Phitthaya Wongkun. Bangkok: Withithat globalization series 1.

Suvinai Pornvalai. 1998. *Setthakit fong sabu: bot-rian lae thang rot* (The Bubble Economy: Lessons and Ways to Survive). Bangkok : Thammasat University.

TDRI (Thailand Development Research Institute). 1994. The Thai economy: first step in a new direction. Unpublished paper, 29 December.

TDRI (Thailand Development Research Institute). 1999a. *Kho sanoe phu songsoem thammaphiban thai* (Recommendations for Strengthening Good Governance in Thailand). Report of the working group on good governance. Bangkok: TDRI.

TDRI (Thailand Development Research Institute). 1999b. *Ekkasan prakop kan sammana wichakan pracham pi 2542 setthakit pho phiang* (Papers from the 1999 annual seminar on the sufficiency economy), held 18–9 December 1999 at Ambassador City, Jomthien.

TDRI (Thailand Development Research Institute). Macroeconomic Policy Program. 1999c. Financial reforms in Thailand. *TDRI Quarterly Review* 14 (4), December.

Thai NGO Support Project. 1995. *Thai NGOs: The Continuing Struggle for Democracy*. Bangkok.

Thai Rak Thai. 1999. *Khana tham ngan phu tit tam kan patipat ngan khong ratthaban* (Working Group to Monitor the Government's Work). Bangkok: Thai Rak Thai Party.

Thirayuth Boonmee. 1993. *Chut plian haeng yuk samai* (The Turning Point of the Era). Bangkok: Winyuchon.

Thirayuth Boonmee. 1998. *Thammarat haeng chat: yutthasat ku hayana prathet thai* [National Good Governance: Strategy to Rescue Thailand from Disaster). Bangkok: Saithan.

Thongchai Winichakul. 1994. *Siam Mapped: A History of the Geo-Body of a Nation*. Honolulu: University of Hawaii Press.

Thongchai Winichakul. 1999. Thai Democracy in Public Memory: Monuments and their Narrative. Keynote speech at 7th International Conference of Thai Studies. Amsterdam, 4-8 July.

Tsai, Pan-Long. 1995. Foreign Direct Investment and Income Inequality: Further Evidence. *World Development* 23.

Ukrist Pathmanand. 1998. The Thaksin Shinawatra Group: A Study of the Relationship between Money and Politics in Thailand. *Copenhagen Journal of Asian Studies*, 13.

UNCTAD. 1996. *Trade and Development Report, 1996*. New York and Geneva: UNCTAD.

UNCTAD. 1998. *Trade and Development Report, 1998*. New York and Geneva: UNCTAD.

Unger, Danny. 1998. *Building Social Capital in Thailand: Fibers, Finance and Infrastructure*. Cambridge: Cambridge University Press.

Wade, Robert and Frank Veneroso. 1998. The Asian Crisis: The High-Debt Model vs. the Wall Street–Treasury–IMF Complex. *New Left Review* 228, March–April.

Warr, Peter. 1998a. Thailand: what went wrong? Unpublished paper, June.

Warr, Peter. 1998b. Growth, Crisis and Poverty Incidence in Southeast Asia. Paper for conference on A Macroeconomic Core of an Open Economy, Chulalongkorn University, 16–18 December.

Westphal, Larry. 1989. *Assessing Thailand's Technological Capabilities in Industry*. Bangkok: Thailand Development Research Institute.

World Bank. 1983. *Thailand: Managing Public Resources for Structural Adjustment*. Country Programs Department, East Asia and Pacific Regional Office.

World Bank. 1985. *Thailand's Manufactured Exports: Key Issues and Policy Options*. Regional Mission in Bangkok, East Asia and the Pacific Regional Office.

World Bank. 1993. *The East Asian Miracle: Growth and Public Policy.* New York: Oxford University Press.

World Bank. 1998. *Social Consequences of the East Asian Financial Crisis.* (An extended version of chapter 5 of East Asia: The Road to Recovery)

World Bank Thailand. 1999. *Thailand Social Monitor: Coping with the Crisis in Education and Health.* Bangkok: World Bank.

World Bank Thailand. 2000. *Thailand Social Monitor: Social Capital and the Crisis.* Bangkok: World Bank.

INDEX

7-Eleven, 223, 243

Abhisit Vejjajiva, 168
ABN Amro, 50, 221–2
Accelerated Rural Development
 Department, 129
Acer, 223
Ad Carabao, 183
ADB (Asian Development Bank), 61,
 63, 141, 227, 231, 232, 238,
 249; social programmes, iv, 73,
 75–82, 92, 95, 97–103, 105
Adisorn Piangket, 149
AFTA (Asian Free Trade Area), 230
agriculture, 4, 12, 19–20, 47, 61, 75,
 82–5, 87, 91–3, 101, 118,
 145–8, 196–8, 203–6, 209, 226,
 232–4, 237–9
Ahold, 223
AIA (American International
 Assurance), 222
AIDS, 236, 251
Akin Rabibhadana, 91
alien business law, 168, 243
Alliance for National Salvation, 172,
 190
Alphatech, 62
Amara Pongsapich, 106

AMC (Asset Management
 Corporation), 53
American Chamber of Commerce, 38
AMF (Asian Monetary Fund), 59, 67
Ammar Siamwalla, 8–14, 37, 115–6
Amnuay Wirawan, 115
Amon Chantharasombun, 111, 114,
 116, 118
amphetamines. *See* drugs.
Anand Panyarachun, 23, 74, 98–9,
 107, 114, 120, 125–7, 133, 154–
 5, 159, 212–3
Anek Laothamatas, 110, 112, 114,
 153, 157, 210–1
Aphichai Phantasen, 198, 212, 214
army, 109, 117, 120, 122, 139, 195
Arom Phromphangan Foundation,
 105
Asia Foundation, 141, 159
Asian Games, 92, 180
Asian model, 5, 17–8, 30–1, 38, 64
Assembly of the Poor, 143–4, 147–9,
 159, 172, 232
Auditor-General, 78–9
automobile industry, 26, 223, 225–6,
 228
Ayutthaya, 174–5, 179, 182–3